HOSPITALITY MARKETING

SOUTH-WESTERN
THOMSON LEARNING ™

DECA
PREP

Kaser and Freeman

VISIT US ON THE INTERNET
www.swep.com
www.thomsonlearning.com

SOUTH-WESTERN
THOMSON LEARNING ™

Australia • Canada • Mexico • Singapore • Spain • United Kingdom • U....

SOUTH-WESTERN

™

THOMSON LEARNING

Hospitality Marketing
by Ken Kaser and Jackie Todd Freeman

Vice President/Executive Publisher
Dave Shaut

Team Leader
Karen Schmohe

Executive Editor
Eve Lewis

Project Manager
Enid Nagel

Production Manager
Patricia Matthews Boies

Editor
Darrell E. Frye

Executive Marketing Manager
Carol Volz

Channel Manager
Nancy A. Long

Marketing Coordinator
Yvonne Patton-Beard

Manufacturing Coordinator
Kevin L. Kluck

Art and Design Coordinator
Tippy McIntosh

Internal Design
Bill Spencer

Editorial Assistant
Stephanie L. White

Production Assistant
Nancy Stamper

Compositor
New England Typographic Service

Printer
Quebecor World, Dubuque, IA

About the Author

Ken Kaser has taught Marketing Education in Texas and Business Education in Nebraska for the past 23 years. Ken has authored four books; written local, state, and national curriculum; and served in professional leadership roles. He has received numerous teaching awards—NBEA, M-PBEA, Nebraska, and Texas Secondary Business Teacher of the Year, and M-PBEA Leadership Award.

Jackie Todd Freeman has taught Marketing Education for more than 20 years, both in Oklahoma and Texas. She coordinated and taught the Hospitality Marketing Internship Program at R. E. Lee High School in Houston, TX. Most recently she has served as a School to Careers Grant Coordinator for the Fort Bend Independent School District in Sugar Land, TX.

For permission to use material from this text or product, contact us by

Tel: 800-730-2214
Fax: 800-730-2215
Web: www.thomsonrights.com

For more information, contact South-Western, 5191 Natorp Boulevard, Mason, OH, 45040. Or you can visit our Internet site at www.swep.com.

REVIEWERS

Kim Galeano
Falls Church, VA

Diane Ross Gary
Bridgeport, CT

Lisa M. Gil-de-Lamadrid
Miami, FL

Thomas D. Griffin
Maple Heights, OH

Mary A. Hollish
Cleveland, OH

LaJuana Hill McKay
Palm Coast, FL

Vicki McKay
Pasadena, TX

Elizabeth S. Pitts
Cartersville, GA

Paul A. Wardinski
Falls Church, VA

YOUR COURSE PLANNING JUST GOT EASIER!

★ **NEW! Hospitality Marketing**
by Kaser and Freeman
In this unique, one-of-a-kind text, traditional marketing concepts are taught in a contemporary fashion within the context of the hospitality industry.

Text	0-538-43208-X
Multimedia Module	0-538-43209-8
Instructor Support Material Available	

★ **NEW! Marketing**
by Burrow
Built around the National Marketing foundations and functions of marketing, this text focuses on professional development, customer service, and technology.

Text	0-538-43232-2
Activities and Study Guide	0-538-43235-7
Instructor Support Material Available	

Sports and Entertainment Marketing
by Kaser and Oelkers
Nothing like it on the market! Learn how key functions of marketing are applied to the sports and entertainment industry.

Text	0-538-69477-7
Multimedia Module	0-538-69478-5
Instructor Support Material Available	

E-Commerce
by Oelkers
Learn the basics of E-Commerce and doing business on the web.

Text	0-538-69880-2
Multimedia Module	0-538-69881-0
Video	0-538-69882-9
Instructor Support Material Available	

Corporate View: Marketing & Sales Support
by Barksdale and Rutter
Engage in realistic online activities typically performed by entry-level employees in the marketing department of a large corporation.

Text	0-538-69154-9
Intranet CD	0-538-69167-0
Instructor Support Material Available	

SOUTH-WESTERN
*
THOMSON LEARNING

Join us on the Internet at www.swep.com

HOSPITALITY MARKETING

CONTENTS

TO THE STUDENT

Welcome to *Hospitality Marketing*. You have decided to embark on an exciting journey. Marketing is the tool that has allowed the United States economy to be one of the most successful in the world. The hospitality industry is an important part of our modern economy. Consumers spend millions of dollars each year on travel and tourism and in restaurants.

You will learn the basic functions of marketing and how these functions are applied to hospitality. Whenever a marketing function is presented in a lesson, it is marked with an icon indicating which marketing function is being used.

MARKETING-INFORMATION MANAGEMENT   FINANCING   PRICING   PROMOTION   PRODUCT/SERVICE MANAGEMENT   DISTRIBUTION   SELLING

To help you on your journey through the world of *Hospitality Marketing,* this text has a number of special features to highlight interesting or unusual aspects of hospitality.

Check In begins each lesson and encourages you to explore the material in the upcoming lesson. Check In also gives you opportunities to work with other students.

Confirmation provides you with an opportunity to assess your comprehension of material. Ongoing review and assessment will help you better understand the material.

Check Out provides exercises at the end of each lesson to reinforce understanding and to provide critical thinking.

Each chapter ends with a review of vocabulary and basic concepts. The **Chapter Review** includes Think Critically exercises which provides opportunities to apply concepts and Make Connections exercises which provide connections to other disciplines.

Deca Prep provides preparation for Deca competitive events in every chapter.

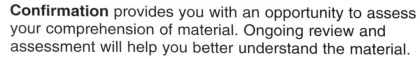

Extended Stay provides an individual or group project for students to apply the marketing concepts in the chapter.

Winning Strategies presents successful strategies used in real-life hospitality business.

Cyber Marketing investigates Internet marketing and how the Internet is a major tool for today's marketers.

Career Spotlight acquaints you with people who have succeeded in hospitality marketing careers.

Marketing Myths explores some common myths that surround advertising and promotion in the hospitality industry.

Judgment Call examines legal and ethical issues that exist in the hospitality industry.

Time Out will introduce you to interesting facts and statistics about hospitality marketing.

Hospitality Marketing will provide you with an interesting journey through the world of marketing. Fasten your seatbelts and enjoy the ride.

CHAPTER 1

WHAT IS HOSPITALITY MARKETING?

LESSONS

1.1 MARKETING BASICS

1.2 HOTEL MARKETING: A COMPETITIVE INDUSTRY

1.3 THE IMPORTANCE OF HOSPITALITY MARKETING

WINNING STRATEGIES

NEW-CENTURY AMENITIES

It has only been a few years since consumers started making hotel room reservations and paying bills via the Internet. Now that method of reserving a room is considered routine. The latest technological development for hotels is wireless Web access in rooms, essentially doing away with the need for dataport connections.

Many hotels are now updating to wireless networks to satisfy the needs of technology-oriented guests. Starwood Hotels and Resorts Worldwide has launched business hotels, referred to as "W" hotels, in Silicon Valley and San Francisco. In addition to innovative Internet services, these W hotels offer network printing, allowing guests to print from their laptops to anywhere in the hotel. All guest rooms have cordless phones. Not everything is strictly business, however. Guests get plush terry-lined bathrobes and pillow-top mattresses for relaxation.

High-tech amenities are advancing, yet other "softer" benefits are important to guests as well. "Boutique" hotels offer extras and frills that may or may not be free, but are often sought by guests with luxury tastes. Soft down comforters and down pillows, Belgian linen bed sheets, and well-stocked gourmet mini-bars are among amenities offered at luxury hotels. The Ritz Carlton in Washington D.C. has a rolling soap tray similar to the dessert tray offered at fine restaurants. Guests select the soap they want to use.

Today's business travelers want more than sleeping space when they reserve a room. Hotels are living up to these high expectations by providing both high-tech extras as well as lavish comforts.

THINK CRITICALLY

1. List at least three technological or luxury extras that a hotel might consider offering business travelers.
2. Why are hotels continually upgrading amenities for customers?

MARKETING BASICS

LESSON 1.1

Describe basic concepts of marketing.

Define the seven key marketing functions.

CHECK IN

In the year 2000, Hilton Hotels announced plans for the first luxury hotel in space. Although it's hard to guess what type of room service might be available, the idea of a space hotel is just an example of the forward thinking of successful hotel marketing. The lodging industry is continually seeking innovative ways to provide a comfortable place to stay for those who are away from home.

Just a century ago, in 1900, there were fewer than 10,000 hotel rooms in the United States. Then, a first-class hotel offered steam heat, gas burners, electric call bells, baths and closets on all floors, barbershops, and liveries. The Lenox Hotel in New York charged $2 and up for a room. In 1990, there were 3,065,685 hotel rooms in the United States, and the average room rate was $58.70 per night. Modern amenities include things unimaginable in 1900.

Work with a group. List at least 15 inventions or technological advances in the last 100 years that have brought major changes to the hospitality industry.

MARKETING CONCEPTS

Marketing is a vital function of business. If you have a job right now, you are involved in marketing. If you purchase any *goods*, items that are tangible, you are participating in marketing. If you purchase something intangible, a *service*, you are participating in marketing. In fact, about half of what you spend on goods or services pays for the cost of marketing. Marketing is far more than just promoting and selling. Marketing also involves research, product development, pricing, financing, distribution, and managing the product or service.

WHAT IS MARKETING?

One definition of **marketing** is all the activities used to plan, price, promote, and sell services or products. Marketing, however, is not limited to those four functions. The American Marketing Association defines marketing as "planning and executing the conception, pricing, promotion, and distribution of ideas, goods, and services to create exchanges that satisfy individual and organizational objectives." As complicated as that sounds, it covers most of what is involved in the marketing process. An easy way to understand marketing is to think of it as all the processes necessary to determine and satisfy the needs of the customer as well as the company involved.

The hospitality industry blends the marketing of goods and services in a unique way. Not only do travelers seek a clean and comfortable room, they also want someone to keep it that way. Not only do restaurant customers want quality food, they want someone to prepare and serve it well. Hotels, restaurants, and other businesses involved in travel and tourism balance basic marketing elements to meet the needs of customers while making a reasonable profit at the same time. This balance is known as the **marketing mix**.

The marketing mix is the way a business combines the marketing elements of product, price, promotion, and distribution.

Product is what a business offers customers to satisfy needs. In the hospitality industry, products include specific items such as double or single rooms or continental breakfasts, and services such as wake-up calls, valet parking, and in-room computer dataports.

Price is the amount that customers pay for the products. In the hospitality business, prices are highly negotiable and often based on supply and demand as well as what consumers consider to be a fair price for the product.

Promotion is a combination of methods used to inform the customer of the business and to encourage the customer to purchase the products or services. Promotion involves advertising, as well as publicity, personal selling, and public relations.

Distribution is the method used to get the product or service to a customer. In the hospitality industry, examples of distributors are travel agents and tour wholesaling companies who put travel packages together.

CONFIRMATION

What is marketing? What are the elements of the marketing mix?

_____

_____

_____

_____

TIME OUT

Many marketing innovations during the twentieth century changed the hospitality industry. The first transatlantic passenger flight in 1939 opened the skies for international travel. The Holiday Inn Corporation opened the first family-oriented motor hotel chain in 1952. In 1955, Disneyland, the first theme park in North America, opened in Anaheim, California.

KEY MARKETING FUNCTIONS

There are seven major functions involved in marketing. Those functions are marketing-information management, financing, pricing, promotion, product/service management, distribution, and selling. At least one of these functions is involved whenever a product or service is marketed.

EXAMPLES OF THE KEY MARKETING FUNCTIONS

Whenever a customer arranges an event or conference at a hotel or restaurant, all of the marketing functions take place. Every time an agent reserves a room for a customer, all of the marketing functions are involved. Because key marketing functions are fundamental to the hospitality industry, examples are abundant.

Marketing-Information Management is gathering and using information about customers to improve business decision making. Many hotels use guest-tracking systems as a means to keep guests happy and ensure their return. The Balsams Grand Resort Hotel in the White Mountains of New Hampshire uses an extensive guest-tracking system to maintain a history of guests' preferences and special requests. The system stores information such as individual guest food and beverage selections, choice of activities, favorite tee times or ski runs, and even the preferred arrangement of furniture in rooms. As a result, the ratio of return guests to this off-the-beaten-path location is exceptionally high.

Financing is acquiring and budgeting financial resources to stay in business. It also means that companies must offer different payment methods to customers for purchasing goods and services offered. Many airline companies team up with hotels and financial services such as American Express to offer benefits and upgrades for their frequent customers. Customers reap extra rewards while companies receive a reliable stream of earnings and revenues.

Pricing is determining the value and cost of goods and services offered to customers. In the travel and tourism industry, supply and demand play a significant role in pricing. Airline prices are usually high during peak travel times. A hotel that caters to business travelers on the nights of Sunday through Thursday will often decrease room rates on Friday and Saturday nights when business is slow. The practice of varying the price of a room based on current demand is known as **yield management**.

Promotion is informing customers about a company's products, services, images, and ideas through advertising, personal selling, publicity, and public relations. In addition to mass media advertising, many hotels

FUNCTIONS OF MARKETING

MARKETING-INFORMATION MANAGEMENT

FINANCING

PRICING

PROMOTION

PRODUCT/ SERVICE MANAGEMENT

DISTRIBUTION

SELLING

offer promotional rates during holiday seasons to increase future business. Many hotels participate in local charity events to publicize their efforts as community benefactors.

Product/Service Management involves designing, developing, maintaining, improving, and acquiring products or services to meet the needs of customers. In order to stay competitive, hospitality managers and owners must continually update the goods and services offered. In an effort to provide privacy, entertainment, and space for vacationing parents and children, some Holiday Inns in Orlando, Florida, developed Kidsuites. Kidsuites have a room specially designed for children within the regular room for the parents. Hoteliers and restaurateurs not only need to modernize equipment they use, but they must maintain and/or redo exteriors and interiors of buildings they occupy. The owner of the Royal Palms Hotel and Casitas in Phoenix, Arizona, brought in 20 interior design teams to assist in an extensive two-year renovation project. The renovation resulted in higher occupancy and higher average room rates.

Distribution is the means of getting a company's products and services to customers in the best way possible. Although many products are critical to the hospitality industry, providing services brings in the majority of a hotel's or restaurant's business. Unlike merchandise, services are not shipped from a warehouse or stored in a back room. Instead, travel and reservation agents, sales personnel, and Internet travel services are the major distribution channels in this business.

Selling is the process of communicating directly with customers to determine and then satisfy their needs. Selling can occur in many different locations. A front desk agent might tell a guest of the availability of a more expensive or larger room than the one originally reserved, a practice called *upselling*. A wait-staff person in a restaurant might use *suggestion selling* when he or she relates the daily special to an undecided customer.

Understanding the seven functions of marketing is fundamental to any successful marketer. Whether you are the CEO of a large company, beginning a dot.com business, or managing a family-owned restaurant, you will be frequently and directly concerned with these functions.

MARKETING MYTHS

Clever promotion and eye-popping graphics are not the key to effective online marketing, according to Accenture (formerly Andersen Consulting). In an age when "Internet everything" seems to hold the key to the future, it is still the customers' total experience with a company or a web site that determines their attitudes. If customers are annoyed by an inefficient site or barraged with advertising, they lower their regard for the company running it.

THINK CRITICALLY
Why is a focus on a customer's total experience especially important for the hospitality industry?

CONFIRMATION

What are the seven major marketing functions? Give an example of each one as it occurs in the hospitality industry.

_____

_____

UNDERSTAND MARKETING CONCEPTS

Circle the best answer for each of the following questions.

1. In the hospitality industry, marketing is
   a. purchasing food and restaurant supplies
   b. suggesting fries to go with that burger
   c. doing what it takes to satisfy the customer and the company
   d. advertising and promoting special room rates to increase business

2. The marketing mix
   a. involves a delicate balance of all seven marketing functions
   b. combines product, price, promotion, and distribution
   c. is the same for every type of hotel or restaurant
   d. involves location, selling, manufacturing, and services

THINK CRITICALLY

Answer the following questions as completely as possible. If necessary, use a separate sheet of paper.

3. **Communication** Think of a recent time when you had a meal at a restaurant, took a flight on a commercial airline, or spent at least a night and a day at a hotel. Describe how each of the seven marketing functions were involved in the activity you selected.

_____

_____

_____

_____

_____

4. **Technology** Find an advertisement for a major hotel chain in a newspaper or magazine, or use the Internet to find a web site of a major hotel. Identify specific ways the elements of the marketing mix are applied in the advertisement or on the home page.

_____

_____

_____

_____

_____

HOTEL MARKETING: A COMPETITIVE INDUSTRY

CHAPTER 1

LESSON 1.2

CHECK IN

The hotel industry is a competitive business that must keep up with the latest trends for survival. Attracting and pleasing the customer is the prime motive of hospitality marketing.

How do you make decisions about which hotel you choose? What are the factors that lead you to consider, evaluate, and select one lodging facility over another?

Work with a group. Identify five advertising campaigns of hotels. Discuss ways those hotels are meeting the high expectations of the modern consumer in their marketing material.

GOALS

Define service marketing and how it relates to the hospitality industry.

Describe hotel amenities and explain why they are important to guests.

TARGET MARKETING

A strong economy, a mobile population, and more disposable income have increased profit potential for the hotel and motel industry. These trends have also increased the competition to secure hotel and motel guests.

Travelers have a wide array of choices for lodging. From metropolitan hotels with fine restaurants and personal service to discount motels offering clean, basic rooms and continental breakfast for a reasonable price, places for consumers to spend their dollars vary widely. Advertising campaigns use radio, television, newspaper, and now the Internet for slogans like *"We'll leave the light on for you,"* and *"Never underestimate the importance of a good night's rest,"* to stay in the minds of consumers.

Attracting hotel guests takes more than a catchy slogan, though. First, the lodging establishment must determine a **target market** or a specific group of people who share similar characteristics as its hotel clientele. What type of hotel serves what type of client? This is a fundamental decision that determines the basic nature of the hotel. Who will stay in a given place? How much are they willing to pay? What do they expect from their lodging? Hotels may cater to repeat business travelers, vacationers and families in particular places, or *transients*, guests who visit an area or stay in a lodging property for only a few

A Crowne Plaza Hotels and Resorts survey found that most business travelers take approximately ten business trips per year, staying an average of four nights per trip. Only about 15% shop around for the best hotel deals. About 22% of those traveling for business are interested in redeeming frequent-flyer miles.

days. Each of these groups has different needs and desires, and makes decisions about how to spend dollars differently.

UNDERSTANDING THE CUSTOMER

In order to compete for those dollars, a lodging establishment must know what its customers want. It can then determine what extras it will offer guests and what prices must be charged to pay for them. Most hotels and restaurants conduct marketing research to determine what customers expect. Hyatt Hotels contracts the Gallup Organization to conduct random surveys of recent guests. The Waldorf-Astoria and Hilton Hotels ask guests to complete a 30-second quality-quiz either at check out time or in the restaurant. The surveys are received and scored daily, with special attention given to customer concerns or complaints. Hotel management pays close attention to **demographics**. Demographics are the characteristics of a target market such as age, income, gender, and level of education. These factors are directly related to choices that hotel management makes about pricing, amenities, and services.

SERVICES WITH A SMILE

The hospitality industry involves **service marketing** because an intangible product is sold to the ultimate consumer. It is true that guests are in direct contact with tangible products as they stay in a room, watch the television, and use the courtesy products provided for them. However, they are not purchasing those products for later use. The intangible "product" that they are really purchasing is the comfortable feeling of the warm, safe, clean room as well as the individual attention given to each guest by the hotel staff. In the restaurant industry it is often put this way: "Sell the sizzle, not the steak." It is usually not just the meal that brings customers back, but the people who present it. Service marketing frequently gets only one chance to make a good first impression. The hospitality industry must maintain high standards to meet the expectations of consumers and ensure repeat business.

Competition is brisk among the different types of lodging establishments. Whatever the type of hotel, the services offered, or the price range, there is another one like it nearby perfectly willing to try a little harder to earn the customer's dollar. Hotel managers are keenly aware of this fundamental economic principle, and pay close attention to service, customer preferences, and staff training.

CONFIRMATION

How do lodging establishments benefit from gathering information about customer preferences?

_____

_____

PLUGGED-IN HOTELS

PRODUCT/ SERVICE MANAGEMENT

Technology has found its way into hotel **amenities**, those services or items offered to guests for convenience and comfort. With the addition of cable television and movies-on-demand, full-size desks, two-line phones, and modem hook-ups at most hotels, many guest rooms have become "branch offices" for the convenience of the highly profitable business traveler. Guests at dozens of Holiday Inns, Embassy Suites, and Hilton Hotels no longer have to worry about long-distance charges or sweat out software glitches and connection hassles. Pay-per-view companies such as On Command already supply almost 1 million hotel rooms, including those at big chains like Hyatt and Marriott, offering movies and other entertainment whenever the guest desires.

ELEGANT EXTRAS

Some hotels believe that an upscale image and impressive extras gain the loyalty of guests—especially in the higher price ranges. Although luxury amenities cost hotels more, they also attract customers willing to pay the added price. The new Hilton Stress-Less room includes a small gurgling "calming pool" rock fountain. A high-tech desk chair waits to deliver massages to stiff backs. Ferns and spider plants dangle from the ceiling to add a feeling of familiarity and warmth. Suites are now packed with PowerBars, exercise equipment, and celebrity videos for fitness buffs. Earplugs and sound boxes that simulate heartbeats are provided for fitful sleepers. These gadgets allow hotels to charge more for the extras that appeal to road-weary business and leisure guests.

Holiday Inn's Fitness Suites have recumbent bikes, abdominal benches, a VCR with exercise tapes, and even flashy mirrored walls. Guests can pay $25 over the standard $125 suite rate for the privilege of a private workout. New York's Fitzpatrick Grand Central Hotel goes a step further by offering a personalized yoga instructor who will work with you for $80 an hour.

CYBER MARKETING

Many lodging establishments have begun putting pictures of their establishments on their web sites. Hotels often show their rooms, while bed and breakfasts and smaller motels may feature an outside view of the property.

THINK CRITICALLY
1. Visit the home page of a major hotel property, a small motel, and a bed and breakfast. Compare the photos and decide what each emphasizes.
2. Why might small motels and bed and breakfasts feature an exterior view?

CONFIRMATION

How do high-tech amenities help hotels compete? What is the trade-off for luxury amenities in hotel marketing?

UNDERSTAND MARKETING CONCEPTS

Circle the best answer for each of the following questions.

1. A target market is
   a. a nationally known mass merchandiser
   b. a group of potential customers with similar characteristics
   c. a professional organization of business travelers
   d. none of the above

2. The hospitality industry involves service marketing because
   a. all employees are trained to be courteous and friendly
   b. extra benefits are provided at luxury hotels
   c. management is concerned with customers' preferences
   d. intangible products are sold to the ultimate consumer

THINK CRITICALLY

Answer the following questions as completely as possible. If necessary, use a separate sheet of paper.

3. **Communication**   Assume you have been asked to design a comment card for guests to complete as they check out of a hotel. List below the questions you would include on the card.

_____

_____

_____

_____

_____

_____

_____

4. **Marketing Math**   Design a scoring system to tally the results of a comment card that guests complete as they check out of a hotel.

_____

_____

_____

_____

_____

_____

THE IMPORTANCE OF HOSPITALITY MARKETING

CHAPTER 1
LESSON 1.3

CHECK IN

Travel and tourism is the third largest retail industry in the United States, behind only the automotive and food-supply industries. In fact, travel and tourism is one of America's largest employers.

There are at least 15 types of businesses involved in travel and tourism, including lodging, airlines, restaurants, cruise operations, car rental agencies, travel agencies, and tour operations. In 1999, one of every seven Americans was directly or indirectly employed because of travel to or travel within the United States.

Work with a partner. Develop a list of companies who are major organizations in the travel and tourism industry. Identify the business area of each company.

GOALS

Explain why travel and tourism is critical to the U.S. economy.

Distinguish between "front-of-the-house" and "back-of-the-house" operations in a hotel or restaurant.

THE FINANCIAL IMPACT OF TRAVEL AND TOURISM

Hospitality marketing is part of a larger industry known as travel and tourism. According to the Travel Industry Association of America (TIA), travel and tourism is the largest services export industry in the nation. In fact, in 29 of the 50 states, travel and tourism is either the first, second, or third largest employer. TIA estimated that more than $582 billion was spent in the travel and tourism industry in 1999. That figure translates to 18 million jobs for Americans. About 7.7 million jobs were directly related to travel and tourism, and 10.3 million employees were indirectly related. As a result of those jobs, $159 billion in payroll income was generated. That's billion, not million.

In the hospitality marketing sector, travelers spent over $50 billion on rooms in lodging establishments in 1999 and more than $23 billion on food while traveling. When you add in shopping, entertainment, and miscellaneous items, travelers dropped a total of more than $235 billion into the accounts of the hotel industry.

You may not be a typical business traveler making about ten trips a year, but chances are you will probably eat out sometime this week. More than four out of ten people ate at a restaurant on a typical day in 1999. In 1999, 11.3 million people worked in some type of restaurant, making the restaurant industry the nation's largest private-sector employer.

Many large metropolitan areas in the U.S. have recently built new professional sports arenas or stadiums. Quite often, private corporations will partially finance the construction of these modern wonders. Other construction and start-up costs are usually covered by revenue from increased hotel or tourism tax rates. That means that many tourists or business travelers who never go to a professional football, basketball, or baseball game have partially paid for the new building. It could also mean many local fans who are avid supporters of the sport have not contributed anything beyond the cost of a ticket or hot dog.

THINK CRITICALLY

1. Do you think travel and tourism-related taxes (hotels, rental cars, and so forth) should be used to pay for a professional sports venue? Why or why not?

2. Do you think customers should be given a breakdown of how hotel taxes are spent? Why or why not?

GROWTH IN TRAVEL AND TOURISM

Travel and tourism is good for the economy. Not only do people in the United States travel within the States, called **domestic travel**, but many international travelers come to America and consequently spend money. United States' travelers spent $81.4 billion while traveling in foreign countries, but international travelers spent more money in America than Americans spent abroad, resulting in a travel trade surplus of $14.2 billion.

Why are more people traveling? With the advent of Internet-based travel services such as Priceline and Travelocity, many travelers are organizing and booking their own travel arrangements. Deregulation of the airline industry often translates to lower airline ticket prices. Because travel agents can no longer depend on ticket sales commissions to support their business, they seek to increase revenue by booking other types of trips such as cruises, motor coach travel, or escorted tours.

Travel has a universal appeal to all ages, and several trends are emerging. An aging Baby-Boomer generation has begun to travel often and book tours. People take their children or grandchildren on trips more often. Young people travel more extensively, often as part of a growing number of families who take shorter, but more expensive, vacations.

Business travelers bring their families along and combine business with pleasure. The business traveler is no longer predominantly male. Female executives make up almost half the executive traveler market.

Travel and tourism is truly beneficial for the economy. During 1999, domestic and international travelers in the United States spent an average of $1.42 billion a day. If that figure seems hard to comprehend, consider it this way: $1.42 billion a day equals $59.4 million an hour, $989,300 a minute, and $16,400 per second.

CONFIRMATION

Explain why travel and tourism is good for our country's economy.

THE NATURE OF THE HOSPITALITY MARKETING INDUSTRY

Hotel employees are responsible for providing a comfortable and enjoyable stay for their customers. Lodging facilities operate 24 hours a day, seven days a week. Large hotels may employ hundreds of people to see to the needs of customers or to maintain efficiency in running the establishment.

MANAGEMENT OPPORTUNITIES

There are many management positions in a hotel.

General managers have the responsibility of overseeing the operations of the hotel.

Front office managers coordinate reservations and room assignments and manage the front desk staff.

Executive housekeepers supervise the work of the housekeeping staff to ensure guest rooms, meeting rooms, and public areas are clean and inviting.

Food and beverage managers oversee all activities involved in planning, preparing, and providing meals and drinks for hotel guests in the hotel's restaurants, banquet or meeting areas, and lounges.

Sales directors supervise the sales staff who may handle corporate accounts, social or special events, conventions and conferences, and exhibits.

Human resource managers not only deal with recruiting and hiring the hotel staff, but are responsible for training and coordinating employee benefits as well.

Operations managers keep the hotel running, literally. They take care of security, heating and air conditioning, electrical and power systems, groundskeeping, safety, and maintenance.

Financial managers supervise procedures involved in tracking a hotel's receipts and expenditures and daily audits.

Keep in mind that entry-level jobs exist in all of the areas listed above as well as management positions.

One-third of all adults in the United States have worked in the restaurant industry at some point in their lives.

A HOUSE DIVIDED

A typical hotel or restaurant has two divisions: the **front of the house** and the **back of the house**. The front of the house involves any area of the hotel to which the general public or a hotel guest has access. That would include guest rooms, meeting rooms, business center, public rest-rooms, gift shop, pool, and restaurants on the property. The back of the house includes those vital departments not usually seen or frequented by a guest or patron. Those departments include areas such as human resources, management, accounting, reservations, operations, house-keeping, and banquet operations.

CONFIRMATION

Name two front-of-the-house and two back-of-the-house departments. What are some of the responsibilities of each department?

CAREER SPOTLIGHT

TOM PARSONS

Tom Parsons may become a hero as big as any sports or entertainment star. He is one of the forces changing the travel industry. He's a marketer, but he's selling discounts, not huge profits.

Parsons got his start in the mid-1980s when he discovered that a co-worker had paid $100 less than he for a ticket on the same flight. From that moment, he has spent his life digging up travel bargains that most other people can't find, and he's glad to tell everything he knows.

Parsons is the publisher of *Best Fares Discount Travel Magazine* and the author of mag-azine articles as well as a new travel-tips book. He is also a frequent guest on many radio and television talk and news shows. You can also check out his web site at www.bestfares.com to learn more about travel deals and travel savvy.

THINK CRITICALLY

1. Look at Tom Parsons' web site, and find costs for two different airline flights to the city of your choice. Then call the toll-free number of the same airlines and ask for their best rates.
2. What did you learn? What would you advise friends and family to do before they travel?

UNDERSTAND MARKETING CONCEPTS

Circle the best answer for each of the following questions.

1. Hospitality marketing is one aspect of which industry sector?
    a. business and marketing
    b. travel and tourism
    c. construction and manufacturing
    d. recreational and sports marketing

2. Hotels and restaurants are generally divided into which two sections?
    a. expenditures and receipts
    b. goods and services
    c. income generation and supportive servicing
    d. front of the house and back of the house

THINK CRITICALLY

Answer the following questions as completely as possible. If necessary, use a separate sheet of paper.

3. Identify five different types of travelers. For each type that you list, name two amenities or services that would appeal to that traveler.

_____

_____

_____

_____

_____

_____

4. **Communication** The advertising manager of a small local newspaper has asked you to write an ad for a new restaurant opening in the community. Tell what type of information you would include.

_____

_____

_____

_____

_____

CHAPTER 1 REVIEW

REVIEW MARKETING CONCEPTS

Write the letter of the term that matches each definition. Some terms will not be used.

_____ **1.** Providing intangible products

_____ **2.** Area of the hotel to which the general public or a hotel guest has access

_____ **3.** Characteristics such as age, income, gender, or education level

_____ **4.** Group of people who share similar characteristics

_____ **5.** The balance of products, price, promotion, and distribution

_____ **6.** Services or items offered to guests for convenience and comfort

a. amenities
b. back of the house
c. demographics
d. domestic travel
e. front of the house
f. marketing
g. marketing mix
h. service marketing
i. target market
j. yield management

Circle the best answer.

7. Assisting in the design and development of new products is
 a. financing
 b. marketing-information management
 c. product/service management
 d. none of these

8. Offering reduced room rates in order to increase future business is an example of
 a. promotion
 b. financing
 c. product/service management
 d. none of these

9. Keeping track of guests' preferences or special requests is an example of
 a. selling
 b. courtesy information
 c. marketing-information management
 d. all of these

10. A target market is
 a. a specific group of people you want to reach
 b. people who have something in common
 c. people who might buy the same services or products if they knew about them
 d. all of these

THINK CRITICALLY

11. You are the general manager of a newly renovated hotel in a large metropolitan area, just across the street from an internationally known luxury shopping center. Who is your target market? Why? Name ways you will appeal to your customer.

_____

_____

_____

_____

_____

_____

12. You are the manufacturer of a new wireless Internet access system. Whom will you contact to sell this product in the hospitality industry? Choose a hotel corporation to endorse your product. Which one did you choose? Why?

_____

_____

_____

_____

_____

13. Using the Internet or travel magazines in your library, find and briefly describe three popular hotel properties. To whom and how are these hotels being marketed?

_____

_____

_____

_____

_____

_____

CHAPTER
REVIEW

MAKE CONNECTIONS

14. **Marketing Math** You are a celebrity who has endorsed a new line of bottled water featured only in restaurants. You will receive 5 percent of the sales of this product. One 12-ounce bottle sells for $1.25. Last month, 6,000 bottles were sold. How much will you earn from the sale of this water?

_____

_____

_____

_____

15. **History** You are a travel marketer in 1849 America. Your job is to promote migration to the West. Research such a trip and write a sales feature describing how your clients will travel, what they will take with them, how long the trip will take, and the dangers they will face.

_____

_____

_____

_____

16. **Communication** You are a travel marketer in the twenty-first century, and you want to praise modern travel. Using the information you learned in question 15, compare the pioneers' trip with a modern-day trip to the same destination. How will your clients travel now? What will they take with them? How long will the trip take by car? By plane? What dangers might they face?

_____

_____

_____

_____

17. **Technology** Imagine you are a travel marketer in the year 2080. As part of your promotion, tell your client about the technological advances your ancestors had at the beginning of the twenty-first century that made travel safer and easier. List at least ten.

_____

_____

_____

QUICK-SERVE RESTAURANT MANAGEMENT ROLE PLAY

http://www.deca.org
/publications/HS_
Guide/guidetoc.html

You are the manager of a nationally recognized fast food restaurant. Your restaurant chain takes pride in serving high quality food and excellent customer service. One of your best customers saw a commercial while vacationing in another state that advertised a new food item for your restaurant. The advertisement was regional and the new product was only being test-marketed in some states. After standing in line for 15 minutes, the cashier informed the customer that the new item was not being offered at your restaurant. It is your responsibility to satisfy the customer in order to not lose their business. The customer is not only unhappy about waiting in line, but has also suggested that false advertising has taken place.

Write down the strategies you will use to keep a good customer relationship. You will be explaining these strategies to the angry customer in this role play.

PROJECT EXTENDED STAY

Your travel marketing firm has been asked by a multimillionaire to create "the adventure trip of a lifetime" for her husband who is turning 50 this year. She will go with him on the trip. Her husband has always wanted to go to Madagascar, but your client is unsure and wants to be sold on that destination. Your boss will give you a large bonus if you can successfully promote this trip.

Work with a group and complete the following activities.

1. With your town or city as a beginning point, discover the quickest route to Madagascar. Include the means of transportation necessary from point to point. For example, if you live in a small town, the first leg of the journey will probably be by car to a city with an airport.

2. Create a map of the world showing the travel route and time for each part of the trip. Use mapmaking software if you have it. Or use a large piece of paper or poster board. Use different colors, and be sure to create a legend.

3. Write an exciting five-page report about Madagascar. Include descriptions of unique plants and animals, delicious foods, scenery, and languages spoken. Be sure to include a section on accommodations and activities available. Do advise your client of necessary vaccinations and other health issues. Include a section on local customs along with any precautions your client needs to take.

4. Provide a simple spreadsheet showing complete costs for the trip, including major transportation (car, plane, train, bus), hotel, tours, and meals. Include recommendations for tips.

5. Write an enthusiastic two-page cover letter telling your client why she'll be glad she and her husband made this trip.

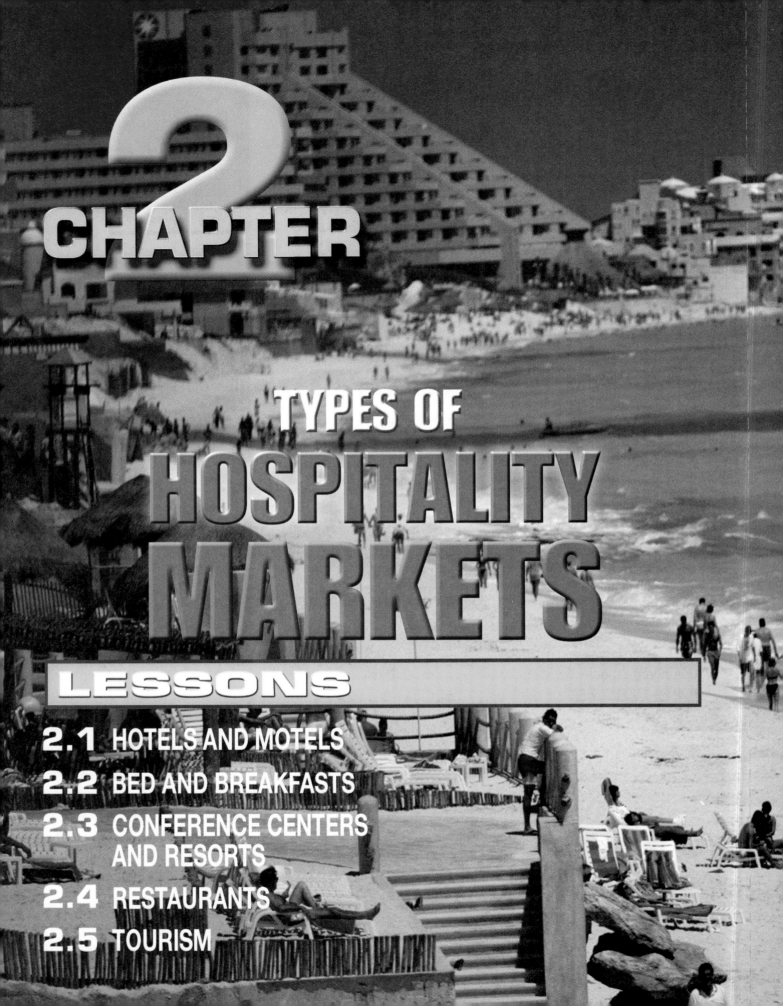

CHAPTER 2

TYPES OF HOSPITALITY MARKETS

WINNING STRATEGIES

CONRAD N. HILTON

Conrad N. Hilton was born in San Antonio, New Mexico Territory, in 1887, the son of the owner of a general store. During the financial panic of 1907, the Hilton home became a modest inn. Each night Conrad went to the train station to attract business. Weary travelers got a clean room, meals cooked by Conrad's mother, and good hospitality for $1 per night.

After the death of his father and service in the Army in World War I, Hilton took his $5,000 savings and inheritance to Texas in 1919, intending to buy a bank. The deal fell through, but Hilton was amazed by the many oil workers looking for rooms in the Mobley Hotel of Cisco, Texas. Hilton purchased the hotel with his savings, help from friends, and a bank loan. From this run-down property, Hilton built the Hilton Hotel chain into a world-renowned hospitality company.

During the Great Depression of the 1930s, 80% of hotels went bankrupt. Hilton lost three of his eight hotels and went $500,000 into debt. He survived hard times by buying distressed hotels at low prices and selling them at a profit. Hilton acquired famous properties such as the Waldorf-Astoria and the Plaza in New York City, the Stevens in Chicago, and the Sir Francis Drake in San Francisco. His empire grew. The 300-room Caribe Hilton in San Juan, Puerto Rico launched Hilton's international operations in 1949.

Hilton was an enthusiastic deal maker who studied properties carefully. Side businesses led him into early forms of the credit card industry. Successful and famous, Hilton led a celebrity lifestyle and authored a book about his career, *Be My Guest*, in 1957. He died in 1979.

THINK CRITICALLY
1. Name three entrepreneurial characteristics possessed by Conrad Hilton.
2. How did Hilton creatively change his business when hotels were failing everywhere?

HOTELS AND MOTELS

GOALS

Define differences among hotel and motel types.

List advantages that each type of hotel or motel has in its particular business.

CHECK IN

Remember the last time you went on vacation? The hotel or motel probably played a large role in the success or failure of your trip. Consumer expectations have risen for the hospitality industry. As competitive businesses that must keep up with the latest trends, the hotel industry looks for ways to expand service. Reserving a hotel room, for example, has become easier than ever. You can call an 800 number, use the Internet, use a travel agent, or dial the hotel directly.

With a partner or in a group, compile a list of things that make an experience at a hotel a pleasure. Make another list of things that will disqualify a lodging from getting your future business.

FULL-SERVICE HOTELS

PRODUCT/
SERVICE
MANAGEMENT

Hotels are multistoried lodging facilities that range in size from a limited number of rooms to hundreds of rooms. Quality of hotels varies widely with price, location, and age. A **full-service hotel** provides a wide range of services, usually including a restaurant and bar on the premises, retail shops, luggage assistance, parking lot attendants, room service, and other amenities such as dry cleaning. Business travelers and convention attendees make up the largest percentage of hotel guests.

The growth and lower rates of limited-service hotels have challenged full-service hotels to offer attractive extras to guests. Many hotels offer suites packed with exercise equipment and other trendy items, such as calming fountains and massage chairs. Fitful sleepers can get earplugs or sound boxes that simulate heartbeats, blackout drapes, or even the BioBrite Sunrise Clock, a device that brightens slowly to simulate sunrise. High-quality, brand-name supplies and amenities, from mattresses and mattress covers to designer soaps and lotions, have become standard.

Many hotels offer high-speed Internet access. Marriott International has about 300 hotels worldwide wired for high-speed access and plans to have an additional 200 hotels online by the end of 2001. Hilton Hotels, Radisson Hotels, and Choice Hotels also plan high-speed access in rooms. The Adam's Mark Hotel in Dallas is offering wireless Web access to business guests who use its meeting rooms.

The number of business trips including children grew 32 percent between 1997 and 1998, so Holiday Inn started offering kids' suites for $115. The rates for these rooms, furnished with bunk beds, Lego play table, and Nintendo, are slightly lower than normal. Even some luxury hotels offer amenities for children.

An increasing number of hotels accept guests with pets. Hotels usually have rules to keep pets and owners controlled. The cheaper the room, the greater the likelihood of paying an additional fee ranging from $5 to $25 a night to cover cleanup costs, or placing a security deposit as a hedge against damages.

As business travelers use the Internet more and more, plugged-in hotels make some form of access one of their amenities. The Century Plaza Hotel in Los Angeles has just the room for demanding, cyber-savvy travelers. The Cyber Suite, complete with voice-activated "butler," virtual-reality headgear, and access to the Internet via NetTV through a wireless keyboard, goes for $2,000 a night.

THINK CRITICALLY
1. Why do hotels find it important to have the latest technology available in rooms?
2. Suggest an example of a future technological advancement for hotel rooms.

AIRPORT HOTELS

Hotels located near airports have often had a reputation for dowdiness and poor service. Recently, millions of dollars have been spent on upgrades. Airy, earth-toned rooms priced from $85 a night contain well-stocked mini bars and features such as spas, dataports, and triple-glazed windows to keep out noise. Weekend rooms often run half the cost of city-center hotels. Airport hotels provide handy accommodations for travelers with early morning flights. Consumers can get a night's sleep—and might save even more by avoiding airport parking lots.

UNIVERSITY HOTELS

Major universities conduct studies to determine whether hotel/convention centers are good for their campuses. Mixed-use hotel and retail conference complexes provide major universities with first-class hotels complete with conference amenities such as bookstores, public atriums, and a diverse range of retail/entertainment shops and restaurants.

CHANGES ON THE HORIZON

DISTRIBUTION

The last decade has seen the expansion and affiliation of many major hotel chains. Summerfield Suites Hotels now franchises its concept, as does Hyatt Hotels Corporation. Although franchise operations expand market penetration, they carry a potential risk if individual franchises fail to live up to standards set by parent companies.

New ideas in customer service will continue at a breathtaking pace. Marriott is in the process of opening 30 upscale full-service Gourmet Bean coffee outlets right in its hotels. New ideas in food service will go further, as will luxury amenities in rooms. Some hotels have begun to maintain guest "profiles" to customize rooms for individual tastes.

CONFIRMATION

What special or unique amenities do full-service hotels offer?

_____

_____

MOTELS AND MOTOR INNS

Motels are lodging facilities usually found on feeder highways and roads, or along lesser-known routes. Motels are usually one-story structures, with parking in front of or near the room. Most motels do not have restaurants, and the owner provides all services.

The term *motel* comes from "motor hotel." The invention of the automobile helped the hotel industry become a booming business in the 1920s. Landowners along major routes built wooden 10-foot by 10-foot cabins easily accessible to weary travelers who could park their cars in front. Owners soon expanded their operations to 15 or more cabins referred to as *tourist courts*.

In the 1930s, the Great Depression devastated the lodging industry. Many smaller motels went bankrupt, and the industry did not revive until after World War II. During the war, troops being transported, workers being transferred to various factories, and families reuniting presented opportunities for new hotels built near major military bases and industrial areas.

At the end of the war, air travel became available to

larger numbers of people. The growing postwar economy saw companies expand with branch and regional offices, and conventions and conferences offered opportunity to the hospitality industry. Vast numbers of business travelers became the most important customers, but people also traveled more for pleasure as they had more disposable income after the war.

Motor inns are the most common lodging facilities found in the United States. Motor inns are usually located near major highways and the interstate highway system, often clustered with other inns. Motor inns range from two to six stories, and usually have a restaurant or bar. Motor inns are becoming hard to distinguish from hotels, offering bellhops, room service, and increasing amenities. Motor inns located near airports are popular for meeting and convention business. Holiday Inn and Comfort Inn are examples of motor inns.

The Superior Small Lodging (SSL) Association is an organization that attempts to ensure tourists receive great value and high-quality accommodations at member properties. Members include small motels, inns, and bed and breakfasts. This organization helps members by associating with Convention and Visitors Bureaus, Chambers of Commerce, and Tourism Destination Organizations. Motels and motor inns have improved their operations, improved their relationships with customers, and become more effective in competing with other hotels and inns.

JUDGMENT CALL

Guests at the Embassy Suites Hotel in Secaucus, New Jersey probably think the copy of *USA Today* left at their door is complimentary. But if they squint at the fine print on their registration forms, they'll find that the hotel is charging them 25 cents a day for their "free" paper. *USA Today* sells loads of discounted bulk rate newspapers to hotels, airlines, and restaurants—an average of 409,980 daily. The hundreds of thousands of people who receive the newspaper free allow *USA Today* to call itself "first in daily readers," though not in paid subscriptions. Hotel guests are often too busy to realize that they are buying a newspaper that they think the hotel is providing for free.

THINK CRITICALLY
1. Do you think it is ethical for hotels to put newspapers at guests' doors and then charge for them? Why or why not?
2. What other hidden costs are a result of increased amenities?

CONFIRMATION

Explain the difference between motels and motor inns.

LIMITED-SERVICE FACILITIES

Rising full-service hotel rates have caused planners to look for meeting sites and lodging that are easy on the budget. Growing numbers of **limited-service properties** provide primarily sleeping rooms without expensive amenities such as food service. **Extended-stay facilities** are limited-service properties offering residential-style units with multi-room plans and kitchen facilities to attract business travelers or those relocating.

Summerfield Suites, AmeriSuites, and Residence Inns by Marriott are examples of limited-service, extended-stay properties serving the meeting market. Training that may last weeks is now often booked at limited-service hotels near major airports. Meeting rooms vary from a small bedroom to a room with a 50-person capacity. Meeting space at limited-service hotels can be as large as 1,250 square feet, and is comparatively inexpensive or may be complimentary. Full-service hotels usually charge between $5 and $10 per square foot for meetings. Limited-service hotels charge flat rates of $50 to $150 for day meetings, frequently including morning and afternoon coffee and soda breaks. Rates go lower when groups book sleeping rooms.

Many limited-service properties offer suites with two bedrooms and two bathrooms. Most business travelers do not like to share one-bedroom rooms. Executives, who realize that most business travelers do not like to share rooms, can give trainees their own bedrooms and baths for $20 less per night than at a full-service hotel.

ECONOMY LODGING IN TRANSITION

The economy segment of the lodging industry faces constant change. Goals for success include a good price/value ratio and guest satisfaction. Added amenities and services result in rising room rates, and the pressure to add amenities is strong. Rates cannot exceed guests' perception of the hotel's value, however, for the business to stay competitive. Major economy hotel chains attempt sophisticated marketing efforts. Consumers remember the "We'll leave the light on for you" tag line that Motel 6 uses. Several chains have automated reservations system interfaces to appeal to travel agents. The bottom line for economy lodging is to offer a lot for a little. Budget Host has more than 180 inns with 7,300 guest rooms located in 37 states and Canada. Amenities offered by Budget Host include king- and queen-size beds, cable television and movie channels, complimentary coffee, microwaves, refrigerators, free continental breakfast, swimming pool, picnic area, suites, at-door and truck parking, and connecting rooms.

CONFIRMATION

What are limited-service hotels? Cite examples of creative marketing used by a limited-service hotel.

UNDERSTAND MARKETING CONCEPTS

Circle the best answer for each of the following questions.

1. Limited-service facilities
   a. cannot compete with full-service hotels for meeting facilities
   b. are rarely able to employ a sufficient number of workers
   c. are often the site of extended stays
   d. are the oldest form of lodging in the United States

2. Dramatically upgraded services and amenities
   a. are available only in full-service hotels
   b. usually indicate an older lodging facility
   c. are a growing trend in all forms of the hospitality industry
   d. rarely return the investment made on them

THINK CRITICALLY

Answer the following questions as completely as possible. If necessary, use a separate sheet of paper.

3. **Communication** Categories of hospitality markets are harder to define than they once were. Why is distinguishing among hotels, motels, and motor inns more difficult than it might have been twenty years ago?

_____

_____

_____

_____

_____

_____

4. **Technology** Use the Internet to review web sites of major hotels, motels, and motor inns in your area. Which web sites do the most effective job of marketing their facilities? Why?

_____

_____

_____

_____

_____

BED AND BREAKFASTS

CHAPTER 2

LESSON 2.2

GOALS

Define the concept of a bed and breakfast.

Explain how bed and breakfasts differ from other types of lodging.

CHECK IN

Remember the last time you took a vacation? Did you return home from your vacation more tired than when you left?

Would you want to be served home-cooked meals or breakfast in bed? A bed and breakfast (B & B) may provide the quiet, restful escape that you seek.

Work with a partner. Discuss what you think would be positive qualities of a stay at a B & B. Also discuss things that some people might not enjoy about staying at a B & B.

TYPES OF BED AND BREAKFASTS

Bed and breakfasts (B & Bs) are lodging facilities that include breakfast in the cost of the room. This concept is common in the United Kingdom and is gaining popularity in the United States. In Europe it is common to rent a room in a single-family household. B & Bs evolved from this concept of renting sleeping rooms in a home with shared common space (living room, dining room, family room, and so forth). Sometimes, bathrooms are shared by several guest rooms. B & Bs began to appear in the United States in the late 1960s. There are now more than 20,000 B & Bs, an increase of 18,000 since 1979. The industry shows an increasing average number of rooms per property, growing occupancy rates, and an increasing number of support services.

There are a wide variety of B & B accommodations available.

B & B homestays are private, owner-occupied residences with up to five guest rooms available to visitors. Breakfast is often the only meal served and is included in the charge for the room.

B & B inns are commercially licensed businesses operated in a building that primarily provides overnight accommodations though the owner may live on the premises. The number of guest rooms for a B & B inn ranges from a minimum of four to a maximum of 25. Breakfast may be the only meal served, or other meals may be available.

Country inns are commercially licensed businesses primarily known for cuisine, usually away from commercial areas. Country inns offer overnight accommodations and a full-service breakfast and dinner to overnight guests and/or the public. The number of guest rooms ranges from a minimum of four to a maximum of 20.

CONFIRMATION

How do B & Bs differ from hotels or motor inns?

_____

_____

APPEAL OF A BED AND BREAKFAST

PRODUCT/ SERVICE MANAGEMENT

Key to the success of B & Bs is that they offer an experience different from that of other lodging. B & Bs appeal to weary travelers who desire personal service from consistent innkeepers as opposed to an anonymous front desk staff. B & B guests often seek a relaxing, private experience different from stays of most corporate travel. Repeat guests sometimes become part of the innkeeper's life. Successful innkeepers learn about travelers' families, their birthdays, and even their food preferences.

BED AND BREAKFASTS AND BUSINESS TRAVELERS

More and more business travelers are seeking out B & Bs as an alternative to the anonymity and sameness of hotels and motels. Corporate guests are sometimes hesitant about staying in an inn, but discover that accommodations are often better than at a hotel and provide the comfort of home. A recent survey of innkeepers and B & B owners indicates that business travelers account for about half of their annual overnight stays. Corporate travelers account for a great portion of repeat business at inns that meet their expectations.

As with other parts of the lodging industry, the key to success is increasing amenities. Private baths are a necessity. Innkeeper Jeff Archuleta, who runs Napoleon's Retreat Bed and Breakfast in St. Louis, says that business travelers won't even consider sharing a bath. Private baths, flexible cancellation policies to accommodate last-minute changes in travel plans, flexible check-in/out times to accommodate flight schedules, private key access so guests can come and go as they please, and policies prohibiting children and pets are key features for attracting business travelers. Other services and amenities desired by business travelers include firm mattresses, desks, private telephones, exercise equipment, dataports, fax machines, and copy machines. Privacy is one of the most important services an innkeeper can offer business guests.

TIME OUT

A successful innkeeper…
1. Is a people person
2. Is healthy, disciplined, aware of and respectful of personal limitations and needs
3. Is attentive to detail
4. Is hardworking
5. Is self-motivated
6. Is a leader in the community
7. Is a motivator who can share a vision with others

CONFIRMATION

Why are more business travelers opting to stay at B & Bs?

_____

_____

UNDERSTAND MARKETING CONCEPTS

Circle the best answer for each of the following questions.

1. The idea of bed and breakfast inns
   a. originated in the American South
   b. was a response to the sameness of corporate travel
   c. evolved from European traditions
   d. was one of Conrad Hilton's early successes

2. B & Bs typically offer
   a. all the facilities of a full-service hotel
   b. privacy, personal service, and atmosphere
   c. dataports, exercise equipment, and fine dining
   d. easy access to major means of transportation

THINK CRITICALLY

Answer the following questions as completely as possible. If necessary, use a separate sheet of paper.

3. **Technology** B & Bs have made good use of the Internet as a marketing tool. Find and share web pages that you think are especially appealing to potential customers. What makes the sites effective?

   _____

   _____

   _____

   _____

   _____

   _____

4. **Communication** If you were opening a B & B, what would be the basis of its appeal? Write text for a brochure for a B & B that you might plan.

   _____

   _____

   _____

   _____

   _____

CONFERENCE CENTERS AND RESORTS

CHAPTER 2

LESSON 2.3

CHECK IN

Think of yourself for a moment as the attendee of a business convention—not the planner. You will attend your meetings, of course, and you'll want that to be accomplished as easily as possible. What other things do you want to see and do or learn about in the city you are visiting?

With a partner or in a group, make a list of the things about a meeting site that make it attractive. Now consider your list from the point of view of a meeting planner. How can you find the best sites for the most reasonable price?

GOALS

Define a conference center.

Explain the main principle of resort lodging.

CONFERENCE CENTERS

A **conference center** is a large meeting venue surrounded by enough hotels to accommodate multiple conventions or conferences simultaneously. Every year, growing cities with good airport hubs discuss the possibility of building convention or conference centers. City leaders realize the revenue potential from a successful conference center. There must be a large number of hotel rooms close to the convention center, efficient public transportation, a wide array of restaurants to accommodate guests, and additional tourist attractions.

The elegant, award-winning Orange County Convention Center in Orlando, Florida will grow to 2.1 million square feet of exhibit space by 2003. This amount of space will accommodate large shows and smaller conferences at the same time. Orlando has plans to add 23,000 additional hotel rooms, increasing the inventory to 99,000 rooms. The prestigious Peabody Orlando will build a 1,000-room, 42-story tower linked to the Convention Center. Universal Orlando will develop hotels, a golf course, and a theme park on 2,000 acres of land.

Transportation, dining, and recreation are important features for a successful conference center. Orlando's International Airport will accommodate 70 million passengers annually by 2003. Nearly 400 restaurants in Orlando provide conference attendees with numerous dining choices. Outlet malls and an upscale Millennium Mall scheduled to open in 2004 add to Orlando's convention-center amenities.

Cleveland, Ohio may seem a less-likely place for a conference center when compared to Orlando, Florida, but the Cleveland Convention Center advertises 20,000 hotel rooms in the greater Cleveland area with 3,200 rooms downtown. The city has a good array of attractions from professional sports to art museums. Rapidly growing Indianapolis has hotels, restaurants, shopping centers, professional sports, and a major airport to meet the needs of most conventions. Indianapolis and Cleveland may not sound as glamorous as Orlando, but both of these cities have what convention centers need to succeed: accessible locations, transportation, hotel rooms, meeting-room space, and community attractions to accommodate a wide array of conferences.

CONFIRMATION

Why do city governments often work to create conference centers?

_____

_____

RESORTS

Resorts are hotels or motels located in popular vacation areas that offer recreational activities related to or in addition to attractions in the area. The resort may provide golf, horseback riding, tennis, skiing, tours, social activities, unique dining, or day trips. Resorts offer deluxe rooms with a wide range of prices. Rooms with a scenic view and more space command higher prices.

Dude ranches, ski resorts, casino hotels, and health resorts are examples of specialized resorts. Resorts may be chains or individually owned. Some resorts are open only "in season," but many resorts are open year-round with indoor pools and big-name entertainment. Resorts offer package deals that vary in price at different times of the year. Warm resort

areas cost more from November through March. Ski resorts charge their highest rates during the winter season. The best rates are offered by resorts during off-peak season (slow business times during the year). Major airlines may work with resorts to offer travelers package deals that include the price of the flight and the hotel.

The growing senior population has changed the focus of some resorts. Branson, Missouri has become a popular resort for senior citizens to visit. Places like Phoenix, Arizona and Georgetown, Texas offer attractive accommodations for senior citizens. Bingo, craft classes, light exercise sessions, and other social activities make resorts fun meeting places for seniors. As Baby Boomers age, they too will affect the nature of resort accommodations.

Condominiums (condos), when considered as a part of the lodging industry, are living quarters owned by private persons that are rented out to the public most of the year. Most condos are apartments in high-rise buildings located at beaches or other recreational areas. Owners consider condos to be good investment properties.

Timeshares involve buying a specific time period (one or two weeks) to spend at a vacation resort. The price of the timeshare depends on the time of the year chosen. February would be a popular season in a warm resort area such as Cancun, Mexico. Timeshare owners can swap dates or property with other timeshare owners.

PUTTING YOURSELF IN THE SHOES OF THE GUEST

Resort and conference-center marketing is a lot more than selling rooms. The central theme is to provide a great guest experience. Guests don't buy a place to stay. They buy the expectation of a great experience. Successful marketers see their property through the eyes of the guests. They try to learn from guests what they really value in a resort or conference center in order to provide great experiences.

THE DISNEYLAND RESORT

Probably no organization has been more successful at marketing dreams and images than Disney. Disneyland Park was the first theme park of the Disney empire, opening in 1955. Today Disneyland is an evolving 85-acre experience featuring more than 60 attractions. The 990-room Disneyland Hotel, with a tropical sandy beach and fine restaurants and lounges, has 120,000 square feet of convention and meeting space. The new Disney's California Adventure Park was designed by Walt Disney Imagineering in the tradition of classic Disney to capture the beauty of California on 55 acres of attractions. Disney's Grand Californian Hotel is a luxurious 750-room hotel located within Disney's California Adventure. Downtown Disney District is a public esplanade of theme dining, shopping, and family-oriented entertainment, located centrally between the Disneyland Resort theme parks and hotels.

Combined with Florida's Walt Disney World, which includes the Magic Kingdom theme park, the Epcot Center, Disney's Animal Kingdom, and Disney-MGM Studios, Disney Enterprises continues to be a giant in the resort industry, and continues to expand with conference business, a cruise line, and interests in many other businesses.

CONFIRMATION

How does a resort differ from a typical hotel?

_____

_____

Resort development doesn't have to go hand in hand with destruction of the environment. Harmony Resort, St. John, U.S. Virgin Islands has been cited as a sustainable energy success story by the U.S. Department of Energy. Developer Stanley Selengut used recycled materials for construction and minimized damage during building. The resort uses only renewable energy sources, while minimizing water use and waste production.

UNDERSTAND MARKETING CONCEPTS

Circle the best answer for each of the following questions.

1. A conference center is a
   a. deluxe hotel or motor inn with meeting space
   b. government-financed meeting and entertainment site
   c. lodging and meeting venue dependent upon climate
   d. complex of meeting sites, lodging, and other attractions

2. The key theme of resort marketing is
   a. marketing the experience more than the space
   b. taking advantage of off-peak rates
   c. effective use of timeshares
   d. presenting an economical package

THINK CRITICALLY

Answer the following questions as completely as possible. If necessary, use a separate sheet of paper.

3. **Communication**   Many cities have discussed the extent to which tax dollars should go toward conference center development. What is your opinion? Should taxpayers fund or partially fund developments that benefit private enterprise?

_____

_____

_____

_____

_____

_____

4. **Technology**   Visit the Disney web site and examine its many attractions and options for travelers. In your opinion, why is Disney so successful in so many hospitality venues?

_____

_____

_____

_____

RESTAURANTS

CHAPTER 2

LESSON 2.4

CHECK IN

Eating out has become one of the most popular social activities in the United States and around the world. Consumers have different expectations for different types of restaurants; however, they expect good food at a fair price from all restaurant establishments they visit.

The economic impact of the restaurant business is enormous. Americans are eating fewer and fewer meals at home, a trend that is likely to continue. Competition is fierce for those dollars.

Work with a group. Brainstorm a list of local restaurants—anything goes, from the hamburger joint to the top of the tower. Then, to help you think more about the food-service industry, attempt to divide your list into various groups. Into what category would you put each restaurant, and why?

GOALS

Differentiate among different types of restaurants.

Identify reasons for the growth of restaurant sales.

DINING OUT

Competition among restaurants gives consumers endless choices for dining. Thousands of restaurants open and close every year. Some of the restaurants are part of well-recognized chains while others are independent operations. Keys to successful restaurants include good food, appropriate prices, strong marketing, and sound public relations.

Dining out has become big business seven days a week. Busy working families find it easier to dine out or have food delivered. Look up restaurants in the yellow pages of the telephone book, and you find a long list of possibilities. No matter what type of restaurant consumers choose, they expect good quality food for the price and excellent customer service. Dining options range from reasonably priced fast food to expensive meals served at full-service restaurants. Higher prices increase customer expectations for the dining experience.

The National Restaurant Association defines three primary types of restaurants. *Table service, quick service,* and *on-site food service* make up the organization's membership. Within these larger groups lies an almost endless variety of menus and prices.

TABLE-SERVICE RESTAURANTS

DISTRIBUTION

Table-service restaurants, as the name implies, are those that serve customers personally at the table. Beyond that large distinction, there are many types of table-service operations.

Fine dining, or white-tablecloth service, provides the highest levels of personal service and more choice of rare food and beverages in a formal or sophisticated setting. The most exclusive restaurants almost always require reservations (if they can be had at all), and may be noted for a particular chef, a unique location, or a long tradition of fine service. Prices for fine dining are usually high, and consumers expect the best—whether the atmosphere is formal or trendy.

Casual dining offers a less-expensive alternative to fine dining, a friendly atmosphere, and more moderate prices. In the last twenty years, national chains such as T.G.I.Friday's, Applebees, and Chili's have established themselves as national leaders, but smaller chains and local establishments attract customers in similar ways. Informal decor, a casual ambience, and a familiar and appealing menu encourage repeat business. These restaurants become regular stops for many people. Casual dining establishments may lack the exhaustive wine list available at a fine dining restaurant, but many beverages are available at reasonable prices. Although there are less expensive restaurants, casual dining places remain popular by selling the sociable mood as much as their menus.

Theme restaurants are a form of casual dining that have also seen the growth of national chains. Many local theme restaurants exist based on such themes as medieval times, old-fashioned parlors, or perhaps most commonly, sports. National chains have brought the consistency of offerings to theme restaurants as well as a distinct experience. Many casual dining restaurants could easily be considered theme restaurants as well.

Ethnic restaurants offer an even more distinct experience, depending upon particular national or regional cuisine to draw diners. Although ethnic restaurants vary as widely as the cultures they represent, in this area, too, national chains have begun standardizing fare. Don Pablo's markets Mexican flavors to a wide audience, and Olive Garden attempts to convey an authentic Italian sense to its food. Restaurant critics might quibble whether these chains offer genuine ethnic food, but they bring a wider variety of tastes to the American palate than were previously available. Prices for most ethnic restaurants, including the national chains, vary as well, but most fall within the same range as casual dining. With changes in population characteristics, many experts predict growth in this field.

MARKETING MYTHS

Have you ever wondered why so many restaurants keep refilling your soda, tea, or coffee for no extra charge? Do you think that the restaurants are losing a lot of money by pouring so many free drinks? Restaurants make their highest percentage of return from beverage sales. A soda that costs the customer $2.00 actually costs the restaurant only 3 or 4 cents. A lot of refills can be poured, and the restaurant still makes a handsome profit.

THINK CRITICALLY

1. If you ran a fast-food restaurant, would you let the patrons refill their own beverages, or would you be in charge of refills? Why?

2. Why does it cost a restaurant so little for the beverages it serves to customers?

Family restaurants, such as Bob Evans or Denny's, offer even more moderate prices and cater to the entire family. Although casual dining establishments usually accept children, family restaurants depend heavily upon those customers who bring young children with them. Alcohol is usually not sold, and breakfast, lunch, and dinner menus are standard. Many locally owned family restaurants have wonderful reputations.

Other types of restaurants exist as well. *Cafeterias* were a once-popular type of restaurant that still do well in some areas. *Buffets* offer a similar type of service, sometimes with a single price for each diner. *Grills* and *diners* cater to the same customers as family restaurants, competing as well in speed of service with fast-food places. In all cases, categories are not hard and fast and there is considerable overlap, and even room for debate. Is Chi-Chi's a casual place, a theme establishment, or an ethnic restaurant?

CONFIRMATION

What types of restaurants make up the table-service category?

QUICK-SERVICE RESTAURANTS

Despite the many types of table-service restaurants, quick-service sales dominate the food-service industry. Fast food is the largest market in the world for restaurant food. Fast food, as we know it today, grew out of old traditions of single-serving vendors and increasing industrialization of food-service operations. Rapid serving times, appealing products, and reliable quality control throughout the world account for the success of fast-food operations. Although there are local places and small chains, the famous international corporations rule the industry. McDonald's is the largest restaurant chain in the world, with more than 24,000 restaurants. Next in sales in the fast-food list is Burger King, followed by Pizza Hut, KFC, Wendy's, and Taco Bell. Tricon, Inc., owns Pizza Hut, Taco Bell, and KFC, but its combined sales still are less than McDonald's.

PROMOTION

The quick-service industry is fiercely competitive, and battles for the convenience-oriented consumer take many forms. New menu items, special pricing promotions, toys for children, and immense advertising campaigns are techniques the fast-food giants use to compete for the huge market. Almost everyone can recite the slogans or even sing a jingle. Still, as fast-food restaurants approach the saturation point in American society, growth in fast food is declining in the United States. The overseas demand continues to grow.

The competition for fast-food dollars is not confined to the United States. According to ChinaOnline.com, the battle for fast-food supremacy in China is between KFC and McDonald's. Although the golden arches are familiar, KFC markets a product more similar to traditional Chinese tastes. McDonald's has added spicy chicken wings to its menu to capitalize on those traditions. KFC ads claim McDonald's is copying them. McDonald's denies the claim.

ON-SITE FOOD SERVICE

An often overlooked area of the restaurant industry is on-site food service. *On-site food service* are those food services in business and industry that include institutional, educational, and corporate food services and may include hotel restaurants as well. Although these are not usually thought of as part of the hospitality industry, many of the same principles for planning and operation apply.

CONFIRMATION

What are the main reasons for the huge size of the fast-food market?

_____

_____

CAREER SPOTLIGHT

VAL AND ZENA WEILER

In 1957 Val and Zena Weiler operated the Campus Fruit Market near the University of Nebraska. It was clear that their business would soon be eclipsed by large supermarkets springing up in Lincoln. Armed with three dozen pizza pans, a recipe that had been in Mrs. Weiler's family for years, and a lot of anxiety, they opened a pizza business called Valentino's.

They took in $60 their first day, and as the restaurant's reputation grew, patrons began to gather and watch through the window as pizzas were made. They would stand in line for an hour or more to sample the Italian specialties created in the original restaurant.

Today, Valentino's has expanded to 44 company-owned and franchised restaurant locations in six states. The recipes and meticulous preparation steps remain unchanged. Valentino's success began with those wonderful family recipes, but there is more than food to the story. The highest quality food, reasonable prices, immaculately clean and comfortable restaurants, and genuinely friendly service led to success.

THINK CRITICALLY

1. What led to the success of Valentino's restaurants?
2. How much competition would you face with this type of franchise business? What marketing techniques could you use to stay ahead of your competitors?

UNDERSTAND MARKETING CONCEPTS

Circle the best answer for each of the following questions.

1. The two main divisions of the restaurant industry are
   a. fine dining and fast food
   b. casual dining and ethnic restaurants
   c. table-service and quick-service
   d. on-site and off-site dining

2. The fast-food business
   a. is a purely American phenomenon
   b. continues to grow at an increasing rate in the U.S.
   c. holds the largest market share of the restaurant industry
   d. avoids innovation in marketing

THINK CRITICALLY

Answer the following questions as completely as possible. If necessary, use a separate sheet of paper.

3. **Marketing Math** In a recent year, McDonald's had sales of $36 billion. What is the average sales per restaurant, then, for McDonald's approximately 24,000 units? What is the average sales per day of each restaurant, calculating with a 365-day sales year?

_____

_____

_____

_____

_____

4. **Research** Find a local restaurant for each of the table-service categories in this lesson. For each, write a very brief description and indicate a price range for entrees.

_____

_____

_____

_____

_____

CHAPTER 2
LESSON 2.5

TOURISM

Explain the ripple effect of tourist dollars.

Identify factors that encourage international tourism.

CHECK IN

Tourism is a big revenue generator for cities, counties, and states. The hospitality industry is booming because everyone wants part of the revenue. Hotels and motels, restaurants, and other shops all benefit from the wanderlust of travelers. Tourism provides jobs.

Miami, San Diego, Galveston, Las Vegas, and Washington D.C. are often associated with the tourism industry. The warm states of California and Florida lure tourists to sandy beaches and year-round amusement parks. Revenue also comes from residents within a state. County and state fairs, amateur athletic events, local celebrations, and concerts are part of the tourism industry, too.

Work with a partner. List recreational trips you've taken in the last five years. Include short jaunts and "road trips" as well as large vacations. Considering all trips, have you spent a greater sum on short trips or on distant vacations?

THE IMPORTANCE OF TOURISM

PROMOTION

Tourism is big business for most states, and sizable amounts of money are spent on advertising campaigns to increase tourism. States pay large sums of money to produce creative promotions aimed at increasing tourism. Web sites, television commercials, brochures, bumper stickers, colorful publications, and coffee mugs are just a few of the publicity items that states have designed to attract tourism. Themes such as "Wake Up to Missouri" or "Tennessee Sounds Good to Me" are now featured in television commercials. Development of a 30-second commercial can easily cost $10,000 or more. Each time the state commercial is shown on television it costs between $100,000 and $1 million, but it's money well spent.

Most people associate sandy beaches or ski slopes with tourism. Florida, California, Colorado, and Texas are frequent vacation spots for spring breaks and family vacations. Increasingly, however, states one might not think of as vacation destinations seek tourist dollars. Many northern states without ski resorts spend their advertising budgets from March through September, realizing that many families take summer vacations. Cities like Ames, Iowa have attracted popular country music festivals. Iowa State's football stadium sells out for the popular music festival and the economy benefits from tourism. Hotels fill with out-of-town guests, and restaurants pump up their volume of business.

Thousands of travelers pass through Nebraska each year and few of them stop as they speed through to South Dakota's Black Hills or Colorado's Rocky Mountains. Nebraska State Senator Roger Wehrbein wants Nebraska to be a destination. He has proposed a bill to annually set aside $1.5 million in general funds for developing Nebraska's tourism industry. Attractions like the Henry Doorly Zoo in Omaha, the Great Platte River Road Archway Monument, Nebraskaland Days, and the Burwell Rodeo could all become more popular tourist attractions with a little extra money for advertising. Iowa, Nebraska's main competitor in the tourism industry, spends $17 million annually on tourism development while Nebraska spends just $2.7 million. Developing the state's tourism industry would lead to new jobs and increased revenue for the state in urban and rural areas.

This example from Nebraska demonstrates the value of tourism to local economies. Multiply that by the fifty states vying for the tourist dollar, and you begin to see the economic impact. Not only are tourist dollars essential for the hospitality industry, there is a ripple effect, as advertising jobs, media development, and travel businesses from airlines to gas stations also depend on the motion of visitors from one place to another.

TOUR & TRAVEL PACKAGES

A **travel package** is a prearranged vacation. Some packages include basic travel services (transportation, accommodations), while others may include a complete travel plan (meals, sightseeing, transfers, and so forth). Usually these packages are assembled by independent tour operators and are sold through travel agents.

Purchasing a travel package has the advantage of convenience and value. A vast array of travel packages can cause confusion, so it is extremely important to read the fine print in advertisements and contracts. All extra charges should be clearly and conspicuously disclosed. It is also important to research tour operators to determine if they are reliable. Recommendations from friends and relatives can provide assurance. The Better Business Bureau may also provide valuable information.

TIME OUT

More Big Red means more green in Lincoln, Nebraska. Mark Essman, director of the Lincoln-Lancaster County Convention and Visitors Bureau, reports that a University of Nebraska home football game gives Lincoln merchants "a captive market of 78,000 people." Essman estimates that football visitors spend $125 to $150 per person each day in Lincoln supporting their beloved Cornhuskers—and the economy of Lincoln as well.

CONFIRMATION

How does tourism benefit state economies?

_____

_____

INTERNATIONAL TOURISM

A strong global economy in 2000 and special events to celebrate the new millennium resulted in a 7.4% increase in world tourism. This growth doubled the increase of 1999. International trips increased by 50 million in 2000. This is the same number of new tourists that major countries such as Spain or the United States receive in the entire year. The

World Tourism Organization (WTO) estimated a record 698 million international travelers in 2000. Receipts from international tourism totaled $476 billion. All regions of the world hosted more tourists in 2000. The fastest-growing regions included East Asia and the Pacific.

The strong dollar and weak European currency attracted record numbers of American tourists to Europe, with Germany and Switzerland enjoying their best results in years. The Middle East was on a fast track of increased tourism before renewed violence cut the flow of tourists to the region.

International tourism goes two ways, of course. Even with a strong dollar, the United States attracted millions of additional international tourists and achieved an 8.7% growth rate. Economic slowdown in the United States and other key locations throughout the world reduces international tourism.

CONFIRMATION

What explains the recent growth in worldwide tourism?

_____

UNDERSTAND MARKETING CONCEPTS
Circle the best answer for each of the following questions.

1. Travel packages include
   a. sightseeing
   b. transportation
   c. accomodations
   d. all of the above

2. International tourism is growing because
   a. passports are easier to get than ever
   b. airline fares continue to drop
   c. Americans have more leisure time
   d. the world economy has been strong

THINK CRITICALLY
Answer the following questions as completely as possible. If necessary, use a separate sheet of paper.

3. **Communication**   How do political events affect tourism? Give both domestic and international examples.

_____

_____

_____

_____

_____

_____

4. **Geography**   Why do you think California attracts more visitors than any other state? Suggest ways states like Oklahoma or Mississippi could attract more visitors.

_____

_____

_____

_____

_____

CHAPTER 2 REVIEW

REVIEW MARKETING CONCEPTS

Write the letter of the term that matches each definition. Some terms will not be used.

____ **1.** Offer residential-style units with multi-room plans and kitchen facilities

____ **2.** A prearranged vacation

____ **3.** Facility with primary features of privacy and personal service

____ **4.** Properties that provide a range of services, usually including a restaurant on the premises, luggage assistance, and room service

____ **5.** Living quarters owned by private persons that are rented out to the public most of the year

____ **6.** Most common lodging facilities found in the United States

____ **7.** Buying a specific time period to spend at a vacation resort

a. bed and breakfast
b. condominium
c. conference center
d. extended-stay facility
e. full-service hotel
f. hotel
g. limited-service property
h. motel
i. motor inn
j. resort
k. timeshare
l. travel package

Circle the best answer.

8. Airport hotels
  a. have reputations for being dowdy with poor services
  b. are spending thousands of dollars to change their image
  c. are becoming more luxurious
  d. all of the above

9. Motels
  a. were first started by farmers along busy highways
  b. usually have more than one story
  c. have parking near the guest's room
  d. A and C

10. A successful conference center must have all of the following except
  a. ample number of hotel rooms
  b. good variety of restaurants
  c. low hotel room rates
  d. good airports

THINK CRITICALLY

11. Spend time with another student to develop a Top Ten List of characteristics possessed by successful restaurants.

_____

_____

_____

_____

_____

_____

12. You have been hired by a struggling full-service hotel to update its amenities in order to attract more guests. Make a list of five solid suggestions to update the hotel in order for it to survive in a competitive marketplace. Don't forget to consider cost.

_____

_____

_____

_____

_____

_____

13. Explain how technology is changing the travel and tourism industry.

_____

_____

_____

_____

_____

_____

CHAPTER 2 REVIEW

MAKE CONNECTIONS

14. Marketing Math   You are in charge of organizing your marketing employer/employee appreciation banquet. You have decided that the Italian buffet best meets the needs of all people attending the banquet. Each meal costs $18 plus 21% for tax and gratuity. How much will each meal cost? What will the banquet cost for 120 attendees?

_____

_____

_____

_____

_____

_____

15. Communication   You are in charge of special tours for the Heritage Club. This group consists of people aged 55 and older who take tours as a group. Use the Internet to find out information about Branson, Missouri. Describe a tour package to Branson, Missouri that you will offer the Heritage Club. Make sure to include information about travel, hotel accommodations, entertainment, meals, and cost.

_____

_____

_____

_____

_____

16. Technology   Lesson 2.1 described technological advancements that hotels are adding to attract customers. Now it is time for you to predict travel and tourism technology for 2050. Don't forget about virtual trips and Internet connections.

_____

_____

_____

_____

_____

_____

http://www.deca.org
/publications/HS_
Guide/guidetoc.html

FULL-SERVICE RESTAURANT MANAGEMENT ROLE PLAY

You are the manager at a popular full-service restaurant. Your restaurant has always taken pride in serving the freshest seafood with the friendliest service. Mother's Day is always a busy time for your restaurant. Accurate reservations are essential for a good business day. A new employee, who did not fully understand the reservations system, overbooked the dinner reservations. Customers with reservations are shocked to learn that they will not be seated until 20 to 45 minutes later than their reserved time. The waiting area in the restaurant is filled with unhappy loyal customers. Some of the customers are leaving angry and vowing to tell their friends about the bad experience. What will you do to cool down this bad situation? What new procedures will you implement to make sure this situation does not occur again? You do not want to lose loyal customers. This role play involves satisfying a frustrated customer.

PROJECT EXTENDED STAY

You are the marketing manager for a new restaurant in a city with a major convention center. Your restaurant serves fine seafood and steaks. Prices charged by your restaurant are high since you offer only the freshest seafood and the best service. Your restaurant has a dress code that requires business attire.

Work with a group and complete the following activities.

1. Design a menu that represents the entrees and prices for your elite restaurant. (Do research to establish prices.)

2. Create a news release for the newspaper that highlights the fine food and service of your restaurant. You may want to highlight the high caliber of your chefs and servers.

3. Create a color advertisement for the local travel magazine that is placed in all hotel rooms of the city where your restaurant is located.

4. Your restaurant also caters events at the major hotels near the convention center. Determine what meals you will make available for catering, prices you will charge for the meals, and special services you will offer for the catered event. Give reasons for each of your decisions.

5. Your restaurant has been losing business to competitors who offer a wider variety of menu items with a price range from $8 to $20. You have been called upon to create a marketing strategy and restaurant update to meet the challenges of the competition. Explain five changes that you propose for the restaurant. Make sure to defend each of your ideas.

CHAPTER 3

KEY PLAYERS IN HOSPITALITY OPERATIONS

LESSONS

3.1 HUMAN RESOURCES DEPARTMENT

3.2 FRONT-OF-THE-HOUSE OPERATIONS

3.3 BACK-OF-THE-HOUSE OPERATIONS

3.4 DIVERSITY ISSUES IN THE HOSPITALITY INDUSTRY

WINNING STRATEGIES

ALAIN DUCASSE

Alain Ducasse, the only chef in the world to hold an eight-star rating, owns restaurants in France, Great Britain, and Monaco. When he decided to open a restaurant in the United States, he chose to locate his new venture in the Essex House, a luxury hotel in New York City, located near Central Park. The restaurant, Alain Ducasse New York (ADNY), opened in June 2000.

The renovation of the hotel to accommodate the new restaurant cost more than $2 million. The size of the kitchen was doubled to make room for the 3,000-pound, induction-cooking electric stove imported from France. The dining room was also redesigned with a window from the dining room to the kitchen to allow guests to watch their food being prepared.

No restaurant that serves more than eight guests would be able to provide food personally prepared by its famous chef, so Ducasse brought in 15 staff members as well as Didier Elena, a 12-year Ducasse Paris veteran, as chef. Ducasse has spent some time in the restaurant, but believes his staff understands the nature of his philosophy. The entire staff for the restaurant numbers 55.

ADNY opened to reviews generally critical of its excessive luxury and high prices, but that hasn't stopped the well-connected and well-to-do from filling all 65 of ADNY's seats. In French style, the table is booked for the entire evening. With appetizers costing as much as $50, entrees $80 and up, and a high-priced wine list, the tab for dinner for four may easily reach $1,000. Reservations are booked six months in advance.

THINK CRITICALLY

1. How can the Essex House benefit by having a world-renowned chef open a restaurant on its property that bears not the name of the hotel, but the name of the chef?
2. What is the appeal of a restaurant like ADNY?

CHAPTER 3
LESSON 3.1

HUMAN RESOURCES DEPARTMENT

GOALS

Describe basic responsibilities of the human resources department.

Identify types of employee compensation and recognition.

CHECK IN

The Cincinnati Marriott Northeast has created a guest-service program designed to treat each guest as if he or she were "part of the family and on a visit to your home." The program has 12 points by which employees pledge to abide.

Among the 12 points are establishing eye contact within 20 feet of a guest and escorting a guest to his or her destination instead of merely pointing it out. The guest-service program has increased occupancy and brought numerous awards and top ratings in guest satisfaction surveys to the hotel. Continual training and employee recognition programs reinforce the commitment of employees to the service pledge.

Work with a partner. Develop a 10-point program that lists ways for employees to make hotel guests feel welcome. Describe how you would implement the program.

HUMAN RESOURCES—THE PEOPLE FACTOR

Hospitality marketing is about people. Guests in a hotel, diners in a restaurant, or passengers on a cruise ship are the customers of the travel and tourism industry, but those who are employed in the industry are its lifeblood. Employees in a hotel or restaurant begin their tenure at the *human resources (HR) department*, and when they leave, it is their last stop. This department, however, does more than hire and fire. The **human resources (HR) department** is responsible for recruiting, inter-

viewing, hiring, training, development, compensation, benefits, supervision, employee evaluation, and separation. The size of the HR department usually depends on the number of employees who work for the company. There may be a *director of human resources* who oversees several departments, with each area being responsible for a specific aspect of human resources. In smaller companies, a *human resources specialist* may handle all or most of the department's activities.

HR RESPONSIBILITIES

Recruitment is essential to finding potential employees. With a labor shortage affecting the hotel industry, human resources departments must be creative in finding potential employees. Most hotels advertise in newspapers, but many also use the Internet, attend college job fairs, or have a job hotline.

There is more work to be done after an applicant is found. References are checked, interviews and placement tests are given, and sometimes drug testing is administered. After an applicant is hired, he or she attends *orientation* to learn the procedures, policies, and philosophies of the company. In addition, a new hire will also require specific *training* or instruction in basic skills that pertain to his or her department and job description. A mentor may be assigned to teach or assist the new employee individually as he or she learns the ropes. Time spent in orientation and training often sets the tone for an employee's entire tenure. This is the time when he or she begins to learn and implement the mission statement of the company, gets acquainted with fellow employees, becomes familiar with routine operating procedures, and learns written and unwritten rules. Professional development and on-the-job training to keep employees updated are important, as rapid changes in business often require employees to learn new technology or improve their customer-service skills. A good training program increases productivity, boosts morale, and creates loyalty to the company.

An increasing number of businesses require drug testing for prospective employees. Some professions long have required employees to consent to such tests, but the practice is growing in many industries.

Although few object to testing in cases in which public safety is a direct concern, such as an airline pilot or an operator of heavy equipment, some feel that widespread testing is an invasion of privacy. They argue that such issues are legal ones, not a company's concern. What business is it of the company's what a housekeeping employee does on his or her day off?

THINK CRITICALLY

1. Do you think drug testing of employees not responsible for public safety is an appropriate practice? Why or why not?

2. When is an employee's private life a legitimate concern of his or her employer?

CONFIRMATION

Name three responsibilities of a human resources department and explain the importance of each.

In an effort to maintain consistency throughout its properties and retain experienced employees, Four Seasons Hotels have "designated trainers" in each department to teach and coach new employees. The trainer is carefully selected based on ability, patience, and communication skills. The program has reduced labor costs and training time and has improved the quality of service in Four Seasons' properties.

SHOW ME THE MONEY

Perhaps the one aspect of human resources most immediately important to employees is **compensation**, which includes benefits as well as salary. It is the task of the HR department to ensure that every employee receives a fair and equitable *remuneration*, or payment for work. Compensation managers stay informed of salary rates within their industry. They compare their compensation amounts with competitors' rates. They may work with staff specialists to design employee incentive plans or reward systems. Sometimes they are directly involved with employee performance evaluations. They also manage employee benefits. *Employee benefits* include health insurance (such as major medical, dental, vision, and long-term disability) and retirement plans (including profit sharing, savings and thrift plans, and stock ownership). Many companies are adding other extras such as parental leave, child or elder care, flextime, and employee assistance and wellness programs.

Knowing that everyone wants to feel significant, successful managers work with the human resources team to implement *employee recognition programs*. Some of the rewards are tangible: inexpensive holiday-related gift baskets for each employee, free amusement park passes, movie or theater tickets, gift certificates, or complimentary meals or hotel accommodations.

Other rewards may not have a direct impact on the employee's wallet, but certainly have a positive effect on morale and thus employee productivity. Special employee award pins, congratulatory notes or articles featured in the hotel or restaurant publication, free English classes for employees who speak English as a second language, and plaques or trophies of recognition are all examples of ways that employees are rewarded and made to feel valued.

CONFIRMATION

Name examples of employee benefits.

_____

_____

UNDERSTAND MARKETING CONCEPTS
Circle the best answer for each of the following questions.

1. The responsibilities of the human resources department in a hotel include
   a. sales, job interviews, and special events
   b. employee benefits, accounting, and reservations
   c. remuneration, event planning, and maintenance
   d. recruiting, training, and employee compensation

2. Employee recognition
   a. requires training programs to implement
   b. is a way to build loyalty
   c. is a costly way to improve productivity
   d. is a form of remuneration

THINK CRITICALLY
Answer the following questions as completely as possible. If necessary, use a separate sheet of paper.

3. List two tangible and two intangible benefits that you have received from a job or a volunteer activity. Describe how these benefits might be included in the human resources activities of a hospitality management company.

_____

_____

_____

_____

_____

_____

4. Research   Interview four people about reward and recognition programs in their jobs. Describe what you learn about those programs.

_____

_____

_____

_____

_____

CHAPTER 3
LESSON 3.2

FRONT-OF-THE-HOUSE OPERATIONS

GOALS

Describe basic activities of front-of-the-house operations.

Identify employee positions in food and beverage outlets.

CHECK IN

Country Inns & Suites, midscale hotels owned by Carlson Hospitality, have developed a "co-branding" strategy with separate restaurants located next to, rather than in, the hotels. The hotels are often located next to a T.G.I.Friday's or Italiani's. Hotel guests can order room service from the restaurants or charge their restaurant meals to their rooms.

Occupancy and room rates are higher at Country Inns & Suites that are located next to the restaurants. In addition, the hotel can forgo the cost of building a restaurant in the hotel. The restaurants gain lunch and dinner business from the hotels, which provide up to 20 percent of their business. Customers get brand-name quality, and see the restaurant as an extra not offered by similar hotels.

Work with a partner. Create a list of other hotels and restaurants that might also benefit from this same co-branding strategy. Combine hotels and restaurants with similar economy levels.

IN FRONT!

Hotels and restaurants have both front-of-the-house and back-of-the house operations. Front-of-the-house operations include areas to which the general public has access, such as guest rooms, meeting rooms, public restrooms, gift shop, pool, and restaurants on the property. These areas are critical areas of hospitality management, for they are the ones with which customers have the most direct experiences.

THE FRONT DESK

SELLING

The front desk and lobby area are the first places most hotel guests see. Therefore, each employee is responsible for making a positive first impression.

Front desk agents are employees who register incoming guests, communicate with guests during their stay, and check guests out of the hotel. Agents must have good communication and organizational skills. A front desk agent needs to know check in and billing procedures thoroughly and must always be courteous and helpful.

The front desk agent determines if the guest has a **reservation** (an agreement that a hotel will hold a specific type of room for a certain day or length of time), or is a **walk-in** (a potential guest without a reservation). If the guest is not already in the hotel's guest database, he or she will need to complete a *registration card*, which asks for information such as the guest's full name, address, business, and payment method. A front desk agent may also inform the guest of the availability of a room with better accommodations or amenities, which is known as **upselling**.

Agents should be professional and friendly, addressing guests by name when appropriate, and informing them of special services and locations and times such services are available. Agents also introduce guests to bell attendants when present, or direct guests accurately and discreetly to their rooms.

The front desk agent is also responsible for accepting payment from the guest. When a guest is checking out, the same rules of etiquette apply. The front desk agent as well as the guest should review the account, called a *guest folio*, for accuracy. The **guest folio** is a summary of all fees charged to a room during a guest's stay. The desk agent then receives payment and provides a receipt. Many hotels offer express check out services either through an electronic system accessible through the guest's television monitor or a machine similar to an automated teller machine located in a central area.

CYBER MARKETING

In 2000, $6 billion worth of hotel business was booked online. In 2001, hoteliers expect to receive anywhere from $20 to $30 billion. Ninety percent of hotel companies have web sites. Almost all have detailed photos of the property, and most have maps. Yet, in 1999, only 39 percent allowed users to book a room online.

THINK CRITICALLY
1. Why you think such a small percentage of hotel web sites allowed online bookings in 1999?
2. Do you think more hotels will offer online bookings in the future?

CONFIRMATION

What does a front desk agent do?

_____

_____

FOOD AND BEVERAGE OUTLETS

The restaurant in a hotel is a major part of the front-of-the-house operations. Bringing celebrity chefs or specialty restaurants to a hotel property are two ways hotels are improving the image of hotel restaurants.

Food and beverage outlets provide guests products to eat and drink, and include restaurants, banquet and meeting rooms, coffee shops, cocktail lounges, pool-side snack bars, and even vending services. Food and

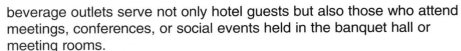

beverage outlets serve not only hotel guests but also those who attend meetings, conferences, or social events held in the banquet hall or meeting rooms.

Some hotels own and operate the restaurant on their property. Some have **licensing agreements**, which allow them to use a brand name and concept in exchange for a fee. Others lease space to independent food service providers who pay a rental or usage fee.

SERVERS

Employees in the front part of the restaurant have direct contact with and serve food to guests. Typical positions include the following.

Maitre d'hotel, from the French for "master," manages reservations, greets and seats guests, and handles complaints.

Cashier accepts payment from guests and balances the register by matching the register tape with the cash, check, credit cards, or direct billing receipts at the end of the shift.

Wait staff, or servers, are the main connection between the customer and the food production staff. They must have solid understanding of the food and beverage operations and standards, excellent interpersonal ability, good sales skills, and problem-solving abilities.

Bus staff assists waitpersons in serving food, refilling beverages. cleaning tables, and re-setting tables for the next customers.

TYPES OF MENUS

Different restaurants offer different types of menu services.

Short order menus feature items that can be prepared quickly and easily.

A la carte menus, from the French for "by the bill of fare," list and price items separately, and remain the same from day to day.

Table d'hôte menus, from the French for "table of the host," have fixed prices for meals normally consisting of appetizer, salad, soup, entrée, dessert, and beverage. This type of menu is used for banquets.

Menus du jour, from the French for "of the day," offer a different specialty each day.

TYPES OF SERVICE

Serving standards and procedures may vary from one hotel to another, but there are basic differences in certain styles of service.

American service places the food on the plate in the kitchen before it is brought to the table by the waitperson or server.

English service employs large serving dishes that remain on the table throughout the meal. A waitperson passes plates that have been filled by the host to the guests. This serving style is referred to as "family style" in the United States, but a waitperson is rarely used to pass the filled plates. Guests serve themselves, passing the serving dishes to the right.

French service is fairly elaborate, involving several waitpersons or table captains serving food from a chafing dish or rolling cart brought to the table.

Russian service has all food dished into the serving dishes in the kitchen and brought to the table and served by one waitperson. A busperson may deliver the food to the table, but the waitperson serves the food.

Banquet service is used for large events and is often a combination of any of these services.

CONFIRMATION

What is the difference between American service and English service?

_____

_____

_____

CAREER SPOTLIGHT

EMERIL LAGASSE

BAM!!!! With that exclamation, a giant dash of pepper, paprika, and other spices crash into the simmering liquid that is the next culinary masterpiece created by Emeril Lagasse. With his other signature proclamation, "Kick it up another notch!," Lagasse now hosts two popular TV shows, owns six successful restaurants, and is fast becoming one of the most popular chefs.

Lagasse began making bread and pastry in a neighborhood bakery in Fall River, Massachusetts. He chose culinary arts over music and worked in Paris and Lyon before returning to the United States to work in several fine restaurants in Philadelphia, Boston, and New York. Ella Brennan, a leader of the New Orleans cuisine scene, persuaded him to come to New Orleans to preside over the legendary restaurant, Commander's Palace.

From the time he opened his first self-named eatery, Emeril's Restaurant, he has been congratulated and praised by well-known food critics, culinary magazine writers, and national magazines such as _Esquire_, _Condé Nast Traveler_, and _Travel & Leisure_. Next came NOLA, which opened in New Orleans' French Quarter in 1992, and Emeril's New Orleans Fish House at the MGM Grand Hotel in Las Vegas in 1995, followed by the classic Delmonico's in New Orleans in 1998. In 1999, Emeril's Orlando at Universal Studios and Delmonico Steakhouse in Las Vegas were added to Lagasse's list of successes.

THINK CRITICALLY

Investigate three other celebrity chefs using the Internet or hotel and restaurant trade publications. Good web sites to begin with are www.foodtv.com, www.restaurant.org, or www.lodgingnews.com. What type of education, apprenticeships or internships, and experience led to their success?

UNDERSTAND MARKETING CONCEPTS

Circle the best answer for each of the following questions.

1. A guest's account record at the front desk is called the
   a. reservation
   b. itinerary
   c. stayover
   d. folio

2. Which of the following is NOT the responsibility of a front desk agent?
   a. greeting and welcoming the guest
   b. carrying guest luggage to the room
   c. entering guest information into the hotel guest database
   d. informing the guest of services available

THINK CRITICALLY

Answer the following questions as completely as possible. If necessary, use a separate sheet of paper.

3. List two benefits customers receive from upselling. List two benefits of upselling to the hotel.

_____

_____

_____

_____

_____

_____

4. **Technology** Design a spreadsheet or database form with column headings of pertinent guest information for a hotel to keep as part of its database and guest-tracking system.

_____

_____

_____

_____

_____

_____

_____

BACK-OF-THE-HOUSE OPERATIONS

CHECK IN

The Boulders, a resort in Carefree, Arizona, has brought a team concept to the previously solo job of housekeeping. Three people on a self-directed team work together on one room, interchanging duties as they choose. The teams are also responsible for their own room inspections. Each team is multicultural, thus assisting staff members who are learning English and encouraging employee interaction.

Start-up and training costs were high, and initial productivity was discouraging. In spite of the difficulties, the new idea of self-directed housekeeping teams has proven successful. Guests are happier, the staff is more stable, and morale among room attendants has improved.

Work with a group. Discuss ways the self-directed team concept could be implemented in other departments of a hotel, such as the front desk area or in a food and beverage outlet.

GOALS

Identify back-of-the-house operations in a typical hotel.

Describe positions in the housekeeping department, engineering department, and kitchen of a typical hotel.

BACK OF THE HOUSE

Back-of-the-house operations include those vital departments not usually seen or frequented by guests or patrons. Departments such as human resources, management, accounting, reservations, operations, housekeeping, and banquet operations often perform their functions invisibly, but they are the engine that keeps the hospitality industry humming.

HOUSEKEEPING

The housekeeping department is mainly responsible for the daily cleaning and care of guest rooms, the front desk and lobby areas, restaurants, banquet and meeting rooms, restrooms, and other offices or rooms on the property. The cleanliness and physical

upkeep of the hotel strongly affect how guests perceive the property. The guests not only judge a hotel by its cleanliness, but also by attitudes shown by the housekeeping staff.

Executive housekeepers are in charge of planning and coordinating the activities of the housekeeping department, including the linen and laundry areas. The executive housekeeper is also responsible for ordering, receiving, and storing supplies; maintaining the lost-and-found department; and reporting the status of guest rooms to the front desk.

The executive housekeeper continually updates the front desk about status and availability of rooms so that the front desk can assign rooms to guests as they arrive. Every morning, the executive housekeeper receives a **room status report** from the night auditor listing the projected status of the rooms. The room conditions are often classified in these four ways.

Check out (C/O)   Guest has checked out, but the room has not been cleaned yet

Stayover (S/O)   Guest will spend another day in the hotel; the room needs cleaning

Vacant ready (V/R)   Room is clean and ready to be occupied

Out of order (OOO)   Room is not available due to a maintenance problem or renovation

CONFIRMATION

What does the executive housekeeper do?

_____

_____

_____

_____

THE ENGINEERING DEPARTMENT

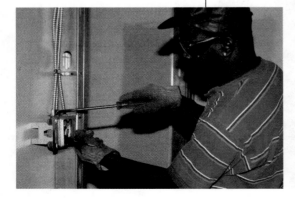

The housekeeping department and the engineering department work closely together to maintain the image of the hotel property. The engineering department takes care of mechanical equipment and the physical upkeep of the hotel. The size of the hotel determines the number of employees in this department. Generally speaking, the **facilities director** (or _chief engineer_) manages this department. The position requires a solid knowledge of the heating, ventilation, and air conditioning (_HVAC_) systems, and the electrical, plumbing, mechanical, and environmental systems on the property. The manager of this department also needs to be able to read blueprints and building schematics. Communication and interpersonal skills are also vital, as this person not only supervises the other department employees but also has direct contact with general management and other department managers. Preventive maintenance, repair, and trouble-shooting skills are also necessary for any member of this department.

Heating, ventilation, and air conditioning (HVAC) services are crucial to the operation of a hotel. Some hotels may have their own boiler and steam-generating equipment, while others may purchase their heating power from a utility company. Refrigeration and cooling systems must constantly be monitored, not only for guest comfort but to avoid food contamination or spoilage. Ventilation systems must be continually monitored and kept clean to perform efficiently. Electrical service work involves maintaining and repairing wiring, appliances, electrical motors, and lighting in guest rooms and public areas. Plumbing services take care of guest baths, public restrooms, plumbing fixtures in food preparation and service areas, and outdoor pools and fountains. Carpenters, painters, and flooring experts may be full-time employees of an engineering department or may be contracted services as the needs arise.

Landscaping and building exterior maintenance is crucial to maintaining the visual appeal of the property. Before guests even speak to or see a hotel employee, they judge the hotel by what the outside looks like. Landscaping maintenance involves planting and taking care of trees, shrubs, and flowers; cleaning and caring for pools and fountains; cleaning public sidewalks; and lawn mowing and maintenance. The continual care of the building exterior involves painting window frames and entry doors; repairing sidewalks and stairs; and cleaning and maintaining storage areas, trash receptacles, and parking areas.

Energy conservation, recycling, and other environmental issues often fall to the engineering department. Most hotels use extensive water conditioning systems to cut down on the amount of water used as well as to reduce wear and tear on pipes and fabric. While the efficient use of

energy is everyone's responsibility, the engineering department takes the lead in implementing and educating others about conservation procedures. The chief engineer needs to stay updated on current equipment, regulations, and procedures designed to protect the environment.

With the increased use of technology, computer skills are a major requirement of the facilities director. A computer program usually controls air conditioning and heating systems. Most departments throughout the hotel use computer hardware, software, and cabling that must be serviced and repaired. Sometimes these high-tech services are contracted out by the lodging facility, but the director still must be knowledgeable enough to engage in that process.

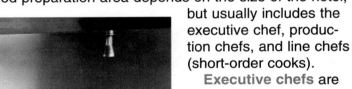

CONFIRMATION

What is HVAC, and why is it important to the smooth operation of a hotel?

_____

_____

THE KITCHEN

Another division of the back-of-the-house operations is the kitchen, where food is prepared to serve to guests. The kitchen provides food for not only the on-site restaurants but for special events, conferences, meetings, room service, and the employee dining room. The number of employees in the food preparation area depends on the size of the hotel,

but usually includes the executive chef, production chefs, and line chefs (short-order cooks).

Executive chefs are responsible for training and managing the kitchen staff and operations. The chef also supervises the kitchen staff and the general food production. An executive chef has an extensive background in culinary arts, through a combination of training, apprenticeships, and experience in food-service production.

Sous chefs, from the French word for "under," are assistant chefs who report directly to the executive chef. The sous chef oversees the day-to-day food production process.

Production chefs, also referred to as station chefs, are responsible for specific categories of food. For example, a pastry chef prepares pastries and bread, sometimes in a special area that is purposely kept cooler than the rest of the kitchen. The *garde manger*, a title taken directly from French, is responsible for cold food production such as salads or fruits. Other production chefs may be exclusively in charge of vegetable, sauce, or meat production. These chefs may only be responsible for preparing large amounts of food for banquets, luncheons, special events, or meeting breaks.

Line chefs are responsible for preparing food that has been ordered by a customer in the restaurant or from room service. The line chef must know a variety of cooking methods in order to prepare the items featured on the menu.

The executive chef spends a large percentage of time planning and purchasing supplies, ingredients, food, and beverages to be used in preparing food. The chef must be able to estimate future sales based on past records or trends. The chef frequently meets with the banquet and restaurant managers to stay informed about upcoming events. The chef must also keep accurate track of items in dry storage (food stored between 40 and 80 degrees Fahrenheit) and cold storage (food stored below 40 degrees Fahrenheit). Logging or recording food as it is received and issued provides a **perpetual inventory**, or ongoing inventory. A **physical inventory** may be conducted weekly by counting perishable and dry food items.

CONFIRMATION

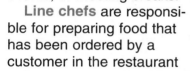

What is a sous chef, and what are his or her responsibilities? For what type of food is a *garde manger* responsible?

UNDERSTAND MARKETING CONCEPTS

Circle the best answer for each of the following questions.

1. The executive housekeeper's responsibilities include
   a. maintaining the lost-and-found department
   b. updating the front desk about status and availability of rooms
   c. ordering, receiving, and storing supplies
   d. all of the above

2. Which of the following is NOT the responsibility of the engineering department?
   a. maintaining electrical appliances in the kitchen and guest rooms
   b. monitoring the amount of towels and linens necessary to stock the hotel
   c. keeping air-conditioning ducts clean
   d. maintaining and repairing wiring

THINK CRITICALLY

Answer the following questions as completely as possible. If necessary, use a separate sheet of paper.

3. **Marketing Math** If the linen required for a double room in a hotel is 4 sheets, 4 pillows and pillow cases, 4 bath towels, 4 hand towels, 4 washcloths, and 1 bath floor mat, how many of each item would be necessary for a hotel with 313 double rooms?

_____

_____

_____

_____

_____

4. **Interpersonal Skills** List at least five ways that the housekeeping department, the engineering department, and the kitchen work together to accomplish the goals of a lodging establishment.

_____

_____

_____

_____

_____

DIVERSITY ISSUES IN THE HOSPITALITY INDUSTRY

CHAPTER 3

LESSON 3.4

In an increasingly global economy, successful hoteliers must become aware of cultural differences. What is acceptable in one country may be considered in bad taste or even rude in another. For example, tipping is expected in some countries but not even considered in others. Price negotiations are an accepted way of business to some, while others see "haggling" as distasteful. Different cultural attitudes about punctuality, courtesy, gestures, and eye contact or the lack of it can result in major misunderstandings with guests as well as an increasingly diverse workforce.

Work with a group. Identify cultural differences that may exist between students in your school or between international business partners. Discuss and explore the origins of the cultural differences you have listed.

GOALS

Explain how diverse cultures affect the hospitality industry.

Discuss ways hotels are making opportunities available for minorities.

VIVE LA DIFFERENCES

PRODUCT/ SERVICE MANAGEMENT

The United States has been touted as a melting pot for a wide array of people. This diversity has contributed to the success of the country, while at the same time creating challenges for the workplace and complicating marketing strategies. Hotels must be sensitive to the needs of a diverse workforce in order to recruit and retain effective employees. As target markets also expand and diversify, it is important for hotel managers to know about and respect other cultures and their beliefs while running a profitable business. Hotel training programs must prepare workers to accommodate a diverse group of customers and to work on a diverse team.

Successful hotel chains have diversified by owning differently priced lodging properties to capture a larger market segment. Hotels have made adjustments to meet the needs of a diverse population. Major hotel chains now offer luxury hotels, timeshares, extended-stay suites, and lodging accommodations at establishments like Holiday Inn Express that could be described as upscale motels.

In 2001, African-Americans, Hispanics, and Asian-American/Pacific Islanders made up 26 percent of the population in America. By 2020, that percentage is expected to rise to 36 percent. In 2050, these three minority groups will likely make up 47 percent of the national population. Hotel companies and franchises offer a wide range of programs to develop minority managers through networking, mentoring, and internship programs. Hotels

The stereotype of the business traveler is the busy male executive or salesman. By the end of the year 2000, though, females represented almost half of all business travelers in the United States. Some predict that women will outnumber men as business travelers in ten years. As the number of female travelers increases, hotels are offering more personal service, increased security, express check-in and checkout, and improved in-hotel restaurants to appeal to them.

THINK CRITICALLY
What are other ways hotels could cater to female business travelers?

Hyatt, Marriott, and Hilton have all been listed on *Fortune* magazine's list of "America's 50 Best Companies for Minorities." Hyatt, 13th on the list with 62.5% of the overall workforce and 36% of its managers as minorities, leads other hotels in minority representation. Marriott ranked 37th and Hilton, making the list for the first time, came in at number 41.

across the nation are incorporating hospitality programs for high school students into their training programs. Hoteliers should see a wealth of opportunity in hosting, hiring, and helping people from all walks of life.

MULTINATIONAL HOTELS

Many major hotel brands are now *multinational companies*. These companies have hotels located in more than one country. To succeed, these hotels have to maintain a uniform standard of service while working in and employing personnel of varying cultures. In addition, the location of some hotels requires that special diversity needs be met. For example, many Japanese tourists vacation in Hawaii. Major hotels in Hawaii must be prepared to accommodate international guests with menus and pertinent information written in Japanese as well as English.

TO KNOW ME IS TO LOVE ME

"I am unique…just like everyone else." This seeming paradox holds a key to success in hospitality management. People have different backgrounds, ambitions, personalities, and talents. Successful hoteliers make wise use of these differences by developing diverse teams or creating multi-ethnic mentor programs. Travel companies send agents to different countries to explore and learn about different cultures. A group of employees may take courses in foreign languages. Sometimes hotels or restaurants provide English classes for those whose first language is not English. Training and information about different cultures, values, and traditions are invaluable ways to promote positive relationships among guests and employees.

Marriott Hotels maintains an extensive database of minority suppliers. The list contains product and geographic information on minority- or women-owned companies. When a hotel needs equipment or supplies, the database can provide information about local and community vendors.

Many large hotel companies work with minority colleges to develop internships and training programs. Minority membership of management teams or diversity councils work to develop action plans to increase education and experience opportunities for women and minorities.

CONFIRMATION

Name two ways the human resources department of a hotel can address diversity issues.

_____

UNDERSTAND MARKETING CONCEPTS

Circle the best answer for each of the following questions.

1. A multinational hotel is one that
 a. has an international guest
 b. employs citizens from foreign countries
 c. addresses the needs of multicultural groups
 d. has a property in more than one country

2. In order to meet the needs of diverse cultures, hotels have
 a. established minority internships and networks
 b. offered language classes
 c. used minority companies as suppliers or vendors
 d. all of the above

THINK CRITICALLY

Answer the following questions as completely as possible. If necessary, use a separate sheet of paper.

3. Communication List at least three customs or phrases that are unique to your own locality, state, or country that might be misunderstood by a person with a different cultural background.

_____

_____

_____

_____

_____

_____

4. Research Write a welcome phrase in four different languages below.

_____

_____

_____

_____

_____

_____

CHAPTER 3 REVIEW

REVIEW MARKETING CONCEPTS

Write the letter of the term that matches each definition. Some terms will not be used.

_____ **1.** A summary of all fees charged to a room during a guest's stay

_____ **2.** Potential guest without a reservation

_____ **3.** Includes benefits as well as salary

_____ **4.** A continual or ongoing count of products, supplies, or merchandise

_____ **5.** Informing a guest of the availability of a room with better accommodations

_____ **6.** Agreement a hotel will hold a specific type of room for a certain day or length of time

_____ **7.** Responsible for recruiting, interviewing, hiring, training, development, compensation, benefits, supervision, employee evaluation, and separation

_____ **8.** Manages the engineering department

a. compensation
b. guest folio
c. human resources (HR) department
d. facilities director
e. licensing agreement
f. perpetual inventory
g. physical inventory
h. room status report
i. reservation
j. upselling
k. walk-in

Circle the best answer.

9. A menu that remains the same from day to day with items listed and priced separately is referred to as
   a. du jour
   b. a la carte
   c. short order
   d. counter

10. A guest who has not asked the hotel to hold a room until his or her arrival is a
   a. new customer
   b. walk-in
   c. risk-taker
   d. none of these

11. The employee responsible for informing the front desk about the condition and availability of guest quarters is
   a. the chief engineer
   b. the line chef
   c. the executive housekeeper
   d. the human resources specialist

12. Employee recognition programs
   a. may consist of tangible or intangible rewards
   b. are government regulated
   c. cause employee jealousy and discord
   d. occur once every three months to keep costs at a minimum

THINK CRITICALLY

13. Find a classified advertisement in a newspaper for three job openings or positions at local hotels or restaurants. Compare each job by listing the title, requirements or qualifications, hours of employment, and compensation. Identify each position as either back-of-the-house or front-of-the-house. Which jobs appear to offer the best opportunities? Which would you most like to have?

_____

_____

_____

_____

_____

14. You are the owner of a newly renovated hotel in a large metropolitan area. You want to use a famous brand restaurant in your hotel. Explain which national or local restaurant you would choose, your target market, the theme, the price range, and the type of menus and service you will offer.

_____

_____

_____

_____

_____

15. How will the changing population demographics affect hospitality management in the next 30 years in these areas: customer relations, recruitment and retention, and training. What do you regard as the greatest challenge posed by diversity in the workplace? Why?

_____

_____

_____

_____

_____

CHAPTER 3 REVIEW

MAKE CONNECTIONS

16. Marketing Math A major hotel is located next to a large theme park that caters to young families with small children. The park leases space for a small gift shop that sells souvenirs and tickets for the theme park. The hotel receives a percentage of profit from merchandise and 0.5% of the season tickets sold. Last year, season ticket prices were $59.95. A total of 1,000 season tickets were sold. How much money did the hotel receive as a result of season ticket sales?

_____

_____

_____

17. Communication Interview managers of nearby corporations about their companies' diversity efforts toward employees and customers. Focus on hospitality companies if possible. Summarize their programs.

_____

_____

_____

18. Research Many tourists keep a journal or diary as they travel. Using the Internet or other reference sources of your choice, create a fictional "journal" of an imaginary five-day trip you take to a city or cities in Africa, Asia, or South America. Describe places you visit, the culture around you, the hotels you stay in, and the challenges you face as a stranger in a culture with which you are unfamiliar.

_____

_____

_____

19. Science Write a minimum one-page report about environmental issues facing either (1) the travel industry in general, or (2) hotels or restaurants specifically. Include water usage, food waste, product recycling, electricity, heating/air conditioning, landscaping and indoor plant care, type of paint and building materials, ventilation, and so forth.

_____

_____

_____

MARKETING MANAGEMENT ROLE PLAY

You are the manager of a five-star hotel that takes pride in exceptional customer service. One of your regular guests, Mrs. Green, has a busy schedule and appreciates the extra attention she has received. Today has not been a good day for Mrs. Green who was expecting a 5 A.M. wake-up call to make her 7 A.M. flight. The hotel desk attendant called the room at 7 A.M. and apologized for missing the 5 A.M. wake-up call. Mrs. Green is irate because the next flight is at 9 A.M. and her business meeting in the destination city is scheduled for 9 A.M. Mrs. Green is frustrated that she will miss one of her largest business opportunities. You have the responsibility of apologizing and doing whatever you can to accommodate the needs of Mrs. Green. She has threatened to take her annual $20,000 of business to another hotel. Let Mrs. Green know what your hotel will do in the future to avoid similar situations.

http://www.deca.org
/publications/HS_
Guide/guidetoc.html

PROJECT EXTENDED STAY

Your human resources consulting firm has been asked to write a "New Hire" information package for a completely renovated and remodeled hotel. It is a five-star luxury hotel in a large metropolitan area, in walking distance of a world-famous shopping area and tourist attraction. It has 350 rooms, three pools, four different types of food and beverage outlets, seven large banquet or meeting rooms, and a spa and tennis courts.

Work with a group and complete the following activities.

1. Develop the section that includes the divisions of the human resources department. Include the responsibilities of the HR employees in each division; how HR assists employees; and how HR works with management to recruit, select, hire, train, and release employees. Estimate the total number of employees of the hotel.

2. Calculate the rough square footage of the hotel, including both front-of-the-house and back-of-the house areas. Conduct research about an appropriate HVAC system for a hotel of this size.

3. Create a floor plan of the front of the house. Include the front desk, lobby area, food and beverage outlets, and banquet/meeting rooms.

4. Select a theme for the main restaurant of the hotel. Create a typical menu to include soups, salads, entrées, beverages, and desserts. Include at least ten a la carte items and at least two du jour items for Monday through Friday. Include appropriate pricing.

5. Create three table d'hôte menus for banquets. Include appetizers, salad or soup, entrée, side dishes, and desserts. Describe typical events for each menu (wedding, buffet lunch for business meeting, gala, charity luncheon, and so forth). Include appropriate pricing.

6. Develop an organization chart for a chain of command for the housekeeping and engineering departments and the kitchen staff.

CHAPTER 4

SELLING HOSPITALITY

LESSONS

WINNING STRATEGIES

WOMEN IN HOSPITALITY

Three trends combine to make it likely that the role of women in hospitality management and marketing will grow. The first is that women are rising in management in all areas of business life. A third of all businesses in the U.S. are owned by women, and women now make up 46 percent of the total workforce. That percentage is expected to rise in the coming years.

The second trend is that the hospitality industry needs good managers. With almost half the labor force female, the industry's constant search for effective managers provides opportunities for talented women. Founded by Dorrit St. John, Susan Spalding, and Shelia Lohmiller, The Network of Executive Women in Hospitality, Inc., is an organization that strives to encourage women in every facet of the hospitality industry. Providing communication, job forums and listings, continuing education, and professional development, NEWH also offers scholarship programs and competitions. Encouraging students to pursue hospitality as a career, NEWH has awarded almost $800,000.

A third trend is that customers are more and more likely to be women. Nearly half of all business travelers are female. Women with insight and experience can build outstanding careers. Dixie Eng of MeriStar Hotels & Resorts rose through the ranks, beginning as a desk clerk in the Washington, D.C. area, then becoming a concierge, then eventually a general manager of the Latham Hotel and the Georgetown Inn. In January 2001, she became the general manager of the prestigious Hilton Washington Embassy Row, which has undergone a multimillion-dollar renovation.

THINK CRITICALLY

1. What hindrances to their careers might women encounter in hospitality management?
2. What steps might the hospitality industry take to develop the potential of female employees and managers?

CHAPTER 4
LESSON 4.1

MARKETING THE HOTEL OR RESTAURANT

GOALS

Identify several roles that contribute to the hospitality marketing effort.

Describe the impact of the Internet on hospitality marketing.

Explain strategies for increasing sales in hospitality businesses.

CHECK IN

Have you experienced the excitement and responsibility of leading a social or professional organization? Leaders of professional organizations often organize important meetings and conventions. Could you handle the details for a convention attended by 5,000 people?

Meeting planners and hotel sales departments offer plenty of help. The hospitality industry wants to provide experiences that produce repeat customers. Number of hotel rooms, room rates, number of meeting rooms, special equipment needs, exhibit hall use, and meal functions are some of the issues that must be considered. Part of choosing the best deal involves deciding what location is most useful and attractive to those who will attend.

Work with a partner. List ten cities in the United States that would be good locations for national conventions accommodating 5,000 to 10,000 attendees. List at least two reasons for each selection.

MARKETING HOSPITALITY PROPERTIES

SELLING

Selling a hospitality facility involves more than renting rooms or tables. The sales team must first determine what image the hotel or restaurant will project. The ranking of hotel or restaurant properties is usually associated with price. Most ranking systems use a star or diamond ranking. Five stars or diamonds refer to the highest quality, best-in-class accommodations. Hotels and restaurants that boast a five-star or five-diamond ranking can usually charge higher prices, but must offer services and amenities to justify the cost. Four stars or diamonds represent excellent service, while three stars or diamonds are associated with very good hospitality properties. Good hotels and restaurants are given two stars or diamonds, and lesser or budget properties receive one star or diamond. Hospitality properties may be ranked by governments, private organizations, and guide books. Some governments rank hotels as part of the licensing process. Many hotels and restaurants proudly display the number of stars or diamonds awarded to the property. Fodor's Travel Guides use dollar signs to denote a price range for the hospitality property. A legend, or key, explains the dollar-sign system.

Hotel and restaurant sales teams involve more than the individuals hired specifically to generate business traffic. Providing satisfying customer experiences for hotel and restaurant guests begins with the front desk clerk and the restaurant host. A beautiful facility does not assure guest satisfaction. The hotel desk clerk is usually the first person that the guest encounters at the hotel. A bad experience will result in an unhappy customer who will tell potential customers about being dissatisfied. The housekeeping crew also leaves a lasting impression on hotel guests. Clean rooms and customer satisfaction go hand in hand.

Some restaurants have guests who are willing to wait for an hour to be seated. These restaurants have gained a reputation for excellent food and great service. A friendly greeting by the restaurant host begins the customer satisfaction process. Catering sales are enhanced by delicious hot food and top-notch service.

CONFIRMATION

Explain the relationship of hotel image and cost. Why might some beautiful hospitality facilities not be successful?

INTERNET IMPACT

The Internet is having a huge impact on how individuals conduct their lives and businesses. It took 38 years for television to get into 50 million homes. Within five years, the Internet has made an equal impact. Four out of five consumers online believe that the Internet is a more important invention than television. Six in ten of these online consumers prefer e-mail over paper mail for business correspondence. Twenty-five percent of online consumers check their e-mail while they are on vacation.

The Internet is redirecting customer attention to new sellers of products and services and away from traditional relationships. Traditional approaches used by hospitality businesses are changing due to the Internet. Reservations taken over the Internet are projected to increase to 9 percent of total volume. **Infomediaries**, third parties used to make reservations on the Internet, are replacing travel agents by providing information and access.

MARKETING MYTHS

Futurists widely predicted increased leisure time for modern society. It has turned out that there is actually less leisure time available for people today, and time-related stress is a common characteristic of life. Service businesses that cater to consumers who want to free up time and relax are growing, another way in which marketing opportunities arise from current conditions.

THINK CRITICALLY
What services can hotels and restaurants offer to reduce their customers' time-related stress?

Using software to develop matches between buyers and sellers, infomediaries have begun to allow consumers do-it-yourself access to hospitality businesses. The Internet has made price information widely available to consumers. Internet business models and web sites affect products and services offered, pricing, distribution, and long-term information capabilities.

Thus the balance of marketing power is shifting from sellers to buyers, making the importance of high-quality service, convenience, and value for money even more compelling. In other parts of the industry, hospitality businesses also use the Internet for communication with vendors for speed and efficiency in keeping properties supplied.

WHAT CUSTOMERS EXPECT

Customers want convenience and consistency from the hospitality industry. They also want information fast. Hospitality companies that don't deliver convenience will be eaten up by the competition. Internet-alert hoteliers will provide in-room technologies and high-speed Internet access to further complicate or liberate guests' lives. Customers determine brand value by the consistency of hospitality services.

CONFIRMATION

What are infomediaries? How can the Internet help consumers get what they want from the hospitality industry?

CHANGING RULES IN HOSPITALITY MARKETING

The operating environment for hospitality companies is changing. New rules of conduct, new relationships, and new standards for success are evolving. There are numerous opportunities and risks in a changing environment. Business traits that separate success from failure include speed, flexibility, and consistency.

Speed in response to changing conditions is necessary in all businesses, and especially in the hospitality industry. Well-informed, restless, and frequently fickle customers have less brand loyalty than previously. Quick response to trends is critical. New, or "start-up," companies must establish themselves quickly or they won't survive. Flexibility is necessary to respond to sudden competitive threats. New competitors can disrupt established customer relationships in the hospitality industry almost instantaneously. Still, in this turbulent environment, consumers require consistency and won't tolerate unstable or unpredictable service.

NEW RULES FOR RESOURCES

The hospitality industry faces challenge in the recruitment, training, and development of human resources. Successful hotels display entrepreneurship, visionary leadership, strength in sales and marketing, and a strong commitment to customer-relationship management. Creativity and risk taking may replace analysis and procedures in the hospitality industry. The rapid growth of infomediaries may require hospitality businesses to upgrade technology constantly, so a whole new field of professionals in the hospitality industry may be emerging. Finding, training, and keeping the kind of people who can respond to the demanding environment of the hospitality business is one of the greatest problems in the industry. Successful managers will be those who can creatively and consistently please the people who please their customers.

TRADITIONAL SALES TECHNIQUES

PROMOTION

Selling a hotel or restaurant can be enhanced through the use of brochures, mailings, and bulk distribution. Brochures must convey a message of quality that matches the prices charged. Brochures should be strategically located throughout the property. The registration area, bell captain's or travel desk, and public areas (restaurant, shops, cocktail lounge) are high traffic areas for promotional materials. Brochures should include property highlights while promoting special guest room packages. Managerial and sales staff should carry brochures wherever they go. This includes sales calls, blitzes, civic meetings, and any place where a potential meeting planner may be encountered.

Hotels use qualified lists of people, companies, and organizations for targeted mailing. Mailing lists may include previous guests or travel departments of companies that set up accommodations for traveling executives. Special promotions frequently revolve around golf, tennis, honeymoons, and family weekend packages, either as part of or in addition to regular business trips.

Bulk distribution means junk mail to most individuals, however, reciprocal trade of brochures with other noncompetitive properties (chambers of commerce, shopping malls, rest areas, departments of tourism, and supermarkets) can reap great results.

The Return Special Value Program (RSVP) is a successful strategy designed to provide an incentive to meeting planners and convention participants to return to Abbey Group Resorts as leisure guests. Abbey will honor the group rate for up to one year from the date of the group function, subject to availability of rooms.

TRACKING QUALITY

MARKETING-INFORMATION MANAGEMENT

The hospitality sales department realizes the direct relationship between customer satisfaction and repeat business. Hotel guests measure service value by more than check-in/out experiences. Information, breakfast, recreation, and courtesy calls provided by the hotel add up to customer satisfaction. Value of the physical facilities is based on cleanliness, maintenance, ambiance, and in-room amenities. Successful hotels examine previous notable marketing strategies to identify particular types of people and what they like, called **psychographic information**. Hotels also compile data on ages, home locations, and spending habits of consumers, called *demographics*. The registration card or a more sophisticated customer database is key to the success of monitoring customer demographics. Short survey questions can be included on the hotel or restaurant bill to gain more information about customer demographics. Some hospitality businesses reward customers for completing surveys with restaurant coupons or discounted hotel room rates.

Once a marketing strategy is chosen, the hard work of turning the strategy into an action plan, complete with a budget, begins. Sales tools based upon financial and human resources must be selected for each market segment during the calendar year to have resources and necessary preparation in place during different times of the year. Holiday specials for December, for example, must be advertised in October and November.

All staff must be aware of the sales strategy and important execution details. Employees must be attentive to where guests are coming from, why, and what they are doing while in the area. Personal attention and service based on customer knowledge separate success from failure.

RESTAURANT SALES

SELLING

Many of the same principles of marketing for hotels apply to restaurants. Sales strategies for restaurants are dictated by market trends, changing tastes of customers, and competition. Success today does not assure success in the future. Customers expect excellent food, friendly service, and a clean restaurant, and go elsewhere when they are not getting value for money spent. Although individual restaurants depend on local repeat business, the overall marketing strategy of restaurant chains or even local ones depends on making choices about the type of food offered, the facility in which it is offered, and the service of the staff. Planning and executing determine everything.

CONFIRMATION

Name three traditional hospitality sales tools. Why is targeting repeat business a key part of a marketing effort?

_____

_____

UNDERSTAND MARKETING CONCEPTS

Circle the best answer for each of the following questions.

1. ____?____ are third parties used to make reservations on the Internet.
   a. Infomercials
   b. Infomediaries
   c. Reservation clerks
   d. Bell captains

2. Which of the following is a traditional sales technique used by the hospitality industry?
   a. brochures
   b. bulk distribution
   c. mailings
   d. all of the above

THINK CRITICALLY

Answer the following questions as completely as possible. If necessary, use a separate sheet of paper.

3. **Technology**   Use the Internet to look up a web site for a hotel and a restaurant. You will probably be more likely to locate chain hotels and restaurants. What information is included on the web sites? What information could be added to enhance the web sites?

_____

_____

_____

_____

_____

4. **Communication**   The months of June and July are slow for your hotel property. Design a brochure that offers a Weekend Getaway Special during the two months. A luxury room that normally rents for $150 per night will cost $89 per night with the Weekend Getaway Special. Your hotel is a full-service property located near a museum, a zoo, good shopping centers, and the local university.

_____

_____

_____

_____

CHAPTER 4

LESSON 4.2

HOTEL RESERVATIONS

GOALS

Identify different ways to make hotel reservations and explain different types of reservations.

Describe the impact of technology on the reservation business.

CHECK IN

Most students have a week off for spring break, a great time to take beach or skiing vacations. Many spring breaks across the nation occur at the same time, making it essential to book hotel rooms well in advance.

Many consumers use the Internet to compare prices of hotels and to actually reserve rooms. Credit card fraud keeps some consumers from sharing their credit card numbers over the Internet. Some consumers are even suspicious about giving credit card numbers to 800-number hotel reservationists.

Work with a partner. Make a list of security precautions for the use of credit cards over the telephone or on the Internet.

RESERVING A HOTEL ROOM

DISTRIBUTION

There are a variety of ways for guests to make hotel reservations. Individuals can make direct reservations by mail, telephone, fax, e-mail, face-to-face, or through a web site. Most hotels and motels have 800/888 telephone numbers available to reserve rooms. In the case of chain hotels, sometimes a direct call to the individual unit will turn up a room when an 800 number can't because of a cancellation or other change. Consumers can also book lodging through a travel agent or tour operator. Increasing numbers of hotel guests choose to book their reservations on the Internet.

Reservation centers, third parties, Internet, and direct customer contact are the most popular means for reserving rooms. Travel agents and tour operators are examples of third parties used to make reservations. Fees or commissions are paid by the lodging establishment to the third-party reservationists.

How do travelers determine where to stay? Recommendations from friends and acquaintances, advertisements in newspapers, magazines, and broadcast media, tour brochures, travel guides, hotel reference books, and the Internet are all sources of hotel information.

TYPES OF RESERVATIONS

Reservations may be made anywhere from one day to years in advance. Regular and guaranteed reservations are two basic types of reservations. A **regular** (or *non-guaranteed*) **reservation** is held usually until 6 p.m. on the date of arrival. If the guest does not arrive by 6 p.m., the room is made available for other prospective hotel guests or walk-in customers who rent the room without an advance reservation. A **guaranteed reservation** requires the guest to pay for the first night prior to the guest's arrival. A credit card number or advance payment guarantees that the hotel room is held until check-out the next day. All advance payments must be posted on guests' folios. Reservations can be confirmed by telephone, e-mail, fax, or letter. Most guests feel more secure with a confirmation holding their room no matter how late they arrive at the hotel.

Availability of rooms can easily be determined with computerized reservation systems. A computer printout shows the number and types of rooms available. This same system shows which rooms are ready for occupancy, because housekeeping keys in the information as soon as a room is cleaned. Rooms not yet ready are shown as C/O, checked out but room has not been cleaned yet.

Accuracy in room reservations is critical. No one is angrier than a tired, late-arriving traveler who discovers that the room he or she had been assured was reserved is not available. Customers also expect without fail the type of room they have reserved. Non-smoking guests will not return to hotels that force them into rooms reeking of stale smoke, and guests who smoke won't appreciate being prohibited from smoking in the rooms they rent. No family wants to discover they've been erroneously booked into a room with one bed, and single travelers don't want to pay for space they don't need. Hotels lose customers forever by botching reservations, the first and maybe most important point of contact with the customer. Goodwill is hard to maintain but easy to lose.

Group reservations are frequently made months in advance to accommodate conferences or special events. A hotel's sales department may offer a group of rooms at a discounted rate for convention meetings or family reunions. Convention organizers negotiate room rates with hotel management. Because hotels near convention centers compete for conference business, pricing strategies are based upon the actions of competitors. Simply offering the lowest rates is not always the best strategy, however, because higher rates can be charged if surrounding hotel properties are completely filled. Competing hotels keep track of their competitors' occupancy rates.

CYBER MARKETING

Priceline.com gives consumers the power to negotiate prices for goods and services. Customers use the web site to bid prices on airline tickets and hotel rates they are willing to pay. Today's marketplace is more customer-driven than ever. The same principle of negotiating price on the Internet can also apply to in-person dealings.

THINK CRITICALLY
1. Why have consumers become more powerful price negotiation agents?
2. Under what circumstances might a negotiated price be good for both the hotel and the consumer?

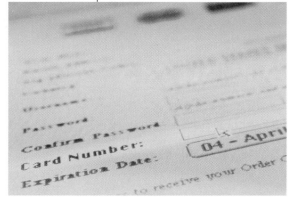

CANCELLED RESERVATIONS

Courteous travelers call the hotel when they do not plan to use a reservation. Cancellation numbers are assigned so billing will not be incorrectly made, and the rooms are changed to available status. Non-guaranteed reservations are normally revoked or "pulled" at 6 P.M., opening additional rooms for walk-in guests.

Stayovers (or *overstays*) are persons staying longer than the length of their reservation. These individuals are charged accordingly for the additional time they rent the room. People expected to check out today are sometimes classified as **due-outs**.

CONFIRMATION

Explain the difference between regular and guaranteed reservations.

_____

_____

THIRD-PARTY RESERVATIONS

Travel agents and the Internet are third-party distribution channels upon which hotels have become more dependent. From 1994 to 1999, travel agent commissions and reservation expenses grew at a rate of 14.1 percent. Did hotels receive benefits equal to the increase in payments? It appears that there has been a diminishing "return on investment" for these expenditures. Room revenue for the six-year period grew at a compound rate of 6.1 percent. Hotels actually had a 0.5 percent decline in the number of rooms occupied. Payments made to distribution channels grew faster than increased sales volume of rooms, so the net benefit to the average hotel was very small.

Projected limited growth in hotel revenues makes it important to control expenses in order to maintain or increase profits. Most major hotel chains have added a room-booking capability to their web site. Customers can use the web site to check availability and rates in order to make reservations directly with the hotel. According to a PhoCus Wright presentation at the October 1999 Travel Forum, approximately $600 million in hotel sales were booked through hotel web sites during the year. The number is expected to increase to nearly $2 billion in 2001.

Technology may be expensive for a hotel. However, it is more reasonable when the hotel can reach a consumer directly instead of paying commissions to third-party intermediaries.

THE IMPORTANCE OF COMMUNICATIONS

MARKETING-INFORMATION MANAGEMENT

The business of receiving and processing reservations is a large and growing part of the hospitality industry. Increasingly, the reservation process is also linked to the data-gathering part of the business, as the same tools that record reservations compile data about the people who are making them. Advances in technology, shortages of clerical employees, and consumers' growing willingness to seek the best deal on their own make a focus on easy, accurate, and economically competitive reservations essential to hospitality managers.

CONFIRMATION

What are two types of third-party distribution channels for hotels? Why is technology increasingly important in the reservation process?

CAREER SPOTLIGHT

HOTEL WEB DESIGNER

The hospitality industry is extremely competitive. Hotels using the latest technology for advertising and hotel reservations will survive in a technology-driven society.

Estep Engineering prepares systems and software for a wide array of industries. The Web Crew is a part of Estep Engineering that provides resources for designing hotel web pages. Mr. Estep became interested in designing hotel web pages when his wife, a freelance hotel sales management agent of change, emphasized the competitive advantage that good web pages give to hotels. The Web Crew has a user-friendly web site that provides general information on web sites, lists of satisfied customers, and steps to creating an effective web site. Among its recommendations, the Web Crew advises including photos and maps, choosing a "theme" for the site, and keeping the site regularly updated.

THINK CRITICALLY

1. How does Estep's career illustrate the way technology has created both new opportunities and challenges for the hospitality industry?

2. What might be examples of "themes" for a hotel web site?

UNDERSTAND MARKETING CONCEPTS

Circle the best answer for each of the following questions.

1. Customers
    a. usually prefer guaranteed reservations
    b. now have more power to negotiate hotel room prices
    c. expect unfailing accuracy in the reservation process
    d. all of the above

2. Which of the following is not a type of room reservation?
    a. regular
    b. guaranteed
    c. group
    d. due-out

THINK CRITICALLY

Answer the following questions as completely as possible. If necessary, use a separate sheet of paper.

3. **Marketing Math** Reservations made over the Internet are expected to grow from $600 million in 1999 to $2 billion in 2001. What is the percent of increase?

_____

_____

_____

_____

_____

4. **Technology** Your hotel has developed a good system to keep track of customer profiles. Some of the information in a profile includes type of room the guest normally rents, favorite music, and favorite food. How could you pleasantly surprise a frequent guest who is scheduled to check into your hotel this evening? Explain your strategy thoroughly.

_____

_____

_____

_____

_____

SALES AND EVENT PLANNING

CHECK IN

Most cities realize the financial importance of tourism. Many growing cities with good airports seriously consider building convention centers and hotels to attract convention and other hospitality business. Voters often determine in ballot issues whether convention centers are built. If an issue passes, different types of taxes may increase to pay the interest on bonds used to build the center. Sometimes these ballot issues are heated contests.

Work with a group. Discuss why voters might be hesitant to pass bond issues to fund convention-center development. What are arguments both sides might use in their campaigns?

GOALS

Define hospitality event marketing.

Identify markets for potential group sales.

List sales strategies for event marketing.

THE BIG BUSINESS OF HOSPITALITY

Hospitality event planning is big business. The most successful operations have aggressive sales strategies to attract the business of large conventions and banquets. Major cities understand the financial value to the entire city of having convention centers and hotels that can handle conventions, banquets, and other business meetings simultaneously.

Many communities seek tourist dollars through the use of a **Conference and Visitors Bureau (CVB)**. Businesses that benefit from tourism pay dues to this organization and form joint efforts to attract more travelers to the area. Typical members include accommodations facilities, special attractions (amusement parks and museums), restaurants, and tour companies.

Group sales involve renting multiple hotel rooms and meeting rooms. A group sale might involve a country club catering a 150-person awards banquet at its facility. Hotels count on group sales for a large percentage of their business. Large convention centers work hand in hand with surrounding hotels to accommodate large groups like the International DECA Career Development Conferences. Group sales may also involve social events such as wedding and graduation receptions.

SALES STAFF

Most large hotels seeking convention business have a sales department to plan strategies for convention and banquet business. A small hotel property might have one person in charge of sales, while large properties have three or more people actively selling. The sales department at a hotel is responsible not only for selling rooms but also the entire hotel product, including food and beverage, meeting space, and recreational facilities. Goals for sales departments include keeping occupancy rates high, knowing when to adjust rates up or down, and increasing repeat business.

ADVERTISING AND RESEARCH

Advertising, direct mail, publicity, and public relations are key elements necessary for selling hospitality. An advertising campaign may be developed in-house, or a sales agency may be hired to create sales promotions. Hospitality businesses also actively watch for publicity opportunities. Positive publicity in the newspaper or on the local television newscast can equal thousands of dollars in sales. One example of favorable publicity occurs when a popular athlete or movie star stays at a hotel and the name of the hotel is printed in a news release about the star. Radio and television stations should be notified of special events such as trade shows. Major renovations or personnel changes at hotels and convention centers are usually sent to the newspaper.

Sales departments depend on marketing research conducted by the city, general manager, and professional organizations to determine the best days during the week and months of the year for business. Once the sales staff determines the heaviest business times, it can design special promotional packages for slow times. Hotels frequently offer special room rates during weekends when business tends to slow.

The hospitality industry must maintain records for rooms rented, convention business, walk-ins, and meals sold in order to make future projections called **forecasts**. Computer programs keep daily records of hotel room and catering business. Forecasts are necessary for staffing, purchasing food, and ordering linen supplies. Hotels also conduct research to determine why guests choose their lodging. The information obtained helps to develop appropriate marketing strategies. Gaining valuable guest information can be as simple as a desk clerk or waiter asking the customer where they heard about the property. Questionnaires allow the guest to rate the service they received. The best hotels use the results of these surveys for formal programs of continuous quality improvement.

CATERING FOR HOSPITALITY EVENTS

The catering or banquet department usually plans directly with the client to organize meal functions. Whether planning a wedding reception or an awards banquet, customers want good food and service. Customer expectations rise with prices. Cold, unappealing food, small portions, and slow or sloppy service are fatal to acquiring repeat business. A catering department helps the customer decide on a meal that meets budget and taste. Important details include the number of people to be served, table placements, linens, decorations, and technical set-up. Customers may decide to have a cash bar that allows guests to purchase beverages. Generally, a buffet is less expensive than individually served meals. Sometimes catering departments subcontract other services, such as a disc jockey, floral arrangements, or special equipment.

CONFIRMATION

Why are group sales so important to hospitality marketing?

POTENTIAL MARKETS

The market for hospitality event business is vast. Every meeting or convention has a unique personality with its own special needs. A Richard Simmons Seminar would likely be quite different than a conference for certified public accountants. The group may be large or small, but all participants expect high-quality service from the hospitality industry. What organizations are holding all of these business conventions or conferences? There are thousands of professional organizations around the world. Nearly every industry has a trade association. Professional associations normally have at least one major convention during the year. Larger companies are having more meetings than ever. Wal-Mart held a major convention for all of its employees during the entire month of January 2001 in Kansas City, Missouri. Each week during January, a different group of Wal-Mart employees from a particular section of the country came to Kansas City for a week-long conference. Kansas City was the beneficiary of a substantial amount of convention revenue.

Top sales representatives for some companies are awarded with **incentive travel** or vacation awards that are presented at sales meetings. Fraternal organizations such as Kiwanis International and Lions Clubs, and college sororities, fraternities, and alumni associations are other sources of conference and banquet business. Common-interest groups like garden clubs, single parents, or antique automobile owners are another source of hospitality revenue.

Professional organizations for lawyers, doctors, teachers, or other skilled professionals hold annual conventions that include trade shows. Trade shows give vendors a chance to show and sell their latest products. Exhibit halls in convention centers and hotels provide the space for vendors, and the professional organization holding the meeting decides how much rent it will charge each exhibitor.

Political conventions large and small are good markets. Politicians have a history of spending lavish amounts of money on meals, parties, hotel rooms, and other special events during conventions. Hotel space in the chosen city for a political convention is sometimes reserved years in advance. Hotels realize that all rooms will be rented during the political convention, so room rates will rise for the occasion.

Special events like the Kentucky Derby fill all hotel rooms in Louisville, Kentucky. Some individuals rent their homes near the track during the Kentucky Derby week.

CONFIRMATION

Identify four types of potential markets for meeting or convention business.

_____

_____

SALES STRATEGIES

SELLING

L arge hotels routinely send effective brochures to prospective group businesses. Many hotels use the Internet to advertise. As well as learning about rates and availability, customers can take virtual tours, which allow them to see what hotel rooms, meeting rooms, and restaurants look like.

Mailing lists of professional organizations are regularly updated and sold by companies that maintain such databases. Local chambers of commerce and state tourism offices can also help hospitality sales departments by identifying meetings or events that could attract visitors. Civic organizations may help make presentations to persuade large groups to book an event. Large meetings requiring more than one hotel may use the Convention Bureau as a housing bureau for referring or handling reservations.

Close contact with tour operators is profitable for package tour business. Trade fairs held by tour operator associations provide good exhibit venues for hotels, convention centers, and other hospitality businesses. Careful attention to local newspaper stories helps hospitality sales departments to contact key people with the Lions Club, Kiwanis International, or other local organizations. A sales department must be creative enough to turn a lead into a profitable end result.

Once the sale is closed, contracts must be prepared showing room arrangements, menus, and projected number of guests. The customer signs a contract that specifies cancellation procedures and fees. All hospitality employees must work as a team to create an experience that will result in repeat business. Successful group functions at hotels depend upon all departments from sales to wait staff to housekeeping performing well.

CONFIRMATION

Name three sales strategies used by hospitality providers to attract group sales.

_____

_____

UNDERSTAND MARKETING CONCEPTS

Circle the best answer for each of the following questions.

1. ___?___ are important to plan for future hospitality business.
   a. CVBs
   b. Forecasts
   c. Guest questionnaires
   d. (b) and (c)

2. The sales staff of a hotel is responsible for selling
   a. meeting space
   b. rooms
   c. recreational facilities
   d. all of the above

THINK CRITICALLLY

Answer the following questions as completely as possible. if necessary, use a separate sheet of paper.

3. **Research** Check your local newspaper or with your local Chamber of Commerce for information on an upcoming group meeting or convention in your area. How many attendees are expected? What hospitality services would you expect to be needed?

_____

_____

_____

_____

4. **Marketing Math** You are catering a meal at your local country club. Your client has chosen chicken, baked potato, steamed vegetables, chocolate cake, and soft drinks for the meal. The price per plate is $21. A trip to the upscale grocery store has a chicken breast priced at $1.50 and the potatoes and vegetables costing approximately $1.00 per person. The chocolate cake costs an additional $1.00 per person, and the soft drink costs $0.20. What percentage of profit are you making on each meal?

_____

_____

_____

_____

CHAPTER 4 REVIEW

REVIEW MARKETING CONCEPTS

Write the letter of the term that matches each definition. Some terms will not be used.

_____ **1.** Particular types of people and what they like

_____ **2.** Vacation awards

_____ **3.** Renting multiple hotel rooms and meeting rooms

_____ **4.** Promotes tourism and convention business

_____ **5.** Future projections

_____ **6.** Guest expected to check out today

_____ **7.** Holds the hotel room until check-out the next day

_____ **8.** Third parties used to make reservations on the Internet

a. Conference and Visitors Bureau (CVB)
b. due-out
c. forecasts
d. group sales
e. guaranteed reservation
f. incentive travel
g. infomediaries
h. psychographic information
i. regular reservation

Circle the best answer.

9. A five-star hotel is rated
    a. good
    b. very good
    c. best in class
    d. excellent

10. The Internet
    a. has made a slower impact on society than television
    b. offers infomediaries to reserve hospitality and tourism services
    c. has very little impact on the hospitality industry
    d. has not proven to be an effective sales tool

11. The sales strategy for a hotel
    a. is the sole responsibility of the sales department
    b. must forecast future trends
    c. is the responsibility of all hotel employees
    d. (b) and (c)

12. A customer with a guaranteed reservation
    a. can sometimes negotiate their hotel room rate
    b. receives priority over walk-in customers
    c. can be accommodated easily with a large number of stayovers
    d. is not required to pay until they check out of the room

THINK CRITICALLY

13. You are in charge of a Spring Home and Garden Trade Show. List ten vendors you want as exhibitors, and give reasons for each of your choices.

_____
_____
_____
_____
_____
_____
_____

14. Select any city and design a brochure to attract tourism and convention business. List items here that highlight the strongest features of the city.

_____
_____
_____
_____
_____
_____
_____

15. Use the Internet to locate as much information as possible about a hotel chain. Does the hotel have a web site? Can you reserve a room directly from the web site? Does the hotel chain promote its facilities to large groups? If so, how?

_____
_____
_____
_____
_____

CHAPTER 4 REVIEW

MAKE CONNECTIONS

16. **Marketing Math**   Your hotel property has 200 rooms with an average room rate of $125 per night. A 60% occupancy rate is necessary to reach the financial goals of your property. There are 365 days in the year. What is the gross sales goal from hotel room sales for the year?

_____

_____

_____

_____

17. **History**   Conduct research about the Internet. Write an interesting one-page paper about the history of this fascinating technology. Make a brief outline here.

_____

_____

_____

_____

18. **Communication**   You are an event planner for a major five-star hotel. A large percentage of your sales depends on repeat business. Design a frequent-user program to reward your best customers. Give explicit details for your plan.

_____

_____

_____

_____

19. **Technology**   Your hotel has asked you to hire a web page designer to design a virtual tour of your hotel and restaurant property. Give clear instructions to the web page designer to let them know what you want included in the virtual tour.

_____

_____

_____

_____

HOSPITALITY AND RECREATION MARKETING RESEARCH EVENT

You have been hired by a major hotel chain to conduct customer research. The purpose of your research is to determine customer expectations and satisfaction with your hotel properties. You will design a survey, develop a budget for your research, conduct the survey with a target market, and report your recommendations to the hotel chain.

http://www.deca.org/
publications/HS_
Guide/guidetoc.html

Follow this outline when you write your entry.

I. SUMMARY MEMORANDUM

II. INTRODUCTION

III. RESEARCH METHODS USED IN THE STUDY

IV. FINDINGS AND CONCLUSIONS OF THE STUDY

VI. BIBLIOGRAPHY

VII. APPENDIX

PROJECT EXTENDED STAY

The American Marketing Association's annual meeting will be held in Anaheim, California, the first week of August. You have been asked to design a tour package for the attendees from Nebraska. The tour package should include airfare, hotel, convention registration ($150), transfers, and possible amusement park tickets.

Work with a group and complete the following activities.

1. Determine the best flight rates from Omaha and Lincoln to Orange County (John Wayne Airport). The flights must leave Nebraska on Tuesday afternoon or evening (first week of August) and return on Sunday. Use the Internet, travel agencies, and 1-800 numbers to locate the best rates. List these on a spreadsheet.

2. Use the Internet or 1-800 numbers to contact hotels near the Orange County Convention Center to find out their special group rates. List the hotel rates for five hotels near the convention center on your spreadsheet.

3. Use the Internet or contact the Convention Center to obtain information about area attractions. Research at least five different attractions (amusement parks, beaches, and so forth) for entertainment. Include these five options and the prices in your spreadsheet.

4. Design an attractive brochure that explains your tour package. Make sure your tour package includes the registration price as well as information and prices for air travel, hotel accommodations, and area attractions.

CHAPTER 5

HOSPITALITY PROMOTION

LESSONS

WINNING STRATEGIES

THE NEW ICE AGE

You might expect to see a bar in a hotel that accommodates about a hundred guests. A movie theater, a chapel, and an art gallery in the same hotel are unusual touches, but nice. What about walls and ceilings made of huge chunks of ice, though? This is a hotel that's really cool.

Since the winter of 1998, the Ice Hotel in the Swedish Lapland town of Jukkasjärvi has opened its doors to over 60,000 visitors. The hotel is made entirely of ice and snow with small rooms containing ice-block beds. Each bed is equipped with arctic-rated sleeping bags atop deer pelts.

A sister hotel in Quebec, Canada, opened a few years after the Swedish bed and breakfast. Ceilings are 16 feet high, and furniture is made of ice blocks. The Grand Hall entryway is supported by ice columns and features a sparkling ice candelabra. The Ice Hotel takes five weeks to build and is open from January 1 to March 31. At the end of the season, the hotel is dismantled, with some parts left intact for tourists to view. During open season, the hotel offers opportunities for tourists to visit, stay overnight, or stage special events such as product promotions or weddings. In addition to the Grand Hall, the hotel has two art galleries featuring original art and carved ice walls.

The Quebec Ice Hotel has room for 600 guests. Rates vary from $200 to $914 a night. Activities available for guests include hikes and ecological treks, snowshoeing, cross-country skiing, and ice skating. For the more adventurous, special activities such as dog sledding or a class in igloo construction are also available. The Ice Hotel turns a cold piece of land into a warm and inviting place to visit.

THINK CRITICALLY

1. Name three market segments to which you could promote either the Canadian or Swedish Ice Hotel.
2. Choose a location in a tropical climate and tell how you would create a hotel that is as much a part of its warm climate as the Ice Hotel is of its cold one.

DEVELOPING PROMOTIONAL STRATEGIES

CHAPTER 5
LESSON 5.1

GOALS

Define the promotional mix.

List the steps involved in personal selling.

CHECK IN

Every employee is a sales associate at the Holiday Inn Express in Cripple Creek, Colorado. Establishing a company culture that emphasizes selling as everyone's responsibility began in 1994 when a new owner and manager took over the hotel. As a result of the personal selling emphasis, the occupancy rate has risen from 55 percent to an average of between 76 percent to 80 percent.

The first item on the job description of each position in the hotel is that every employee must be sales promotion minded. Management provides each employee with information about occupancy costs and operating profits as well as the importance of interacting with guests one-on-one. A semiannual promotion encourages all employees to be the first to initiate a conversation when they come in contact with a guest. Flyers in guest rooms state that any guest who is not greeted first by a hotel employee when the two parties meet will be given a free night at the hotel. For such a strategy, all employees must share the courtesy-as-sales-promotion philosophy.

Work with a partner. List incentives you might provide for employees who promote sales successfully.

STRATEGIES FOR SUCCESS

PROMOTION

The hospitality industry is intensely competitive. Companies constantly vie for the attention and money of weary, wary, and well-informed customers. Many businesses in travel and tourism develop partnerships with related corporations to make it easy for consumers to choose their products and services. Hilton Hotels partners with no fewer than 55 airline companies, as well as car-rental agencies, cruise lines, and rail lines to offer incentive points for members of Hilton Honors, a reward program for guests who stay frequently at Hilton Hotels. The Marriott Corporation offers Marriott Rewards, its version of the frequent-guest incentive program, and partners with companies such as VISA, Hertz, AT&T, American Express, and Diner's Club.

Hotels and other businesses in travel and tourism also team up with businesses that buy, sell, or arrange sales of products. These businesses, called **intermediaries**, offer special promotional packages. Examples are travel agents and tour operators.

Travel agents sell lodging and tourism products to the final consumer. An agency or an agent may sell a travel package that includes not only lodging, but transportation, meals, and entertainment or sightseeing opportunities as well. The agent charges the hotel a sales commission of up to 15% of the total room rate charged to the guest during the trip.

Tour operators also develop packages, but usually sell in large volume to either travel agents or consumers.

Hotels continually promote their properties in order to sell room space. A web site of a major hotel chain recently listed the following promotions.

- Family getaways

- Breakfast-lovers specials

- Romantic weekend getaways

- A trip around the world contest

- Senior living for short term stays

- Palm Pilot contest for those booking a meeting

Did you notice how many different market segments were targeted by the list above? Hotels, restaurants, and other travel-related industries offer special promotions to customers of every age, gender, income level, and occupation.

No matter how good a promotion is, if customers don't know about it, they can't participate. That's why promotional strategies are important. In Chapter 1, you read that promotion is an important part of the marketing mix. Each hotel, restaurant, or other travel or tourist business has an individual formula for promotion to market product lines successfully. The combination of advertising, public relations, personal selling, and sales promotion make up the **promotional mix**.

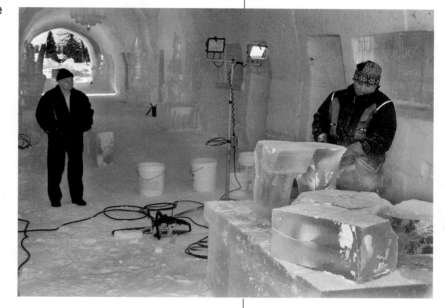

CONFIRMATION

List three strategies that travel and tourism businesses use to increase sales. What is the promotional mix?

_____

_____

_____

TIME OUT

PERSONAL SELLING AS PART OF PROMOTION

SELLING

Personal selling is the individual, one-on-one effort made by a representative of a company to persuade a customer to purchase goods or services. In the hospitality industry, sales associates work with businesses, event planners, and travel agents to sell rooms, parties, conferences, or travel packages. In addition, wait staff, guest service agents, reservationists, meeting or social event planners, bell staff, and concierges all represent the company and are thus involved in personal selling every day.

Marriott International has several sales-related strategies to increase sales and improve occupancy rates.

The Internet has redefined selling in the hotel industry. The Travel Industry Association of America reported that, in 1997, 5.4 million people used the Internet to make reservations at a hotel or with an airline. In 1999, that figure jumped to 16.5 million. Hotels are now using Global Distribution Systems to keep updated information available for hotel employees and customers.

THINK CRITICALLY
1. What is the advantage of a Global Distribution System for an individual hotel?
2. How does this type of information help consumers and encourage sales?

- Marriott sponsors a "Hotel Excellence" program to train travel agents on how to sell a hotel room effectively. The course shows agents how to determine the right hotel for each type of client.

- Marriott uses the **single-image inventory**. The same inventory of rooms is always available to anyone making a reservation, whether the reservation is through an agent, a direct call to the hotel, or the Internet. This allows the salesperson to have fast, updated information to meet customers' needs.

- Marriott has a specific sales and marketing department that focuses on the **Global Distribution System (GDS)**. The GDS is a computerized link between hotels and other travel-and-tourism-related companies and Internet sales from Marriott's web site.

- Marriott also has account associates who represent the company across the world, even in areas where Marriott has no properties. These employees have specific accounts, sell any economic level of a Marriott hotel, and represent all of Marriott's properties.

- Marriott assigns other salespeople to a specialty salesforce that is "customer-centric," which means they focus on the needs of the customer rather than the features of the hotel.

THE BASICS OF PERSONAL SELLING

Characteristics of a successful sales associate include honesty and integrity, enthusiasm and motivation, solid product knowledge, belief in the product, the ability to empathize, and willingness to spend the effort and time it takes to succeed. A good sales associate thinks ahead to determine what the client may need or want, and decides how to provide for those desires.

1. **Pre-approach** the client by preparing. Research the company or client, call to set up an appointment, and gather necessary *collateral materials*, such as product information, brochures, photographs, property descriptions, and rate information.

2. **Approach** the customer by arriving on time, dressed professionally, with appropriate sales material and professional attitude.

3. **Determine needs** of the client by asking questions such as the date and purpose of the event, the number of people involved, services desired by the client, and the client's intended price range.

4. **Present sales information** in a well-organized, clear, and personable way. Use the client's name, but be respectful. Describe **features**, or characteristics of a product or service, to demonstrate **benefits**, ways to help the customer meet needs. For example, a restaurant may have a large private dining area the customer can use for a meeting or an event. The *feature*, the size of the dining area, leads to the *benefit*, the ability of the customer to hold the meeting successfully. A sales presentation may be as simple as showing collateral materials, photographs, and prices, or as involved as taking a client on a tour of the property.

5. **Handle objections** as they arise. An *objection* is a true concern that the client may have about a product, property, or price. The salesperson should not see an objection as a rejection, but as an opportunity to address the needs of the customer.

6. **Close the sale** by asking the client to approve the product and sign a contract. The final closing may not always occur during the initial sales call, as a customer may need to gather more information or secure authorization. The salesperson maintains contact with the client during this decision-making interim. Staying in touch during the booked event as a contact point or a troubleshooter helps assure repeat business.

7. **Suggestion selling** occurs throughout the sale as a salesperson offers different services, room upgrades, or extra amenities to meet the needs of the client or the client's company.

CONFIRMATION

Describe the personal selling process.

_____

_____

_____

UNDERSTAND MARKETING CONCEPTS

Circle the best answer for each of the following questions.

1. Personal selling is
   a. a promotion or set of promotions to encourage customers to buy products
   b. a one-on-one presentation to encourage a customer to buy a product or service
   c. creating and maintaining extensive partnerships with other companies in the same industry
   d. none of the above

2. The elements of the promotional mix are
   a. promotion, pricing, personal selling, and advertising
   b. product planning, advertising, pricing, and promotion
   c. purchasing, personal selling, advertising, and promotion
   d. personal selling, sales promotion, public relations, and advertising

THINK CRITICALLY

Answer the following questions as completely as possible. If necessary, use a separate sheet of paper.

3. Think of the last time that you had a one-on-one experience with a salesperson. List the steps of personal selling that the salesperson actually completed during the time you were making a buying decision.

_____

_____

_____

_____

_____

4. **Communication** Find the web site of a hotel or restaurant. List at least five features of the establishment. For each feature that you list, identify a potential corresponding benefit.

_____

_____

_____

_____

ADVERTISING AND PUBLIC RELATIONS

CHAPTER 5

LESSON 5.2

CHECK IN

Travel and tourism has a giant effect on the restaurant business. The National Restaurant Association reports that approximately one-third of the annual revenue for table service restaurants comes from tourists. Travelers whose total bill is less than $25 account for almost one-fourth of sales. About half of the revenue at table service restaurants where the check totals $25 or more comes from tourists. As the amount of the check increases, so does the percentage of revenue.

In 2000, the National Restaurant Association developed a program for the purpose of promoting dining out as a memorable experience during family vacations. The strategies of the 2000 Tourism Promotion Plan included increasing media coverage, using the Internet to target consumer and corporate audiences, developing working relationships with tourism groups to promote restaurant business, and helping Association members market to summer travelers.

Work with a group. Identify travel and tourism businesses that would logically work with restaurants to increase business for all companies represented in a partnership. Include company names, images created by advertisements, and the market segment being tapped.

GOALS

Define advertising, and describe different advertising methods.

Discuss the differences between public relations and publicity.

ADVERTISING

PROMOTION

Advertising is the most familiar component of the promotional mix. **Advertising** is a paid presentation of a product or service with an identifiable sponsor. A successful advertisement will catch the *attention* of a reader, viewer, listener, or Web surfer. The ad must then continue to keep the potential customer's *interest*, while invoking a *desire* to purchase or further investigate the product or service. The ad must motivate the new customer to take whatever *action* is necessary to purchase the product or service. All these functions must occur in approximately five to ten seconds before the potential customer is distracted by another ad. Advertising falls into three main categories: print, broadcast, and specialty advertising.

PRINT ADVERTISING

Print advertising involves those ads featured in newspapers, magazines, billboards, or direct mail. Successful print ads include a short, easy-to-read

and attention-grabbing *headline* to draw the customer into reading the rest of the ad. The text or *copy* of an ad describes the product or service. The reader can clearly understand the benefits, features, and product description in the copy. The words should encourage the reader to try the product. *Illustrations*, which may be drawings or photographs, not only attract attention, but may serve to explain the product as well. The *logo*, the symbol used to identify the product or company, is always present in a successful ad. Nike's famous "swoosh" logo and McDonald's golden arches are two highly recognizable examples.

Newspapers are used by advertisers to promote a product or service because they can target readers in specific geographic regions, including national, regional, or local publications. The promoter can also select a specific day of the week to advertise, too. Usually when there is a travel section in the Sunday newspaper you find many ads for hotels, restaurants, travel agents, travel packages, airlines, and travel Internet sites. There are some drawbacks to newspaper ads. Newspapers have a short life span, print on low-grade paper, and are sometimes limited to black-and-white photographs. Cost can become an issue for large or colorful ads, and small ads must often compete with many nearby similar ones.

Magazine advertisements feature bright, colorful photographs on higher-grade paper. *Trade magazines* are periodicals that focus on specific aspects of travel and tourism. For example, *Lodging News* is the monthly publication of the American Hotel and Lodging Association. The articles, ads, and special offers are mainly of interest to hoteliers. *Consumer magazines* are geared to the general public or to specific markets such as travelers, business people, or recreation or adventure-seekers. The main drawbacks to magazine advertising are cost and the extended lead times required. The deadline for ad submission may be months before the actual publication date. However, magazines are usually read at a leisurely pace, have a long life span, and can employ powerful and colorful illustrations.

Direct mail advertising goes to potential customers through the mail. Direct mail can be used to reach specific market segments to promote new business openings, seasonal deals, or weekly specials. In order to capture the reader's attention, direct mail advertising must be colorful and creative. The results of direct mailings can be easily tracked by coding the mailed items and requesting the code when a customer makes a purchase or calls for a reservation. The main drawback to direct mail is that often customers see it as junk mail and toss it before reading it. Some consumers resent it as environmentally wasteful, especially when they get duplicate copies of the same unwanted ads.

For all the advertising you may see about special meals for holidays, such as Thanksgiving, the restaurant industry does best at other times. The most popular month to eat out is August. The next three most popular months are, in order, July, May, and June. Although Mother's Day is in May, the high traffic at restaurants in these four months are direct results of their being the busiest travel months of the year.

OUTDOOR ADVERTISING

Another form of printed advertising is outdoor advertising, which includes billboards and transit advertising. The advantages of outdoor advertising are the ability to reach customers in a specific location and the use of a clear, easily understood message.

Billboards are commonly used by hotels and restaurants to attract those who are traveling to or within a specific area. Billboards must be located in a highly visible spot, must have large print, and must be able to be read and understood in a time span of three to five seconds. A successful billboard shows the property name and address, location of the property, and any special features or promotions.

Transit advertising is found on buses, on the back of taxis, and in air, rail, and bus terminals. Transit ads carry the same information as a billboard. Sometimes a phone with a direct line to the advertised hotel property is located in the arrival area of a terminal.

OTHER PRINT ADVERTISING

Directories are another form of print advertising. Telephone directories, consumer guides, travel books and magazines, and trade directories all carry vital information about hotels, restaurants, car rental agencies, and local tourist attractions.

Counter cards and brochures strategically placed at front desks, in guest rooms, or at restaurant tables are proven ways to inform customers of local eating places, attractions, or recreational theme parks.

Collateral materials, which include press releases, photographs, product specifications, and price lists, are given to potential clients as part of a sales kit or promotion package.

BROADCAST ADVERTISING

Until the last decade of the twentieth century, the two forms of broadcast advertising were radio and television ads. When the Internet came on the world scene, web sites and links began to revamp the way the travel and tourism industry promotes products and public images. Global Distribution Systems, web sites, and connecting links are increasing in number and speed. Yet, television and radio advertising remain integral parts of promotional plans for hotels, restaurants, and other travel and tourism industries.

Television advertising sends audio and visual messages in a time span of 10 to 60 seconds. Television advertising can generate huge responses because of the size of the potential audience. Television ads, whether on a national, regional, or local network, must be simple, atten-

MARKETING MYTHS

When the Internet and World Wide Web began to offer on-line reservations for hotels, airlines, cruise lines, car rental agencies, and even restaurants, many travel agents and agencies feared extinction. Do-it-yourself bookings, they worried, would end their business. Such has not been the case, however, and many travel agencies have developed creative ways to promote their value to the traveling public, including establishing their own Internet sites. Corporate services, vacation packages, tour specials, and large volume discounts are examples of ways that travel agents and agencies promote their services. Agents can provide one-stop shopping for all travel needs.

THINK CRITICALLY
What personal added value can a travel agent bring to booking a trip or tour that might not be available on the Internet?

tion grabbing, and frequent to be effective. Television ads can be targeted to specific markets by broadcasting the ads during different times of the day or the week. The main problem with television advertising is expense. Commercials on a national network can cost millions of dollars per minute every time the ad is shown. Smaller businesses often cannot afford television time, even in local markets. High-quality television advertising can be expensive to produce, and any ad must compete with a constant stream of others, as well as with the restless viewer with one finger on the remote button.

Radio advertising is not as expensive as television advertising and is often used to reach large groups of potential customers. People listen to radios in their cars, at work, at home, or at play. Radio advertising allows for effective targeting of a market based on the type of station an ad is aired upon, and radio advertising is less expensive. Messages can change frequently and easily. A disadvantage of radio advertising is that many market segments may mean many separate contracts. Another disadvantage is that some listeners have short attention spans and switch channels quickly, especially when ads come in blocks.

SPECIALTY ADVERTISING

Specialty advertising involves a variety of events and materials to keep a company name in the public eye. The most common forms of specialty advertising are promotional items with a name or a logo on them. The list of such items is endless, from ball caps and T-shirts to key rings and refrigerator magnets. Although such items rarely have space to communicate much of a message, they build and maintain a brand awareness that may help bring a particular company to the consumer's consciousness.

CONFIRMATION

Define advertising. Name different types of print and broadcast media.

_____

_____

_____

PUBLIC RELATIONS

While advertising promotes goods and services, public relations promote an image. Advertising is always purchased. Publicity, one type of public relations, is not.

Public relations are activities or events in which companies participate to help promote a business and to enhance its image or reputation. For example, a hotel may sponsor a special Earth Day event to introduce the public to all its environmentally friendly policies. Hotels and restaurants often sponsor athletic events, support social or charitable causes, or coordinate food drives. Many hotels and restaurants donate linens, paper goods, and food to assisted-living facilities or shelters.

Publicity is a large part of public relations. When a new restaurant opens and is featured in the dining guide of a newspaper, that's publicity. When two airline companies merge and the national news networks report the business merger, that's publicity.

Press kits containing photographs, news articles, or celebrity biographies may be sent to news media.

News (or press) releases are articles about special events sent to members of the media prior to the event, hoping it will be newsworthy and generate attention.

Media dinners are events held specifically for reporters and editors to display some feature of a business as well as promote it.

JUDGMENT CALL

Some businesses go to great lengths to get publicity, since publicity can be a valuable form of free advertising. Sometimes, though, an ethical line can be crossed. What is seeking publicity and what is seeking to manipulate information for your own advantage?

Suppose the family of a seriously ill child were coming to your restaurant. The child, his parents, and his extended family from around the nation are all gathering to be together at a difficult time. The child, whose prospects are dim, will see many relatives and probably be given presents and the most pleasant time possible. You think it would be a nice gesture if the restaurant picked up the tab for the family. You also know a reporter for the local paper who is always looking for human-interest stories.

THINK CRITICALLY

1. Would you call your reporter friend and suggest that she bring a photographer and cover the event?
2. What ethical guidelines would you observe about seeking publicity? What is fair and legitimate activity, and what is not?

CONFIRMATION

Explain public relations and publicity. How do they relate?

_____

_____

_____

UNDERSTAND MARKETING CONCEPTS

Circle the best answer for each of the following questions.

1. Advertising is
   a. an article in a newspaper describing the grand opening of a restaurant
   b. a paid presentation, with an identifiable sponsor, for a product or service
   c. an event presented to inform prospective customers about a company
   d. an activity sponsored or supported by a company to enhance its image

2. The elements of a successful print advertisement are
   a. headline, copy, article, and logo
   b. headline, byline, tagline, and illustrations
   c. headline, copy, illustrations, and logo
   d. headline, illustrations, sponsor, and address

THINK CRITICALLY

Answer the following questions as completely as possible. If necessary, use a separate sheet of paper.

3. **Research** Find three advertisements in a newspaper or magazine. Identify and label the four major parts of each ad. Describe how each aspect contributes to the success of the advertisement.

_____

_____

_____

_____

_____

4. **Research** Find a news article (press release) in a newspaper, magazine, or on a web site. Compare and contrast the publicity item to any one of the ads you found in the assignment above.

_____

_____

_____

_____

_____

SPECIAL PROMOTIONAL STRATEGIES FOR HOTELS

CHAPTER 5
LESSON 5.3

CHECK IN

"We'll leave the light on for you" is probably the most-recognized advertising campaign in the lodging industry. The warm, folksy voice of Tom Burdett promises low prices, friendly hospitality and a homespun atmosphere for all who want an economical place to stay.

The campaign for Motel 6 began in 1986 as a plan to increase occupancy and create an appealing image for the brand. When the radio ads first aired, occupancy increased by eight percentage points in a short 18 months. For ten years, the campaign used only radio spots, but now includes television. The original campaign emphasized appealing value. In later years, the spots have highlighted upgraded amenities while maintaining downhome appeal and value.

Work with a group. Identify other travel and tourism advertising campaigns that evoke specific images. Include the company name, the image created by the advertisements, and the market segment being tapped.

GOALS

Define sales promotion.

Describe different sales promotions used in the lodging industry.

SALES PROMOTION

PROMOTION

The fourth component of the promotional mix is sales promotion. Any activity, other than advertising, public relations, and personal selling, that increases sales is considered **sales promotion**. Typical examples are sales incentive contests, two-for-the-price-of-one meals, discount coupons, or sweepstakes. When customers lined up at the counters and cars jammed the drive-through windows of McDonald's to buy miniature Ty Beanie Babies, people were not looking for a quick meal. They

The Farmington Inn, in Connecticut, uses story books to promote the hotel. The books are a combination of fact and fiction that introduce the reader to local history and nearby tourist attractions. A book is placed on the pillow in each room, so guests can read about the local area. Each book, such as *The Farmington Lady,* takes about 30 to 40 minutes to read. Guests are encouraged to take the books with them, resulting in a highly successful marketing tool. Similar books have been developed for other properties.

were buying the product to get the promotional item. The highly collectible stuffed animals took McDonald's sales through the roof.

KNOWING THE MARKET

The sky's the limit for a good promotional activity, and creativity and target marketing are the keys. Successful promotional activities get the right products to the right customer at the right time for the right length of time and for the right price. Hotels, restaurants, airlines, cruise lines, and travel agencies are forever creating packages and partnerships to do just that. There is a chain effect involved in traveling. Customers arriving in a city away from home need ground transportation, food, and entertainment or sightseeing opportunities. Hotels, airlines, car rental agencies, restaurants and entertainment or theme parks often provide package deals that include a little bit of everything the traveler needs. Effective sales promotions not only draw business, they create goodwill in the consumer which brings in repeat business, the ultimate goal of the hospitality industry.

Other companies are developing products to lure customers away from the traditional attractions of theme parks or land resorts. Royal Caribbean built the $500 million Voyager of the Sea that has everything you would normally find on land. The ship has an opera house, a 1,350-seat state-of-the-art theater, an indoor ice skating rink, an 18-hole golf course, 36 bars and restaurants, and a 30-foot rock-climbing wall.

Hotels offer not only vast accommodations and activities, but also creative packages to attract an expanding market of customers. The Travel Industry Association of America reports that 72 percent of all vacations in 1998 were family oriented. Among travelers, children influence 50 percent of the choices of accommodation and dates of travel. Sixty percent of the time, destinations are influenced by the traveling children. Rooms

and suites geared to children's interests have increased the number of children traveling to resort areas where they are no longer ignored. Imagine the ease of selling a room and entertainment package at Sun International's Atlantis Paradise Island in the Bahamas. The resort offers the world's largest open-air aquarium with an encased water slide that gives riders a safe and fast trip through the "shark-infested lagoon."

PROMOTIONAL ITEMS

Another promotional activity involves **specialty advertising merchandise**. When a sales associate calls on a business to set up an event or conference, he or she may leave clients promotional items like pencils, key chains, or coffee mugs bearing the company name. Specially items are often given away at community events or trade shows. Typical specialty items include pencils, key chains, matchbooks, and cold drink holders. Some promotional items can be expensive, but they are worth it if they build brand loyalty and generate repeat business. In some cases, promotional items are for sale as souvenirs. Many hotels have plush terry cloth robes, coffee mugs, or T-shirts with company logos available in the hotel gift shop. A desirable promotional item can also add directly to sales revenue, as well as becoming a traveling form of free advertising. Think of the countless Hard Rock Café and Planet Hollywood T-shirts that have been sold.

CONFIRMATION

How does sales promotion differ from advertising? What are the keys to effective sales promotion?

CAREER SPOTLIGHT

TAUCK WORLD DISCOVERY

Arthur Tauck started out as a salesman who traveled in a Studebaker across New England in 1925. Enamored with the beautiful countryside and rich history of the area, he started to bring friends along on his trips. He arranged the accommodations and itineraries and served as historical tour guide. By 1929, he was operating a tour company that offered the best hotels and finest restaurants as part of an all-inclusive package.

By the late 1940s, Tauck offered trips to Florida and Niagara-Ontario in addition to New England. When Arthur Tauck, Sr., retired in 1958, he turned the presidency of the company over to his son, Arthur Tauck, Jr.

Tauck's travel destinations soon expanded to the western United States thanks to air travel. Prior to the late 1950s, most leisure travel was mainly by rail. Jet air travel changed that, and Tauck added a new dimension to the company. In the mid-1970s, Tauck offered helicopter journeys to such faraway alpine areas as the Canadian Rockies. "Heli-hiking" still remains as one of the unique offerings.

In June 2000, the company changed its name from Tauck Tours to Tauck World Discovery, reflecting the company's expanded offerings. It has expanded trips to Europe, Australia and New Zealand, China, and Southeast Asia. Tauck World Discovery offers a Treasure Series to the Western Mediterranean area, Greece and Turkey. (Consider taking a trip on the Christina O, the multi-million-dollar yacht, formerly owned by Aristotle Onassis and named after his daughter.) In 2000, Antarctica expeditions guided by scientists and polar explorers became another voyage possible through the company. With the addition of African adventures in 2001, the company offered packages and excitement on all seven continents.

THINK CRITICALLY

Look at Tauck's web site and review some of the trips and adventures offered. Compare the prices, the itineraries, and the educational and adventure aspects. What makes Tauck World Discovery unique among travel companies?

UNDERSTAND MARKETING CONCEPTS

Circle the best answer for each of the following questions.

1. Sales promotion is
   a. an advertising campaign designed to promote a company, product, or service
   b. a newspaper article describing a travel editor's Alaskan cruise adventures
   c. a sales associate presenting information to a client about a hotel property and the banquet and conference facilities available
   d. any activity other than advertising, public relations, or personal selling that works to increase sales

2. Which of the following is NOT an example of specialty advertising?
   a. an umbrella with the name of a famous golf course
   b. a billboard of a beachfront hotel
   c. a ball cap with a resort logo on it
   d. a T-shirt with a restaurant's slogan on front and back

THINK CRITICALLY

Answer the following questions as completely as possible. If necessary, use a separate sheet of paper.

3. Name four sales promotions that you have seen recently. Describe how effective each was in increasing sales.

_____

_____

_____

_____

_____

4. Design a specialty advertising item for a local hotel or restaurant. Describe how you would use this item to increase the hotel's or restaurant's sales.

_____

_____

_____

_____

_____

REVIEW MARKETING CONCEPTS

Write the letter of the term that matches each definition. Some terms will not be used.

_____ **1.** Hotels and other businesses in travel and tourism that team up with businesses that buy, sell, or arrange sales of products

_____ **2.** The combination of advertising, public relations, personal selling, and sales promotion

_____ **3.** Paid presentation of a product or service with an identifiable sponsor

_____ **4.** Activities or events in which companies participate to promote the name of the business and to improve its image or reputation

_____ **5.** Computerized link between hotels and other travel-and-tourism-related companies

_____ **6.** Ways to help the customer meet needs

_____ **7.** Individual, one-on-one effort made by a representative of a company to persuade a customer to purchase goods or services

_____ **8.** Characteristics of a product or service

a. advertising
b. benefits
c. features
d. Global Distribution System (GDS)
e. intermediaries
f. personal selling
g. promotional mix
h. public relations
i. publicity
j. sales promotion
k. single-image inventory
l. specialty advertising merchandise

Circle the best answer.

9. The system that keeps the same inventory of rooms available to anyone making a reservation, whether the reservation is through an agent, a direct call to the hotel, or the Internet, is known as a
 a. central reservation system
 b. technical reservation inventory
 c. single-image inventory
 d. computerized inventory

10. Sponsoring a charity fun run or golf tournament is an example of
 a. public relations
 b. product and service planning
 c. ad purchasing
 d. presentation

11. The part of personal selling in which one sets an appointment to see a client and prepares information for that client is known as the
 a. approach
 b. presentation
 c. investigation
 d. pre-approach

THINK CRITICALLY

12. Work with a partner to review the characteristics of a successful salesperson. For each characteristic, list examples or situations that require a salesperson to exhibit those traits.

_____

_____

_____

_____

_____

13. Why should selling be a part of every employee's job description and training?

_____

_____

_____

_____

_____

14. Why is personal selling considered part of the promotional mix?

_____

_____

_____

_____

15. Explain how members of a hotel's housekeeping staff are involved in personal selling.

_____

_____

_____

_____

_____

CHAPTER 5 REVIEW

MAKE CONNECTIONS

16. **Marketing Math**   You are a sales associate for a large metropolitan hotel. Your annual salary is $57,250 plus 5 percent commission of your sales. Last year, your work brought in $379,250 in total business to the hotel. What was your gross annual income last year?

_____

_____

_____

_____

17. **History**   Research a local historical landmark, tourist attraction, or event. Outline or create a description of a fictional short story that features the landmark, tourist attraction, or event; fictional characters; and "real-life" history.

_____

_____

_____

_____

18. **Communication**   Now develop a brochure or one-page ad promoting the landmark, tourist attraction, or event you selected in 17.

_____

_____

_____

_____

19. **Technology**   Create a PowerPoint presentation telling your story and promoting the landmark, tourist attraction, or event. Give the presentation as if you were presenting a marketing plan to a client you selected in 17.

_____

_____

_____

_____

BUSINESS SERVICES MARKETING ROLE PLAY

http://www.deca.org
/publications/HS_
Guide/guidetoc.html

You are the front desk manager of a major 1,000-room hotel that is the choice for numerous national conventions. Your hotel is located in Houston, Texas and the two major airports are located 35 miles from your hotel. Cab service from the airport to your hotel costs $49 and the airport shuttle that runs sporadically costs $25. Many hotel guests have complained about the service and cost to and from the airports. You have scheduled a meeting with the hotel general manager to convince them of the need for free shuttle service to the airports provided by the hotel. You feel that the cost can be absorbed in higher room rates since your hotel was recently remodeled and upgraded. Be sure to emphasize the importance of the service you are proposing.

PROJECT EXTENDED STAY

Your hotel wants to work with a travel agency to promote vacation packages, trips, and special weekend rates to increase its occupancy rate. You have been in the sales department for two years and have worked successfully with meeting planners, event directors, and group sponsors. The hotel general manager is seeking your help in developing information to provide the travel agents.

Work with a group and complete the following activities.

1. Using the Internet or your local Chamber of Commerce as a resource, research local attractions that you might wish to offer in your packages. Include at least six, reaching as many market segments as possible.

2. Create a brochure that promotes your hotel. Include features, benefits, photographs or clip art, and other vital information such as phone numbers, location, reservation information, logos, and so forth.

3. Write a press release describing the vacation packages and special promotional offers. Include information regarding the savings resulting from the special packages as compared to purchasing the various elements separately.

4. Develop a folder of collateral materials, including items such as descriptions of the rooms, photographs of the property, menus for the food and beverage outlets, and recreational opportunities.

5. Plan a dinner and tour of your property for at least 20 travel agents in your area. Include the dinner menu as well as the specific features of your hotel that you plan to include in the tour. Create an agenda for the dinner meeting. Identify personal selling techniques for use in the presentation.

CHAPTER 6

PROMOTING TO TARGET MARKETS

LESSONS

BOUTIQUE LODGING:
A NEW TREND

A trend called "boutique lodging" is bringing a new style of luxury hotel to American cities. In Washington, D. C., the 139-room Hotel George is a hip hotel located on a quiet street in Capitol Hill's business district, near the Smithsonian and the new Sculpture Garden. Stainless steel and glass with retro furnishings in jewel-bright shades, the city's first modern boutique hotel plays on its name with huge neon silk-screen dollar bills adorning every room.

Contemporary French cuisine is served at the super-chic bistro, Bis, run by one of the city's top chefs. The restaurant is gorgeous, with high ceilings, metallic wall coverings, and a soft-glass window on the open kitchen so you can see the chefs at work. The Hotel George provides an irreverent breath of fresh air in conservative Washington. Standard rooms at the Hotel George range from $225 to $285 per night, with suites costing $475 to $675, and has attracted celebrities such as John Malkovich and Christina Aguilera.

In Houston, the Red Lion Hotel, located near the famous Galleria, will become Houston's first boutique hotel, the Hotel Derek. Designer Danya Lee plans a total transformation of the 319 rooms, including pink up-lighting behind mahogany platform beds, custom linens edged in black piping, armoires with mirrored glass shelves and removable wooden boxes, and unique lamps attached to the bathroom vanities. A popular restaurant and bar will be the superstar partner in the hotel. Room rates for the Hotel Derek will range from $200 to $260 per night.

THINK CRITICALLY

1. What defines a "boutique" hotel?
2. What marketing strategy could be used by the Hotel George and the Hotel Derek to attract a customer base to this new type of hotel?

CHAPTER 6

LESSON 6.1

CUSTOMER DEMOGRAPHICS

GOALS

Define target market, and list the five elements of market segmentation.

Explain the role of demographics in hospitality marketing.

CHECK IN

Perhaps a retired couple on vacation or college students on spring break are looking for economy hotels. Newlyweds may seek luxury hotels for their once-in-a-lifetime honeymoon. A teachers' convention may require many reasonably priced rooms, while a corporate seminar may demand five-star amenities. Individuals looking for the unique may opt to stay at a boutique hotel.

Hotels and motels must determine whom they wish to have as their clients in order to devise sound marketing strategies. Understanding these target markets is critical to success in the hospitality industry.

Work with a partner. List four distinct target markets that hotels or motels might seek to serve. Subdivide these four markets into at least two specific groups of customers.

MEETING THE NEEDS OF A TARGET MARKET

MARKETING-INFORMATION MANAGEMENT

The hospitality industry must determine the audience to which it sells its services in order to design an effective promotional strategy. **Target market** is the specific group of people that a business intends to reach. The needs and wants of the target market must be determined in order to promote and sell products. Knowing the preferences of a target market helps a business determine what those people will purchase. Successful hospitality businesses acquire specific information about their markets, such as potential customers' age, gender, marital status, income, educational level, and attitudes. These characteristics are referred to as **demographics**.

Niche marketing involves selling goods and services to a smaller, uniquely defined group of people. Hospitality businesses must research both the larger target market and smaller niche markets for the goods and services they sell. Common niche markets for the hospitality industry include men and women in different age groups for business travelers, leisure travelers, international travelers, families, and senior citizens. Different ethnic groups in a diversified society are good examples of niche markets. This diversity opens specialized opportunities for restaurants and other hospitality businesses. One of the most sought after target markets in the hospitality industry consists of senior citizens. This market has a healthy disposable income, attractive to the hospitality industry.

A **market segment** is a group of people within a larger market who share one or more characteristics. For example, millions of people in the United States enjoy country music, but a smaller group enjoys the entertainers at Branson, Missouri. Senior citizens enjoy group travel to Branson because they do not have to drive and they can travel with friends in their age group.

FIVE ELEMENTS OF MARKET SEGMENTATION

Maximum profit can be obtained when the hospitality industry focuses on customer needs.

Geographic segmentation involves dividing markets into physical locations such as the South, Midwest, Central Plains, West Coast, and East Coast regions of the United States or the urban and rural areas of a state.

Demographic segmentation focuses on measurable items such as income, profession, gender, and education. Level of income determines whether marketers will advertise upscale hotels to corporate executives, or less expensive accommodations to those more concerned about traveling on a budget than indulging in the extras offered by a luxury hotel.

Psychographics focus on attitudes and lifestyle choices—things that are harder to measure but have an impact. For example, the hospitality industry takes advantage of revenue brought in by fans of successful athletic teams, and restaurant marketing includes holiday buffets to capitalize on those who want to free up time for a family gathering without the hassle of meal preparation.

Product usage reflects how frequently customers use a product or service. This information allows marketers to promote preferred products and services.

Benefits derived are the value that people attach to a product or service. Enjoyment received from staying at a beachfront hotel and the satisfaction from a pleasant dining experience are examples of benefits derived.

Many businesses offer some type of program to attract senior business. Pender State Bank is located in a small Nebraska community with a population of 1,200. The Heritage Club was formed to provide senior bank patrons with travel packages that don't require them to drive to destinations. The Heritage Club has taken trips to Branson, Missouri; New York City; the Nebraska State Fair; and football games.

CONFIRMATION

What is a target market? What are the five elements of market segmentation?

A CLOSER LOOK AT DEMOGRAPHICS

MARKETING-INFORMATION MANAGEMENT

Demographics play an important role in marketing strategy. For example, hospitality tastes may differ for seniors and business travelers. Age must be seriously considered in planning a marketing strategy. Level of income influences what amount individuals might spend on hospitality. Education level is frequently associated with professional and income levels.

Males and females sometimes have different preferences when considering hotel properties. The growing number of traveling female executives makes it essential for astute marketers to attend to female preferences when possible.

Family travel has increased with the popularity of soccer, baseball, football, swimming, and other sporting events. Connecting hotel rooms, family rates, and family-style meals have evolved to satisfy the needs of traveling families.

MARKETING TO SENIORS

Seniors are a growing segment of the hospitality market. People are living longer and enjoying more active years of retirement. Many senior citizens are successful retired business executives and entrepreneurs who have saved and invested money successfully. These individuals desire to travel and enjoy dining out.

Many seniors feel more secure traveling with people their own age, who may share similar tastes. These "cohort" traits may include a preference for a musical style, for example. Today's seniors might like music from the '40s and '50s, but when Baby Boomers become seniors, they will likely prefer music from the '60s and '70s. Goods and services that appeal to today's seniors will not necessarily appeal to seniors a decade from now.

The current senior population has a disproportionate number of women in ratio to the number of men. The ratio is approximately 4 to 1 in the oldest age category. Living longer, healthier lives, many seniors are in good shape and able and willing to travel and explore the world.

MARKETING TO BABY BOOMERS

Many current seniors are products of the Depression years of the 1930s and the war years of the 1940s. This generation learned to scrimp and save as an absolute necessity, and believed in saving money for financial security. The following generations, raised in more prosperous times, are more prone to use credit to buy what they want and don't fear incurring debt. The number of Baby Boomers, and thus the potential market, is huge. Someone will turn 50 every 8 seconds in 2001. In-line skating, marathons, aerobics classes, and scuba diving are not out of the question for the next generation of seniors. Expensive hospitality venues are more likely to attract baby boomers than today's senior citizens whose practicality and frugality sometimes steer them away from luxury sites.

SELF-PERCEPTION AND REALITY

Adults often perceive themselves as younger than their actual age. Promotional materials such as brochures frequently have pictures of individuals as much as 15 years younger than the target market. These carefully designed brochures thus appeal across strict boundaries of age.

INTERACTIVE MARKETING

Interactive marketing is like a high-tech Yellow Page directory. **Interactive marketing** involves putting information about local history, culture, restaurants, museums, and other attractions and programs on the guest room television. Hotel guests select what advertisements they want to know about at the moment. The hotel guest can even have the television connect a particular advertiser to the guest room telephone in order to make reservations or to obtain more information. Interactive marketing provides a win-win situation for everyone. Advertisers get high-quality advertisements in full color with sophisticated graphics in hotel guest rooms. The advertiser has access to a record of the inquiries, calls forwarded to them, and a focused audience. Travelers increasingly appreciate and use this available technology.

CONFIRMATION

Why is the senior market so important for the hospitality industry? What special services may be demanded by this market?

_____

_____

UNDERSTAND MARKETING CONCEPTS

Circle the best answer for each of the following questions.

1. Which of the following is NOT one of the elements of market segmentation?
   a. target market
   b. demographic segmentation
   c. psychographics
   d. benefits derived

2. The largest percentage of the current U.S. population consists of
   a. senior citizens
   b. Baby Boomers
   c. members of Generation X
   d. children ages 3-14

THINK CRITICALLY

Answer the following questions as completely as possible. If necessary, use a separate sheet of paper.

3. Describe some business promotions for different target markets in your community. To what market segments do they appeal?

_____

_____

_____

_____

_____

_____

4. **Communication** Outline the features of two travel packages you might design: one for senior citizens, another for Baby Boomers.

_____

_____

_____

_____

_____

THE BUSINESS TRAVELER

CHECK IN

Many people think it is glamorous to have a profession that requires a lot of travel. It must be exciting to travel throughout the United States and around the world. Most business travelers, however, do not associate excitement with the travel that is part of their jobs.

Traveling, even to exotic destinations, can get to be a grind. What business travelers want is the simplest, most comfortable stay they can get. Successful hotels pay close attention to the needs of business travelers, because repeat business depends upon living up to their expectations.

Work with a partner. List differences between business travel and recreational travel.

Define business traveler.

Describe the latest trends and technologies affecting business travelers.

THE BUSINESS TRAVELER

Business travelers are on the go for meetings, conferences, and trade shows within the United States and throughout the world. Boarding an airplane is old hat to the business traveler and does not carry the same excitement generated from leisure travel.

Teleconferencing was predicted to dramatically reduce business travel. Experts were sure that thousands of meetings each year would be replaced by videoconferencing. While the use of videoconferencing has increased, business travel has not declined proportionally. Today's number of business travelers is at an all-time high, even with well-established technologies. Hotels and the rest of the hospitality industry must be aware of the current climate in the business travel market in order to offer services and amenities that business people need, prefer, or demand.

WHAT DO BUSINESS TRAVELERS WANT?

MARKETING-INFORMATION MANAGEMENT

Outstanding hotel properties track the preferences and practices of their guests throughout the year. A survey conducted by the William F. Harrah College of Hotel Administration polled 600 business travelers to determine how they spend their time on the road and in their hotel rooms. Results for the 2000 survey, when compared to the 1998 poll, pointed to several emerging trends in communications and technology. Rapid changes in these fields make it necessary to conduct research on an annual basis. The survey measured travelers by gender and generation. What age group is most wired? How much time is spent working in the room? Who leaves the room a mess and who calls home? Do men or women enjoy business travel more? What are the needs of a new generation of business travelers, and how will they impact marketing programs?

CONFIRMATION

Why are hotel rooms more than just a place to sleep for business travelers?

TRENDS WORTH WATCHING

Most business travelers take approximately ten trips per year, with an average stay of four nights per trip. Forty-three percent of a highly mobile work force traveled in 2000 due to a change in job.

Business travelers tend to be less frugal during a booming economy. Only 15 percent shopped for the best hotel deals in 2000. Redeeming miles to save money attracted 22 percent of business travelers. Prosperity and mileage programs make it easier for business travelers to take a spouse along on a trip.

CYBER MARKETING

A high-wired world has 40 percent of business travelers toting a laptop computer and 64 percent carrying a mobile cell phone. Business centers are used by 11 percent of business travelers, while 52 percent check their e-mail while on the road.

THINK CRITICALLY
1. What technology should be included as standard features in hotel rooms?
2. How might the growth of wireless Internet connection affect the hospitality industry?

IMPORTANCE OF HIGH TECHNOLOGY

PRODUCT/ SERVICE MANAGEMENT

Business travelers equip themselves with the latest technology. Hotels and the hospitality industry must be equipped to meet the technology needs of guests. Cell phones and laptops are highly valued by travelers in the 18-to-35 age range. This age group is more reliant on technology than travelers over age 35.

Because of technology, travelers can actually work more on the road. One to two hours are spent each day by travelers working in their hotel rooms. Competitive hotels will be challenged to meet this growing trend. Rooms not wired for the latest technology will not be booked by business travelers. Two telephone lines, voice mail, dataports, and oversized desks in well-lit work areas are needed to accommodate today's business travelers. Only 4 percent of business travelers order an in-room movie—they are too busy taking care of business when they are on the road.

HEALTH TRENDS

Frequent travelers rank "staying healthy" as a high priority. About 50 percent of travelers over age 35 make sure they take a daily vitamin. Only 40 percent of younger travelers take vitamins along. Twenty-eight percent of the up-and-coming business travelers take along medical information, versus 38 percent of the veterans. Exercise is important to the younger generation, with 25 percent using the gym versus 14 percent of older travelers. Hotels must continue to provide health spas and recreational facilities, as a new generation demands state-of-the-art equipment.

DINING STYLES

Travelers listed dining as a favorite benefit of traveling, with 30 percent of men and 22 percent of women enjoying a good dinner. About 13 percent of men and 8 percent of women were likely to have an alcoholic drink, and men were more likely to end a meal with dessert by 23 to 18 percent. Only 31 percent of new business travelers use in-room coffeemakers as opposed to 49 percent of the veteran travelers.

Younger travelers are less likely to eat alone, but 17 percent of young travelers use the mini-bar, while only 9 percent of experienced travelers unlock the mini-bar door. Monitoring statistics like these helps the hospitality industry meet and anticipate what its customers want.

MORE FEMALE EXECUTIVES

Women make up nearly half of the business travel market. Early attempts to accommodate female business travelers were not very effective. Segregating women on all-female floors was quickly rejected as demeaning and discriminating. Women want the same high level of services, security, respect, and recognition given their male counterparts.

Women are driving the trend of combining business and leisure travel. Forty-one percent of women polled enjoyed staying in hotels on business, while only 31 percent of men responded positively. Almost half of the respondents polled added leisure time to their business trips. Forty-two percent of the women surveyed spent time researching the destination and planning leisure activities, while only 27 percent of men followed this practice. A third of women like to take a friend or significant other with them on a business trip, while only 13 percent of men took a companion.

WHAT WOMEN WANT

Surveys reveal noticeable differences between men and women business travelers in what they expect from hotel services and amenities. Successful hotels have responded to the increasing number of women traveling for business. Like any consumers, women want suppliers to provide services and amenities that are important to them. Some of these items may not be important to male travelers.

Women consider responsive service to be the most important factor in selecting a hotel for business stays. Responsive service was ranked

People younger than age 35 have different characteristics than those beyond that age. More people 35 and younger travel with cell phones, carry laptops, check e-mail on the road, and carry pagers. Those over age 35 are more likely to place calls from a hotel room and keep up on current events than their junior counterparts, according to the William F. Harrah College of Hotel Administration survey for the year 2000.

Contrary to earlier belief, few women travel with their children when they are on business. The majority of women separate work and family. They are, however, extremely concerned with how work affects their family relationships.

THINK CRITICALLY

1. What might a hotel do to decrease guests' uneasiness about leaving family at home?

2. How could a hotel's sensitivity to family issues convert business guests to vacation guests?

higher than location and affordable rates. Males chose location as the most important variable. Women are more likely to avoid night travel than men, and pay considerable attention to hotel security. Women are twice as likely to order room service when they are alone on a business trip.

Women tend to prefer special equipment like separate vanities, make-up mirrors, and hair dryers in the room. Women strongly desire airport shuttle service and check-in for their flight at the hotel. Women seem more interested in frequent flyer, hotel rental, and car rental perks than men.

A 1999 survey of 500 business women and subscribers to *Working Woman* and *Working Mother* magazines indicated that women enjoyed exploring different cities to escape office routines, but they are more concerned than their male counterparts about the effects business travel have on family routine. Location, airport shuttle, and in-room checkout are part of convenience, the most important criterion for women's choice of hotels in this survey.

AN EXAMPLE AT WYNDHAM

Wyndham Hotels and Resorts was one of the first members of the hospitality industry to focus on female business travelers. "Women on Their Way" (WTW) is a special Wyndham program that began with a contest in which women responded to a single question, "What's your most important travel tip?" The huge response resulted in a web site, www.womenbusinesstravelers.com, a corporate division with an annual budget of $1.5 million. Wyndham has become the number one choice among women business travelers. Wyndham has a women's advisory board, an annual contest, a strategic partnership with leading business organizations, and an executive position dedicated to the needs of women business travelers. The program has generated improved services for and greater patronage by female travelers. The hotel offers a five-minute room service pre-call, for example, allowing guests time to get ready to receive their room service order. Corporate culture is changing as more women are in decision-making positions, and Wyndham now has 60 percent women among its directors of sales and marketing.

CONFIRMATION

To what hotel services and amenities do women pay particular attention?

_____

UNDERSTAND MARKETING CONCEPTS
Circle the best answer for each of the following questions.

1. Teleconferencing
   a. has replaced almost all international travel
   b. has proved to be more effective than personal contact
   c. has decreased the overall amount of business travel
   d. has not noticeably affected the amount of business travel

2. Female business travelers tend to seek
   a. security and service
   b. separate hotel floors from male business travelers
   c. the same high level of services and respect as male business travelers
   d. a and c

THINK CRITICALLY
Answer the following questions as completely as possible. If necessary, use a separate sheet of paper.

3. Marketing Math A hotel catering to business travelers has 128 single rooms and calculates occupancy based on a 365-day year. In a given year, the single rooms had a 94 percent occupancy rate. Registration records indicated that 52 percent of the occupants of the single rooms that year were female. How many women rented the single rooms at the hotel in the course of the year?

_____

_____

_____

_____

4. Communication You are in charge of the renovation of a major hotel that caters to business guests. What special amenities will you add to meet the needs of female business travelers? How would you decide on these amenities? Design a brochure or computer presentation to encourage female business travelers to stay at your hotel property.

_____

_____

_____

_____

CHAPTER 6
LESSON 6.3

THE LEISURE TRAVELER

Define leisure travel.

Describe the latest trends for leisure travel.

CHECK IN

The calendar flips to May, and you become more eager for summer vacation. Millions of Americans travel each year. Families, senior citizens, and friends look forward to leisure travel as a change of pace from the demanding daily grind.

Leisure travel offers consumers numerous choices ranging from exotic islands to baseball games in a neighboring community. Since there are so many choices, marketers of leisure activities must determine their target markets and design creative strategies to earn their business.

Work with a group. Make a list of possible leisure activities in your area to which visitors might travel. What is a possible target market for each attraction?

LEISURE TRAVEL

Leisure travel is travel taken solely for vacation or pleasure. Family vacations, weekend getaways, cruises, and guided tours are all examples of leisure travel. Leisure travel may involve a vacation to an exotic destination or a trip to a neighboring community for a soccer tournament.

Weekends are made for leisure travel, and the three-day weekends created by national holidays on Mondays allow people to travel more.

All states seek leisure travel revenue. Even for a place like Hawaii, tourism is no longer a sure thing. There is more competition around the world now, and there are many places where the quality of visitor service may be better. Small towns throughout the United States scramble to provide facilities for leisure travelers. Every weekend, families travel for sports activities or brief getaways. Local motels, restaurants, and service stations are financial benefactors from these leisure events.

ADVENTURE TRAVEL

Two categories of adventure travel are hard adventure travel and soft adventure travel.

Hard adventure travel requires physical strength and endurance for whitewater rafting, snorkeling, scuba diving, and off-road biking.

Soft adventure travel includes activities that require less rigorous exertion, such as a cruise ship tour of Alaskan waterways or a bird-watching expedition on the south coast of Texas.

THE POPULARITY OF CASINOS

The gaming industry is large and growing, and it has positioned its venues successfully as destinations for leisure travel. Casino boats and large land casinos earn tax revenues to pay for schools, roads, and other public works, and provide employment for many. Although economic benefits are hotly disputed by opponents of the gaming industry, many cities and states consider gambling a way to boost revenues.

Las Vegas is the premier casino city, and offers other entertainment attractions as well. The largest percentage of the city's revenue comes from the gaming industry. Las Vegas is one of the fastest-growing cities in the United States because of a favorable tax rate, mild climate, and profitable casinos and other attractions — the same qualities that have made it a boomtown of leisure travel for decades. Travel packages, including airfare and hotel, to Las Vegas are reasonably priced. Some packages even include shows and meals. The Las Vegas hotels realize that more income will be generated from gambling at the casinos located in or associated with the hotel properties, and thus keep costs down while still enjoying a solid profit. The city is working diligently to broaden its appeal by projecting an image as a family vacation destination as well. Adding attractions for children and promoting a safe image are two promotional strategies that have been implemented by Las Vegas.

JUDGMENT CALL

Casinos, gambling, and other venues for gaming earn large sums of money for state governments and Indian reservations. Like other forms of leisure industries, casinos and other gaming venues target seniors as a valuable market, offering free transportation and low-cost meals on site. Yet most people who gamble at casinos lose money. Some lose a lot of money, and for those unable to control their gambling or those on fixed incomes, these losses can be disastrous.

THINK CRITICALLY

1. In your opinion, what responsibility does a casino or other gaming venue have toward those who cannot gamble responsibly?

2. What is the most responsible approach to promoting casinos and other gaming venues to seniors?

CONFIRMATION

CONFIRMATION

Why is leisure travel not always to distant destinations? What is the difference between hard adventure travel and soft adventure travel?

LEISURE TRAVELERS' PREFERENCES

SELLING

A recent survey indicated that leisure travelers' first and second preferences for hotel rooms were basic cable television and an iron and ironing board. Surprisingly, the iron and ironing board ranked sixth for business travelers. Other items in the top five for leisure travelers included in-room coffee maker, premium television channels, and pay-per-view television. *USA Today* was the overwhelming newspaper of choice for travelers. Perhaps the easy readability and the color-coded sections of the newspaper were attractive to leisure travelers who were interested in quick and easy reading in a uniform format nationwide. Many hotel chains have made *USA Today* a standard amenity. The top five amenities appreciated by leisure-traveling guests have minimal cost.

THE IMPACT OF SENIOR TRAVELERS

Seniors will soon be one of the largest prospective market segments of the hospitality and travel industries. Older travelers will demand more than discounts to get their travel business. Active, fit, and healthy longer than ever before in history, seniors are rapidly changing the face of tourism. The group now known as seniors, defined as those age 55 and older, is the fastest-growing age group in the United States. As today's Baby-Boomer generation moves into this group, the senior market for leisure travel will be huge.

The growing senior group is quickly becoming a marketing target because its members have greater disposable incomes than do members of other groups. Retired seniors have more time to travel. Seniors can travel any day of the week and at any time of year to fill hotel rooms and restaurants. They have more flexibility to take advantage of meal and hotel specials. These same individuals fill seats on airplanes and tour buses, and fill campgrounds with their RVs traveling throughout the country. From 1990 to 1998, the U.S. population grew by 9 percent, while growth of American travel grew by 36 percent. During the 1990s, travel by the 55+ group grew by 50 percent, mainly in the leisure travel category. This age group is expected to grow by 27 percent in the next ten years.

Seniors travel for many reasons, but their travel patterns have two common traits. Seniors seek experiences that are a combination of education and adventure, and they expect to receive high-quality facilities and service for their dollars. Hospitality businesses that understand these two characteristics of a new generation of leisure travelers have a bright future.

TIME OUT

Here are some facts that show the impact of the senior population.

- Half of the Baby-Boomer generation will live to be 100.
- In 1900, only about a quarter of the population lived past age 65. Today, 80 percent does.
- At the beginning of the twentieth century, average life expectancy was 42 years. Today, it has almost doubled.
- People age 85 and older are the fastest-growing segment of the population.

ALTERNATIVE LEISURE LODGING

PRODUCT/ SERVICE MANAGEMENT

For those who regularly travel to a particular location, sometimes another strategy for lodging makes sense. Two-income professional families are investing in timeshare properties as a second home for vacation. Property taxes and interest paid on the loan for a timeshare property are tax deductible.

Timeshares are lodging properties owned by multiple families and individuals. The property is available to each owner for one week during the year. Timeshare properties at different locations can also be traded by the owners. For example, one timeshare owner might trade a week in Maui for a week in the Cayman Islands.

The key to success, though, is occupancy. Vacation rental bookings, like airline seats, are perishable commodities. Each day that passes with an empty lodging property means missed opportunity for revenues. Some owners who are not happy with their occupancy rates have formed strategic partnerships with Internet-based organizations that target travel agents and consumers. These partnerships follow the model set by the travel industry with airline travel in the 1980s. Deregulation intensified competition, and suddenly the friendly skies had a lot of empty airplane seats. Airlines addressed this problem by offering new pricing schemes through new channels of distribution. Owners of lodging facilities of all types have embarked on similar plans.

INCREMENTAL REVENUE

DISTRIBUTION

Incremental sales are sales to new customers outside the normal distribution channel. These sales are to customers who were typically inaccessible through normal marketing. Two Internet companies, Priceline and Cheap Tickets, for example, sell more than 20,000 airline tickets a day. The only costs to airlines associated with these sales are service expenses incurred in adding the business.

The Internet has drastically altered the landscape of the travel business. By developing strategic partnerships with Internet-based organizations, property managers can showcase the unique benefits of the vacation property rentals which are displayed, reviewed, and booked online by consumers and previously untapped travel agents. The travel agent community controls over 80 percent of leisure travel purchases.

CONFIRMATION

Why does the hospitality industry pay attention to seniors? What are incremental sales?

UNDERSTAND MARKETING CONCEPTS
Circle the best answer for each of the following questions.

1. Leisure travel
   a. usually begins with a business purpose
   b. may include nearby destinations
   c. is less attractive in a business-driven society
   d. is hurt by three-day holiday weekends

2. Senior travelers
   a. make up a huge and growing market segment
   b. are spending less on leisure travel as years pass
   c. avoid both hard and soft adventure travel
   d. are less demanding than business travelers

THINK CRITICALLY
Answer the following questions as completely as possible. If necessary, use a separate sheet of paper.

3. **Technology** Visit priceline.com or cheaptickets.com to see what these web sites offer travelers. Write a one-page paper describing what you find. Then visit the web sites of an airline and a hotel to determine the cost of a seven-day trip to Los Angeles beginning the tenth of next month. Look for the best prices possible. Describe your findings.

_____

_____

_____

_____

_____

4. Make a two-column chart showing advantages and disadvantages of casinos and gaming.

_____

_____

_____

_____

_____

THE INTERNATIONAL TRAVELER

CHAPTER 6
LESSON 6.4

CHECK IN

International travel is on the rise, and the U.S. hospitality industry realizes the benefits to be reaped. Adjustments must be made to appeal to international travelers, and companies that do not do so will miss out on a growing market.

From the point of view of hospitality marketing, it may be more helpful to think of international visitors to the United States rather than dreaming of your own visit to Tahiti or the Taj Mahal.

Work with a partner. List ways that managers can make American hospitality businesses more appealing to international travelers.

Describe the importance of international travel.

Explain special considerations for international travelers.

THE GROWTH OF INTERNATIONAL TRAVEL

Americans are traveling around the world at a growing rate. The number of Americans traveling internationally each year is approaching 100 million people, with the average traveler spending $3,500 per trip. Typical travelers leaving the United States spend 73 days planning the travel, and airline reservations are booked an average of 44 days before departure. During this four-month period of time, travelers face hundreds of questions and decisions about how to travel economically, enjoyably, and productively. International travelers should make sure that passports, visas, immunization records, international driving permits, and other documents, most requiring long lead times, are in order.

International travelers come to the United States as well. In fact, they come here more than anywhere else. The United States receives a larger share of world international tourism receipts than any other country in the world. The U.S. market share of world travel receipts has increased to 16.4 percent, representing $74 billion in travel receipts.

The growth of a global economy, the relative strength of the U.S. dollar, and the growth in the number of leisure travelers account for the growing amount of international travel.

WELCOME TO OUR COUNTRY

PRODUCT/ SERVICE MANAGEMENT

Wise hotel operators realize that international travelers are some of the best customers because they stay longer—almost always an extra day at least—and they are accustomed to paying higher prices. The hotel must work hard to establish a long-term relationship with international guests. The international business traveler is often interested in

long-term commitments by the hospitality industry. Some international companies look unfavorably at hotel sales operations that simply go after the highest bidder. Loyalty is a key factor in maintaining international business. Winning international business may require extra steps not usually part of domestic dealings, including patient and sensitive nurturing of relationships.

MAKING GUESTS COMFORTABLE

Visitors to the U.S. speak hundreds of languages. Printing information in English and Spanish can't accommodate all the international travelers arriving each day. Most hotels print guest information in English, which is an international business language, but they also hire people who can speak more than one language. Hospitality venues whose representatives can speak other languages take the lead in making international friends.

Hotels that want international business must be flexible with arrival and departure times of guests. Most international flights leave the United States in the evening, so hotel check-out should be extended to 4 or 5 p.m. without extra charge. Most flights from Europe arrive between 6 and 7 a.m., making an early hotel check-in attractive to international guests suffering from jet lag. **Jet lag**, a feeling of fatigue and disorientation, is caused by the disruption of the body's normal rhythms, and lasts until the body adjusts to its new location. Early check-in and late check-out times, sound-proof rooms, window treatments that shut out light completely, and noise control within the hotel accommodate the tired international traveler.

WHAT'S FOR DINNER?

International travelers appreciate touches that make them feel at home. A hotel hosting Japanese guests might make green tea available. Guests from the Middle East prefer plain yogurt over yogurt with fruity flavors. European guests may prefer a cold breakfast of fruit, lunch meats, and breads to the hot buffet offered by many American hotels. People in some cultures linger over meals, leave food on plates, eat at different times of the day, or do not eat meat. Some international travelers smoke more frequently than others and do not expect restrictions on their practice. Smart managers of hotels and restaurants make appropriate adjustments when they are aware of a group of guests coming from a specific area in the world. It is hard to please everyone all of the time, but making a dedicated effort will win the golden prize of international travel—repeat business.

CONFIRMATION

Give three examples of special needs for international travelers. Why are there more international travelers today?

BON VOYAGE

Business and leisure travelers going to other parts of the world from the U.S. need to learn as much as possible about destinations to determine the best method of making arrangements. Doing some research can help a lot when choosing travel agents, tour operators, cruise lines, and other professionals, or when planning a trip yourself.

SELECTING A TRAVEL AGENT

A travel agent will cut the hassles involved with international travel. More than 200,000 U.S. travel agents account for almost 80 percent of airline ticket, cruise, and package tour sales. They book more than half of all car rentals and one quarter of all hotel bookings made each year. Travel agents can customize a trip to best fit the international traveler's needs.

Full-service travel agencies make their money on commissions. They provide tailored service and personal attention to their customers.

Specialists or destination agents focus on a specific travel niche, such as business travel, leisure travel, tours of Italy, hiking/camping, cruises, or renting villas.

Rebaters return part of their commissions to travelers, and target those interested in the lowest price available for airfares, hotels, cruises, and package tours. They deal with people who know exactly where and how they are going to travel.

Fee-based agents do not receive commissions from service providers, but charge clients a fee for their service instead.

INSURANCE FOR INTERNATIONAL TRAVEL

Most international travelers think insurance is a good idea. Flight insurance covers death and injury in the event of a crash, collision, fire, or other serious mishap. Baggage and personal effect insurance cover possible damage or loss. Trip cancellation and interruption insurance applies to charter and packaged tour trips. Default or bankruptcy insurance applies if airlines or tour operators go out of business during your long-planned trip. Automobile insurance should be purchased if you plan to drive a rental car in another country. Personal accident and sickness insurance can cover health problems encountered while traveling outside of the United States.

The U.S. Department of Commerce has offices located in every major U.S. city, and within each of those offices you will find staff of the Department's International Trade Administration (ITA). International business travelers should contact the ITA before traveling abroad.

MAKING RESERVATIONS

Booking hotel accommodations through a third party, such as a travel agent, typically doesn't increase cost. Prices are usually the same as if the lodging were booked directly. These professionals generally offer their services at no charge to the traveler, because they are compensated with commissions from service providers such as hotels, car rental firms, cruise lines, and so forth. Rates vary greatly between peak and off-peak seasons.

WORKING WITH INTERNATIONAL HOTELS

Concierges provide personalized service to hotel guests. A concierge can help travelers make up for mishaps, surprises, and inadequate preparation. A good concierge is an important link, providing up-to-date information on sightseeing, transportation, restaurants, entertainment, and other attractions. Concierges can help plan family outings, make reservations, obtain medical assistance, and provide a wealth of other local information.

CONFIRMATION

How does a travel agency typically earn money?

CAREER SPOTLIGHT

SURVIVING INTERNATIONAL TRAVEL

Charlie Colon never dreamt that he would be an international business traveler when he started working for the Gallup Organization in 1991. Hard work and team leadership enabled Charlie to land the Director of Information Systems Global Support position. Charlie quickly learned that international business travel does not generate the same excitement as vacation travel. One of the most interesting challenges in traveling internationally was preparation. From passports to visas to currency, there are a variety of issues that Charlie had to learn. Did you know that an electric razor can start a small fire if you do not switch from 120v to 220v power in international hotels?

Charlie offers three tips as an experienced international traveler. First, make sure that you get a regular night's sleep before flying. Jet lag is real, and the body needs to be rested to help it adjust. Second, make sure to drink lots of water on the plane. Airplane air is dry, and dehydration may occur quickly. Flight attendants offer water about every hour. Drink up! Third, ask for an aisle seat. Snuggling next to a new acquaintance for 15 hours really isn't fun. International business travel is pleasant and productive when appropriate preparation has been made.

THINK CRITICALLY

Research the customs and business practices of a foreign country. What adjustments should a business traveler make for travel to this country? Devise a "Top Ten List of Preparations for International Travel."

UNDERSTAND MARKETING CONCEPTS

Circle the best answer for each of the following questions.

1. Most travel agencies make their money by
   a. charging fees for their services
   b. earning commissions on sales of tickets
   c. persuading consumers to accept higher rates
   d. selling travel insurance sales

2. Jet lag
   a. rarely affects international travelers
   b. is caused by a disruption of the body's daily rhythms
   c. is an international flight more than three hours late
   d. cannot be eased by hotel policies

THINK CRITICALLY

Answer the following questions as completely as possible. If necessary, use a separate sheet of paper.

3. **Communication**   Interview a travel agent to learn exactly what preparations you should make, documents you should acquire, and information you should have for a successful trip to an African country.

_____

_____

_____

_____

_____

4. **Research**   Your hotel will be used by a Japanese group for leisure travel on their visit to the United States. Conduct research to determine what special amenities the hotel should offer the group. Report your findings.

_____

_____

_____

_____

_____

CHAPTER 6 REVIEW

REVIEW MARKETING CONCEPTS

Write the letter of the term that matches each definition. Some terms will not be used.

_____ **1.** Specific group of people that a business intends to reach

_____ **2.** Information on age, gender, marital status, income, educational level, and attitudes

_____ **3.** Selling goods and services to a smaller, uniquely defined group of people

_____ **4.** Vacations and pleasure trips

_____ **5.** Putting information about local history, culture, restaurants, museums, and other attractions and programs on the guest room television

_____ **6.** Provides individual service to hotel guests

_____ **7.** Weariness caused by travel through multiple time zones

_____ **8.** Group of people within a larger market who share one or more characteristics

a. business traveler
b. concierge
c. demographics
d. incremental sales
e. interactive marketing
f. jet lag
g. leisure travel
h. market segment
i. niche marketing
j. target market

Circle the best answer.

9. Increasingly important to the leisure travel industry are
    a. male business travelers
    b. female business travelers
    c. seniors
    d. members of Generation X

10. Niche marketing involves
    a. concentrating on a particular part of a business
    b. international travel to multiple locations
    c. focusing on the widest possible population
    d. avoiding complaints of discrimination

11. Hard adventure travel is
    a. a function of jet lag
    b. booking to out-of-the-way locations
    c. uncertain cultural practices
    d. participating in strenuous sports on vacation

THINK CRITICALLY

12. Spend time with a partner discussing your age group as a target market for the hospitality industry. What special needs must the hospitality industry address for your age group?

_____

_____

_____

_____

_____

_____

_____

13. You are developing a new type of moderately priced hotel for senior citizens. What special amenities will you offer? Present your information in an attractive brochure. Be careful about stereotyping seniors.

_____

_____

_____

_____

_____

_____

_____

14. Use the Internet to look up a popular hotel chain. Does this hotel offer special senior citizen discounts? Does the web site focus on a particular target market? Does the hotel offer special services particularly attractive to female business travelers?

_____

_____

_____

_____

_____

REVIEW

MAKE CONNECTIONS

15. **Marketing Math** Suppose that the Hotel Derek in Houston, Texas, plans to charge $250 per night for a hotel room. This hotel was previously a Red Lion that charged $110 per night. What is the percentage increase for room rates? If the hotel occupancy was filled, how much more revenue would be generated for the Hotel Derek from the 319 rooms for one night, not counting taxes?

_____

_____

_____

16. **History** Research attitudes toward foreign travel and countries from earlier eras, using old magazines, books, or other material. How have American attitudes toward other countries changed? Outline a report that you might present about the changing outlook on people of other nations and cultures as it pertains to the hospitality industry.

_____

_____

_____

17. **Communication** Design a hard adventure travel package brochure for senior citizens. This vacation will involve hiking in the foothills of the Rocky Mountains in Boulder, Colorado. Make sure that the brochure includes all necessary information and emphasizes the beauty of the Rocky Mountains.

_____

_____

_____

18. **Technology** Design a computer presentation for travel to a foreign country. Be sure to give travel tips, and tell about the culture, dining, business practices, gifts, holidays, and dealing with jet lag. The presentation should at least have 12 slides. Write an outline for your presentation below.

_____

_____

_____

_____

HOSPITALITY TEAM DECISION MAKING EVENT

You have 30 minutes to study this situation and to develop an appropriate plan of action.

You and a partner are the managers of a luxury hotel located 1/2 mile from the location of next year's Super Bowl. Weekly hotel room rates are $150 for a single room and $200 for a double room. Super Bowls provide a financial bonanza for hosting cities. You and your partner must determine what room rates you will charge for next year's Super Bowl. All hotel rooms in the city will be rented for the Super Bowl.

http://www.deca.org /publications/HS_ Guide/guidetoc.html

Study the Situation Take 30 minutes to study the situation and outline your marketing strategy for accomplishing the three goals to boost earnings. Organize an analysis of it, using a management decision-making format. During the preparation period, teams may only consult with one another about the management situation.

Present Your Analysis Prepare a 10-minute presentation that describes your analysis of the situation. You may not use printed reference materials, audio or visual aids, and notes made during the preparation time to enhance the presentation. You may use a laptop computer for the presentation.

PROJECT EXTENDED STAY

Design a travel survey for a specific target market, such as female business travelers, senior citizens, families, or others. Your survey should attempt to determine what members of this market want from the hospitality industry in terms of accommodations, services, food, and other appropriate categories.

Work with a group and complete the following activities.

1. Identify a target market. Define the market as accurately and precisely as you can.

2. Design a survey for your target market. Begin by identifying categories and then compose questions for each. The survey should include at least 20 clearly written questions.

3. After your teacher approves your survey, find members of your target market and conduct your research. You should survey at least 50 people from your selected target market.

4. Tabulate and analyze the results of your survey using spreadsheet software.

5. Make specific recommendations to hotels and restaurants for accommodating your target market more effectively. Present your recommendations to the class.

7 CHAPTER

PRICING AND FINANCING

LESSONS

WINNING STRATEGIES

THE FATHER OF FRANCHISING

On a road trip to Washington, D.C., Kemmons Wilson found few options for lodging and was annoyed by the ones he found. Quality was poor in the $6 rooms, and the owners tacked on another $2 apiece for each of his five children. "I told my wife that wasn't right," Wilson said of his journey in the summer of 1951. "I told her I was going to build a chain that would have no charge for children." From this idea grew one of the most famous hotel chains. Wilson built Holiday Inn into a giant of the industry, the first chain to have outlets in all 50 states. In the early 1970s, a Holiday Inn was opening somewhere every two days.

Among Wilson's many innovations, his idea for franchising may have been his best. He built the first few hotels himself, then realized expanding would require more capital than he could raise. He pioneered the idea of licensing the name and standards, and allowing individual owners to own and operate the hotels. The timing was perfect, and as the interstate highway system grew, so did Holiday Inn.

Wilson designed the first few hotels, based on notes and measurements he had taken on that summer trip. He asked a draftsman to render plans, and when the drawings came back, the draftsman had sketched "Holiday Inn" on them, the title of a popular Bing Crosby movie of the time. Wilson liked the name, and so the words and familiar green sign became one of the most famous icons of the lodging industry. Wilson kept his promise about children staying free, and added innovations that revolutionized the industry, such as free parking, cribs for infants, televisions, telephones, air conditioning, swimming pools, and ice machines. He brought comfort at a fair price to America's middle class.

THINK CRITICALLY

1. How did Wilson identify a business opportunity?
2. Visit Wilson's web site at www.kwilson.com and find his twenty tips for success. Which five of these seem most important to you?

CHAPTER 7

LESSON 7.1

HOTEL PRICING STRATEGIES

Define types of room rates in a hotel.

Describe procedures for determining room rates and prices.

CHECK IN

Stylish "boutique" hotels appeal to young, well-traveled consumers more interested in being hip than pretentious. The trend probably started as early as 1981 with the Blakes Hotel in London, a luxury hotel in a property that was once twin Victorian townhouses. No two rooms are the same, and the restaurant is as innovative as the décor.

The term "boutique" suggests a small place, but some have as many as 200 rooms. Individuality is a key, although some things are typical. Instead of standard chintz or damask, you'll find canvas or solid colors, dramatic lighting, candles in lounge areas, and big, bold leather or velvet furniture. One typical feature is a young, good-looking doorman, dressed in all black. Though prices were originally moderate, many of the most recent ventures have high rates. Some of the pioneer boutique hotels are the Triton in San Francisco; the Delano in Miami; the Royalton, the Paramount, and the Mercer in New York; and the Hotel George in Washington, D.C.

Work with a partner. Describe some of the features of a boutique hotel that you might design. Compare your ideas with those of other pairs.

TYPES OF ROOM RATES

PRICING

Simply put, the hotel business sells room space. Room rates are highly variable, and always perishable. If a room remains empty for one night, the opportunity to make money from that room cannot be retrieved. The price of a room in a hotel depends on several factors, including the location and type of property, the services and amenities offered, the target market, and current economic conditions. A major consideration is supply and demand and the business cycle. Hotels that cater to business travel have higher occupancy during weekdays, so rates are higher Monday through Friday. Those same hotels lower rates on Saturday and Sunday and may even offer a promotion to increase weekend occupancy. Hotel prices are also subject to **peak seasons**, when the demand is high and so are rates, and slow or **shoulder seasons**, when the demand is low and the rates go down as well.

ROOM PRICES

Rooms in a hotel sell at different prices during different times and to different groups.

Rack rates are the published rates considered to be standard. These are the prices published in travel directories or quoted to a walk-in guest. Usually the highest rates, rack rates include different ranges quoted in terms of single and double occupancy. These rates are also based on the type of room, size of beds in a room, and location of the room. The term "rack rate" is considered hotel jargon and should not be used when quoting rates to a potential customer.

Corporate or commercial rates are usually 10-15% less than the published or rack rate. These rates are given to companies or businesses that are frequent customers of the hotel. Corporate rates are usually available Monday through Friday and are often determined by the amount of business the company brings into the hotel.

Group rates are available for large groups that reserve ten or more rooms for a conference or special event. Group rates are given because it is easier for the hotel to make a reservation for a large group than for each individual in that specific group. Since hotels usually require advance deposits and penalties for cancellations, groups are considered dependable and often bring repeat sales to the hotel.

Government rates are available for school, state, or federal government employees. These customers usually receive a *per diem*, or daily rate, of expense money from their employers. Money spent beyond the per diem comes from the customer's own pocket. Hotels offer government rates that are within per diem rates to acquire and maintain regular clients.

Senior rates are for guests who are at least 55 years of age or older. Seniors are a large target market and will continue to grow as the Baby Boomers born between 1946 and 1964 age. Seniors are often experienced travelers with a limited income. Most senior discounts are 10-15 percent less than the published rate.

SPECIALTY RATES

Specialty rates are discounts given for several reasons.

Airline rates are those available on properties located close to airports. Airline crews may receive a discount of 30-50 percent and transportation to and from the airport. Hotels may offer special rates to distressed travelers who may be stranded due to weather conditions.

Club or frequent guest discounts are given to loyal customers who return to the hotel on a regular basis. Club discounts usually begin during the slow season to improve occupancy rates and continue through peak times as a reward.

Employee rates are given to employees from the same hotel corporation. The employee rate is usually 50 percent of the published rack rate and serves as a reward and benefit for the employee. In addition, when employees experience other hotels in the same chain, they increase their product knowledge and improve their selling potential.

Travel-agent rates are offered to build a strong partnership with those who are able to sell large amounts of room space. When a travel agent is familiar with a property, he or she is more likely to recommend it to a client.

CONFIRMATION

List five factors that affect the price of a hotel room. Define five different types of room rates.

DETERMINING ROOM RATES

Setting marketable room rates is vital to the profit and success of a hotel property. Limited-service hotels get 98 percent of their profits from room revenues, while full-service hotels usually earn about 80 percent or more of their profit from room revenues, so rates have to be considered carefully. Construction costs, services and amenities offered, size of rooms and type of bedding, competition, and anticipated sales are all considered when room rates are determined. A traditional guideline figures a room charge of $1 for every $1,000 of construction costs and per-room investments. For example, if a hotel cost $200,000 per room to build, the average room rate should be $200.

HUBBART FORMULA

A more formal method, the *Hubbart Formula*, uses specific information to determine profitable room rates. This formula adds the *operating expenses*, or what it costs to run the hotel, to the *desired return on investment (ROI)*, the money a hotel hopes to make. Money earned from other areas of the hotel such as gift shops, restaurants, in-room movies, and so forth is labeled *other income* and is subtracted from the subtotal. That figure is divided by the number of *projected room sales*, derived from forecast information based on past sales, trends, and research. The resulting number is the average room rate. Following is the formula illustrated with example figures.

$$\frac{\text{Operating expenses} + \text{Desired ROI} - \text{Other income}}{\text{Projected room sales}} = \text{Average room rate}$$

$$\frac{\$9,000,000 + \$6,000,000 - \$900,000}{\$100,000} = \$141$$

BREAKING EVEN

It is important for hotel management to know the **breakeven point**. The breakeven point is where revenue, the money from sales, equals the cost of running the property. Revenue beyond that is profit. Successful hotel managers know how many rooms per night must be sold in order to reach the breakeven point. To find this number, first determine the fixed costs and the variable costs. *Fixed costs* are expenses that remain the same from month to month. *Variable costs* are costs that change with the number of rooms occupied, such as housekeeping. Suppose the fixed costs are $200,000 and the variable costs are $63 per room. Use the average room rate of $141, calculated previously. To determine the number of rooms that must be sold to reach the breakeven point, use the following formula.

$$\frac{\text{Fixed costs}}{\text{Average room rate} - \text{Variable costs}} = \text{Breakeven point}$$

$$\frac{\$200,000}{\$141 - \$63} = \begin{array}{l}\text{2,564 rooms per month must} \\ \text{be sold to break even}\end{array}$$

Occupancy rate is a percentage that expresses the ratio of total rooms sold to total rooms available per month. To determine the occupancy rate necessary to break even for a given month, first find the number of rooms available per month.

$$\begin{array}{l}\text{Rooms available} \\ \text{each day}\end{array} \times \begin{array}{l}\text{Number of days} \\ \text{in a month}\end{array} = \text{Rooms available per month}$$

$$134 \text{ rooms} \quad \times \quad 30 \text{ days} \quad = 4,020 \text{ rooms available per month}$$

Then determine the occupancy rate to break even.

$$\frac{\text{Rooms to sell to break even}}{\text{Rooms available per month}} = \text{Occupancy rate}$$

$$\frac{2,564}{4,020} = 0.6378 \text{ or } 64\%$$

Management and hotel industry researchers continually monitor the average room rate (average daily rate or ADR) as well as the occupancy rate of hotels. Another key factor in measuring the success and productivity of a hotel is the amount of revenue per available room (REVPAR), which is the average daily rate multiplied by the occupancy rate. REVPAR measures the revenue generated per available room and, in fact, is the method most widely used in the industry today to measure market position.

YIELD MANAGEMENT

Because prices in the lodging industry change constantly, management must continually analyze past rates, predict future demand, and adjust room rates accordingly to maximize profit. The practice of evaluating demand and setting prices that result in maximum revenue is known as **yield management**. In a slow season, or low-demand time, management often lowers prices or offers special promotional rates to bring in guests. When demand is high, or at a peak, hotels rent room space to guests

In 1861, the Willard Hotel was chosen as the place to smuggle in and protect President-elect Abraham Lincoln from threatened assassination. Lincoln and his five-member family stayed for ten days until his inauguration on March 4. From his first presidential paycheck, Lincoln paid his bill at the Willard, which totaled $773.75. Today, the Willard Inter-Continental offers rooms, restaurants, a business center, and a fitness center. Room rates at the historic landmark have risen, however. Prices range from $425 per night for a single room to $3,600 for a suite.

who are willing to pay higher prices. Fewer rooms are available at a lower rate. A hotel may ask a guest or group to sign up for a specific number of nights, to *block out* rooms. If the demand for rooms is high and a guest wants to stay during that time period, he or she must be willing to stay for the entire time period.

PROMOTIONS & PSYCHOLOGICAL PRICING

Hotels offer special rates and promotional packages to increase business during slow seasons. Weekend packages, family value deals, and coupons are examples of specials offered to entice customers to use a hotel. The hope is that the guests who use the coupons or weekend prices will be pleased with the service and return even when prices are not discounted.

Hotels often use psychological pricing. If a limited-service or economy hotel offers a price lower than its competition, the image of the hotel is one of efficiency and services at affordable rates. A five-star hotel may charge higher rates than competitors to suggest to guests who don't care about cost that its rooms, services, and amenities are more luxurious. Hotels often avoid even numbers when setting prices for room space. If a double room is offered for $59.99, consumers tend to regard the price as being below $60, even though the difference is just a penny.

CONFIRMATION

What information do you need to determine the breakeven point of a hotel?

UNDERSTAND MARKETING CONCEPTS

Circle the best answer for each of the following questions.

1. Factors considered when setting room rates include
   a. services and amenities offered
   b. location and property type
   c. demand, competition, economic conditions, and business cycles
   d. all of the above

2. The breakeven point is
   a. the point at which all rooms are reserved for a given night
   b. the point at which blocked reservations are released
   c. the point at which revenue equals the cost running a business
   d. the point at which a hotel fails because costs exceed revenue

THINK CRITICALLY

Answer the following questions as completely as possible. If necessary, use a separate sheet of paper.

3. **Pricing** Using the Internet, local phone directory, or newspaper, find ads for three different hotels. Compare and contrast the different types of room rates publicized. What accounts for variations?

_____

_____

_____

_____

_____

_____

4. **Marketing Math** Determine the breakeven point during June for a 120-room hotel with fixed costs of $550,000, an average room rate of $275, and variable costs of $132 per room.

_____

_____

_____

_____

_____

CHAPTER 7
LESSON 7.2

RESTAURANT AND TOURISM PRICING STRATEGIES

GOALS

Describe basic concepts of restaurant pricing.

Discuss factors that affect airline ticket prices.

CHECK IN

McDonald's, the king of quick-serve counters and drive-through windows, is experimenting with table service in an effort to capture another segment of the market. A test site in Kokomo, Indiana, offers customers a choice between standing in line at the counter to order food or sitting at a table and ordering via a special phone at the table.

The menu for the diner section has 122 items of traditional American fare, from pancakes for breakfast to meat loaf for dinner. Sandwiches, milkshakes, and desserts are also available. Once the food is ordered using the table phone, a server brings the food to the table. No tipping is allowed. In addition to the dining section, there is also a Diner To Go area, where customers can call in an order and then take it home.

Work with a group. Suggest ways other restaurants could change their methods of serving customers.

FACTORS IN RESTAURANT PRICING

PRICING

What would you charge for a burger? Simple—just figure out how much it costs to make the burger, add the overhead expenses, plus some extra for a fair profit, and there you have the retail price of a meal. That's logical, but the reality is not quite as simple. Many factors are involved in the competitive process of assigning a price to a meal, whether the restaurant is full-service, limited-service, drive-through, or delivery.

A major consideration in determining prices is the *cost of sales*, the cost of food purchased by the restaurant over a specific time period. To calculate the cost of sales, add *purchased inventory*, the amount of food purchased during the time period, usually one month, to the *opening inventory,* the value of food on hand at the beginning of the month, and subtract the *closing inventory*, the value of food in inventory at the end of the month. For example, if at the beginning of May you had $5,000 worth of food inventory, and you purchased $12,000 worth of food during May, you would add to get $17,000. That tells you how much food you actually had in your restaurant during May. However, you sold some of that food, so now you need to subtract the value of food remaining in inventory at the end of May, which is $4,000, to get the cost of sales, $13,000.

Opening inventory	+	Purchased inventory	−	Closing inventory	=	Cost of sales
$5,000	+	$12,000	−	$4,000	=	$13,000

When you subtract the value of food you have at the end of the month from the amount of food that you had when you started plus any extra you purchased, you know how much you sold. That figure is the cost of sales, because you had to buy all that inventory to make your sales.

But that's not all you must figure. You still have other expenses. **Direct operating expenses** are expenses that can be directly attributed to a department. For example, the dining room uses flatware, glasses, and dishes, and the kitchen uses grills, ovens, pots, and pans. In full-service restaurants with an average check per person of $15 or more, linens are the largest direct operating expense. In restaurants where guests typically pay less than $15 a visit, paper supplies and disposable items account for the majority of direct operating expenses.

Indirect operating expenses are costs associated with expenses difficult to charge to any specific area. Examples of indirect expenses include marketing, utilities, administrative costs, and repair or maintenance expenses for the facility at large, such as a roof repair.

There are still more expenses to consider. Payroll is the largest operating expense at most restaurants. Other expenses such as occupancy costs, interest on any money borrowed, equipment and depreciation, corporate overhead or franchise fees, and taxes must also be figured into the price charged for the food sold.

In 2000, two states considered legislation to ban smoking from restaurants. The Washington State Senate voted to ban smoking in all public places, particularly restaurants, where children are frequently present. If passed, the law will go into effect in July of 2003. Businesses where children are not allowed, such as casinos, are exempt from the ban, but must provide better barriers to divide smoking and non-smoking areas.

The Texas legislature considered measures that would make it a misdemeanor for a manager who allowed smoking in any food and beverage establishment that receives 75 percent of its gross revenue from food and beverage sales. The law carries a fine of up to $5,000. Private clubs and those offering outdoor seating are exempt from the law.

THINK CRITICALLY
1. Do you think restaurant and food-service managers should be required to prohibit people from smoking in their establishments?
2. What are positive and negative effects that anti-smoking laws might have on public restaurants?

MENUS AND MARKETING

Marketing is vital to a restaurant's success because it brings customers to tables. An important marketing tool is a restaurant's menu. The menu of a restaurant not only lists the food available and prices, but also reflects the image and character of the restaurant. Managers continually analyze menus to determine which products are profitable and which ones are not. Most restaurants use computer software programs to determine the profitability and success of menu items. Managers use sales figures, cost of food production, and revenues earned to determine whether or not to keep, drop, or add an item. Sometimes restaurant managers use jargon to classify menu items. Those that are *dogs* have low sales and low profit margins. Items that are *puzzles* have low sales but bring high profits. A *plowhorse* has high sales but low profit margins, and everyone wants to see *stars*, with their high sales and high profit margins.

CONFIRMATION

What is the difference between direct operating expenses and indirect operating expenses?

_____

_____

THE HIGH COST OF FLYING

Airline tickets are some of the most negotiable products in the travel business. A plane flying from San Francisco to New York will arrive at the same time whether that plane is full or not; and the opportunity to sell a ticket on that flight is short. A seat on a plane, like a room in a hotel, is a perishable product. Yearly seasons and business cycles affect the supply and demand of airline tickets. Due to deregulation of prices, the airline industry has become more competitive and has significantly lowered the price of the average ticket.

The policies and methods used to set airline prices based on supply and demand are considered *revenue management*. In the airline business, revenue management is not only highly competitive but also extremely confidential. Airline companies use extensive mathematical models and formulas to determine how much you will pay to fly next to another passenger who may or may not have paid the same price you did for a seat.

Just as hotels and restaurants, airlines have basic costs and expenses that must be covered by revenue generated mainly from the sale of the seats on the airplane. *Operating expenses* include the salaries of the cockpit and cabin crewmembers, fuel, maintenance of the aircraft, and equipment used. The largest percentage of operating expenses pays for salaries, wages, and benefits of airline employees. Jet fuel is another major expenditure. The air-line industry spends billions of dollars a year on jet fuel, consuming nearly 20 billion gallons of fuel a year. Ten to fifteen percent of all the money spent by airlines goes to fuel costs. Airlines are extremely safety conscious and spend large amounts of money to keep planes safe and updated. In 1998, $3.3 billion was spent on mainte-nance. More than $2 million per aircraft goes for labor, parts, and service. Other supply expenditures include passenger food, travel agent commissions, advertising and promotion, communications, insurance, and taxes.

Airline tickets pay for more than half of the expenses of airports by covering landing fees and terminal rental charges that the airlines must pay to local governments. The partnership between an airport and an air-line is one of mutual benefit. Airlines can offer service to countless desti-nations around the world because of well-run airports, and thanks to airlines, more than 1.5 million people are employed at airports.

Taxes are another big expenditure for airlines. Types of taxes include income and payroll taxes; ticket and cargo excise taxes; international departure and arrival taxes; fuel taxes; and immigration, agriculture, and customs fees. In fiscal year 1998, United States' airlines and their pas-sengers paid $18.8 billion in taxes and fees.

ANY GIVEN FLIGHT ON ANY GIVEN DAY

Airlines must sell a specific number of spaces in order to cover the oper-ating expenses of the flight. For illustrative purposes, assume that the tickets on a 150-passenger flight all sold for the same price. To make the flight economically successful, 100 of the seats must be filled. The follow-ing table gives an idea how some of the expenses are distributed.

Revenue from...	Covers the cost of...
29 tickets	Employee wages, salaries, and benefits
8 tickets	Fuel
9 tickets	Owning and operating the fleet of aircraft
12 tickets	Airport maintenance
5 tickets	Travel agent commissions
2 tickets	Passenger food
Remaining tickets	Taxes, fees, marketing, administrative, and other costs

CONFIRMATION

Why do airline ticket prices vary so greatly? What are the three greatest expenses for airlines?

CAREER SPOTLIGHT

HERB KELLEHER

Some people thought Herb Kelleher was nuts, but he's proud of his unconventional approach. In 1971, Kelleher and Rollin King decided to start an airline with simple ideas: to get passengers to their destinations on time at the lowest possible fares, and to make sure they had a good time. They started with three planes serving three Texas cities. In 2000, Southwest Airlines owned more than 300 airplanes and flew to 55 cities. Kelleher, former CEO of Southwest Airlines, built a wildly successful airline by doing business in unconventional ways.

Kelleher didn't run his business in a normal way. A creative, fun-loving businessman, he is known for settling a dispute over an advertising slogan in a friendly and well-publicized arm wrestling challenge. Other philosophies of the strong, smart, and passionate leader are to forget fancy business plans, put employees first, customers next, and love one another. He considers advertising campaigns to be celebrations, not gimmicks. The Southwest fleet includes planes painted as Shamu; the state flags of Texas, Arizona, Nevada, New Mexico, and California; and, to celebrate the company's twenty-fifth anniversary, Silver One, with a matching interior.

Conventional or not, under Kelleher's direction, Southwest Airlines won the airline industry's "Triple Crown," with the Best On-time Record, Best Baggage Handling, and Fewest Customer Complaints, more than 30 times. In 1999, *Chief Executive* magazine named Kelleher CEO of the Year. In January of 2001, *Business Week* listed Kelleher as one of twenty-five top managers in the country.

Kelleher stepped down as CEO of Southwest Airlines in June of 2001, but will remain involved in the company as the chairman of its board of directors.

THINK CRITICALLY

Investigate the web site for Southwest Airlines at www.iflyswa.com. What other ways does Kelleher create a unique corporate culture for his company? With a partner, make a list of personal qualities of an effective leader.

UNDERSTAND MARKETING CONCEPTS

Circle the best answer for each of the following questions.

1. The sum of opening inventory and monthly purchases minus closing inventory is called
   a. direct operating expenses
   b. cost of sales
   c. indirect operating systems
   d. revenue yields

2. The largest airline operating expense is
   a. jet fuel
   b. maintenance and safety
   c. marketing and administration
   d. employee payroll

THINK CRITICALLY

Answer the following questions as completely as possible. If necessary, use a separate sheet of paper.

3. Think of a meal you recently purchased. List all the food, supplies, and equipment that were used to promote, prepare, and serve the food. Include costs of everything you can think of, including such things as the furniture and fixtures in the building. Label each item as a direct operating expense or an indirect operating expense.

_____

_____

_____

_____

_____

4. **Research** Using the Internet, a newspaper, or several travel brochures, compare ticket prices and services of three different airlines. Find the price for a round-trip ticket to one destination for a duration of four days during a week one month from today's date.

_____

_____

_____

_____

CHAPTER 7
LESSON 7.3

PURCHASING STRATEGIES

Describe basic procedures used in purchasing.

Discuss the processes of receiving, storing, issuing, and reordering supplies.

MORE THAN JUST SHOPPING

PRODUCT/ SERVICE MANAGEMENT

Purchasing the right products for use in a hotel or restaurant is more involved than most people think. In some hotels or restaurants, the executive chef acts as the purchasing manager. In most hotels, executive housekeepers are usually responsible for ordering cleaning supplies, guest linens, and amenity items. Some businesses have a purchasing manager or department that oversees the ordering and receiving procedures of all items purchased.

Simply stated, **purchasing** is selecting and obtaining goods and services from *vendors*, the companies that supply them. Purchasing involves maintaining a professional relationship with vendors, gathering bids or quotes to determine the best prices available, evaluating products and services for value, developing and following adequate ordering procedures, receiving merchandise when it comes in, storing and issuing supplies, re-ordering, and keeping accurate records of all transactions.

The person who purchases goods, supplies, and services to keep a hotel or restaurant in business must keep several things in mind.

- **What is being ordered?** The purpose of the product being ordered is important. A floor cleaner that makes tile sparkle could easily destroy a fine Oriental rug. A purchaser must be thoroughly knowledgeable in all areas of hotel operations. Wrong materials, unneeded materials, or needed ones not ordered mean waste or poor service. Any of these conditions cost money, not just in purchasing but ultimately in guest revenue.

- **How much needs to be ordered?** *Par level* or *par stock* is the normal stock level that must maintained. A chef must track how much fresh produce he or she needs to meet the forecast or projected sales of vegetables and salads. An executive housekeeper must know how many linens to have on hand to keep guest rooms fully stocked.

- **Where is the best value?** Getting the best quality product at a reasonable price is vital to maintaining the standards of a hotel. Many businesses have specifications, commonly referred to as specs, that serve as guidelines when ordering materials or supplies. Specs may include size, weight, durability, quality for price, quantity for price, texture, or freshness. Purchasing managers constantly seek ever better deals.

- **When will these products arrive?** Delivery time is crucial. Consideration must be given to not only the amount of time it takes for the product to get from the supplier to the buyer, but also the time of day and week it will arrive, so that it can be handled by in-house staff.

MAY I QUOTE YOU?

Many companies require purchasing managers or buyers to secure several price estimates, or *quotes*, for products before buying. Informal purchasing involves getting several verbal quotes from different vendors. More formal procedures entail lists of specifications and written price bids.

Once the best price for the best product is determined, a list of supplies ordered from a vendor, called a *purchase order*, is completed. The purchase order is actually an agreement with the vendor and includes the name of the ordering organization, descriptions of ordered items, number of items ordered, individual prices of items, and the extended price (the price of the product multiplied by quantity).

E-PURCHASING

Online shopping has changed not only the way consumers buy goods, but the way the hospitality industry purchases goods as well. Think of the wide array of goods a hotel must purchase, from light bulbs to linen, pencils to potatoes, and furniture to frying machines. Hotels have a wide variety of items on a long shopping list. Hotels and technology companies are investing large amounts of money into systems that promise to move hotel purchasing to a higher level of efficiency and savings. New *online procurement companies and services* now offer automated approvals and ordering, price quotes, product specification comparisons, and reordering capabilities. In the past, hotels needed to call three vendors to get the best price. If an item was missing from the kitchen's inventory, it was considered a food cost. Today, e-procurement companies can do the shopping, tracking, and reporting for a hotel.

CONFIRMATION

What must a purchasing agent or buyer keep in mind when ordering supplies for a hotel or restaurant?

RECEIVING GOODS AND SUPPLIES

The careful purchase of supplies can be ruined if they are incorrectly tracked or handled when they arrive at the hotel or restaurant. Most receiving areas are part of or next to the purchasing department. When items arrive, the person receiving the goods compares the purchase order to the shipping or packing list to determine that everything ordered was received. Items are also checked for quality and/or damage. If some items are not present but are shown as back-ordered, a notation is made during the check-in procedure.

After the order is received and verified, the purchase order and packing slip can be turned over to management or accounting so payment can be processed. Some companies mail the invoice or bill separately. In such cases, the packing slip or purchase order must be compared to the invoice to ensure that the hotel was billed correctly. After the proper receiving procedures are followed, the merchandise or supplies are delivered to the department that requested them.

STORING, ISSUING, AND REORDERING SUPPLIES

Once supplies are in, they must be stored properly. Housekeeping supplies and linens are stored in a secure area of that department. *Inventory logs* show when products are taken out or put into storage areas. This record keeps a running total of items in the storage area. Food and beverage items are kept in *dry storage*, where temperatures range from 40° to 80° F., or freezers or refrigerated compartments. An inventory log or inventory card may be used to keep a updated count of all items kept in storage. This type of inventory is known as *perpetual*, because it is ongoing.

Managers also conduct periodic *physical inventories*, by actually counting all perishable and non-perishable items in storage.

When new supplies arrive, they must be stored in a way to ensure that the products already there are used before items that just arrived. This method of using the products in the order in which they were received is known as *first-in/first-out* or FIFO. Usually new items are stocked behind other similar items or rotated from left to right. Shelf life, or the amount of time a product can remain in storage before it loses its value, is a major consideration in food preparation areas.

Some businesses have very structured procedures for issuing supplies. Usually, the executive of the department is in charge of the inventory and allows several trusted employees access to the storage areas. When supplies are needed, a requisition form is completed that lists the name of the person requesting the supplies, the item description, and the quantity.

Hotels or restaurants often set a reorder point. When the inventory reaches the level established as the reorder point, the purchasing agent orders more items or supplies. Par levels are established and maintained easily when reorder points are considered.

CYBER MARKETING

Many online procurement companies are coming onto the scene in all businesses. One of the most comprehensive is Zoho, an online service totally dedicated to the hospitality industry. Using Zoho's massive database, a hotel purchasing agent can find food and beverage products as well as maintenance, repair, and operating materials. Through Zoho, hotel management can also find bids for prices, place and track orders, and maintain reports of purchasing trends. Zoho assists with shipping and delivery as well as billing and payments. The entire cycle of supply is covered as Zoho assists with hotel planning and design, purchasing, and even liquidating of equipment and materials.

THINK CRITICALLY
How are online procurement companies changing the way purchasing agents do their jobs?

CONFIRMATION

Explain what the acronym FIFO means and why the concept is important to product storage.

UNDERSTAND MARKETING CONCEPTS

Circle the best answer for each of the following questions.

1. Which of the following is NOT a normal function of purchasing?
   a. selecting and buying products and services
   b. receiving, storing, and reordering materials
   c. evaluating employee effectiveness with supplies
   d. identifying new sources of materials for purchase

2. A purchase order is
   a. the inventory level at which new supplies are needed
   b. a document requesting and agreeing to specified items and prices
   c. a bill the vendor delivers or sends for purchased materials
   d. the sequence of use of supplies in the inventory

THINK CRITICALLY

Answer the following questions as completely as possible. If necessary, use a separate sheet of paper.

3. Think of a recent purchase you have made that required a lot of thought, research, and expenditure on your part. Compare the way you went through the purchasing process to the way a hotel or restaurant would do the same.

_____

_____

_____

_____

_____

_____

4. Why are regular physical inventories a necessary part of purchasing policies?

_____

_____

_____

_____

_____

FINANCING VARIOUS FORMS OF OWNERSHIP

CHAPTER 7
LESSON 7.4

CHECK IN

Imagine a hotel owned by a jeweler—not just any jeweler, but the world's third-largest jeweler. Marriott has partnered with Italian jeweler Bulgari to offer luxury accommodations with a contemporary Italian accent. Bulgari wanted to move into the service industry, so luxury hotels seemed a logical extension of its brand. Bulgari officials approached Marriott with the idea in 1999. A partnership with Marriott would bring hotel know-how to the venture. Bulgari will join Ritz-Carlton as part of Marriott's Luxury Group.

The target market is the "avant garde" customer, attuned to the fashion industry. Bulgari is not only a jewelry company, but also a leading retailer of upper-end leather and silk goods. Therefore, the hotel décor will reflect that style by incorporating leather, metal, and beechwood into the furnishings, seeking a contemporary, clean look. The board of directors of the joint venture is considering potential locations in London, Rome, Paris, New York, Southern California, Miami, and several island resorts. The goal is to build or convert seven hotels in five years.

Work with a partner. List five reasons why a company not in the hospitality industry might want to get into the hotel business.

GOALS

Describe basic types of hotel and restaurant ownership.

List different sources of financing available when buying a business.

HOTEL AND RESTAURANT OWNERSHIP

There's more than one way to own a hotel or restaurant. In fact, if you really want to own a hospitality business, there are several options available to you.

One way to own a lodging property or food and beverage establishment is to invest in a **franchise**, which is a legal agreement to operate a business under the name of an already established business trade name or brand. Kemmons Wilson, the founder of Holiday Inn, was one of the first hoteliers to offer hotel franchising in the 1950s. The *franchisee* pays a royalty and an initial fee for the right to own a business under the name and system of the recognized company. The *franchisor*, in turn, lends the trademark, the trade name, and often the business system to the franchisee. The owner of the hotel, the franchisee, owns and independently operates the business within specific guidelines established by the franchisor, the recognized company. The advantage of owning a franchise is instant brand name recognition, national advertising, assistance with

In 2000, the cost of a new McDonald's franchise ranged from $444,800 to $742,150, with a minimum of $175,000 to start. McDonald's does not sell franchises to partners or investors, so the potential owner must meet financial requirements personally and be willing to devote full time to the daily operation of the restaurant. The franchisee must have no other active business interests when opening the restaurant.

training and development, site selection, marketing aids, and operations manuals. The franchisee is obligated to maintain the quality standards established by the parent company. The hotel or restaurant must use equipment and supplies and provide services that reflect the image of the company. Due to extensive franchising, the restaurant business is one of the fastest-growing areas in our economy. About 76 percent of all fast-food restaurants are franchises.

Sole proprietorship, owning and operating one's own business, is another form of ownership. A sole proprietor accepts all legal and financial responsibilities involved in owning the business. Because the owner accepts the risks, the owner also receives all the profits. The major disadvantage is the liability inherent in this type of ownership. There is no partner to share the work involved in running a business.

A **partnership** is when two or more people own a business and share the risks, responsibilities, and profits. Agreements are established and usually drawn up by an attorney. Every partnership must have at least one *general partner*, who will have unlimited personal liability and full responsibility for the management of the business. Sometimes partnerships are set up so that everyone involved is a general partner. However, sometimes a partnership has *limited partners*, whose liability is limited to their investment. The advantages of a partnership are that it is easy to set up and the partners have full control. However, the disadvantage is the strong possibility of eventual personality conflicts. Each partner can also be held liable for the other partner's actions.

Often a management company will operate a hotel under a *management contract* between the managing company and the owner of the property. The management company does not own the hotel, but is responsible for the daily operations of running the hotel such as controlling expenditures, purchasing goods and services, managing human resources, and maintaining quality standards. The management company receives a fee for expertise and service it provides. Management companies often operate a variety of hotels and other hospitality-related industries. Such a company presents many opportunities for the employee seeking to advance within the company or hospitality industry.

Another form of hotel and restaurant ownership is corporate ownership. A **corporation** is registered or chartered by a state and is owned by stockholders. A corporation must have a board of directors, who elect a

chief executive officer and a chief financial officer. These executives and other management personnel are experts in marketing, operations, human resources, planning, and financing. Any liabilities or operational challenges are under the control of the corporate management. Any profits that are generated by a corporation are distributed among the stockholders. The main advantage of working for a corporation is the vast amount of financial resources and support.

WHAT'S IN A NAME?

A corporation may own several different brands of hotels. A *brand* is one or more hotels with the same name. For example, Omni Hotels is a brand name, as is Hilton, Sheraton, or Marriott. Hotel companies often own many different brands in order to meet the needs of different market segments. According to the American Hotel and Lodging Association, in 2000, Cendant Corporation owned eight different brands of hotels, with a total of 6,410 properties. The brands owned by Cendant Corporation are Days Inn of America, Ramada Franchise Systems, Super 8 Motels, Howard Johnson International, Travelodge, Knights Franchise Systems, Inc., Wingate Inns International, and Villager Franchise Systems.

Major corporations also own restaurant chains. Tricon Global owns several: Kentucky Fried Chicken (KFC), Pizza Hut, and Taco Bell. Brinker International owns Chili's, Macaroni Grill, and Cozymel's, among others.

CONFIRMATION

List four types of lodging property ownership. Give one advantage for each type of ownership.

_____

_____

MARKETING MYTHS

Do you think you have to be a giant corporation to get financing for a business? The Small Business Administration (SBA) is another source for a loan. If the SBA agrees to lend money, it uses a commercial bank to process and release the money. The SBA guarantees that up to 90 percent of the money borrowed will be repaid if the business fails. Most SBA loans are for $150,000 or less and are usually given to veterans or disabled persons. The SBA also licenses privately owned Small Business Investment Companies and Minority Enterprise Small Business Investment Companies to provide financing for beginning businesses.

THINK CRITICALLY
The SBA's guaranteed-loan policy poses some risk to taxpayers, because if the business fails, the government guarantees most of the loan. Is this a good policy for the government? Why or why not?

FINANCING SOURCES

Wanting to own a hotel or restaurant is one thing, but finding the money to buy it is another. The money that is necessary to run a business is known as **capital**. The term capital includes money, real estate, equipment, and tools or goods used to produce goods and/or services. How much money it takes to operate a business successfully depends on the type of business, the location, and the type of ownership. Money to pay operating expenses is usually repaid over a year's time. Larger expenses such as property costs, building or construction costs, and equipment purchases are paid over a longer time period. Several financing options are obvious, such as banks and financial institutions. Other sources may not be the first places you would look.

Banks and commercial finance companies are both sources of *debt capital*. They require the borrower to repay with interest the money he or she borrows to run the business, called *operating capital*. Banks will set up a *line of credit*, which is a certain amount of money available for the company to use, as it needs to, but then pay back on a regular basis. Banks rarely take on much risk, which makes them a rare source for start-up money. Commercial finance companies will take more risks, so it may be easier to get a loan from them. However, their interest rates are higher.

Equity capital sources loan money in return for part ownership, or equity, in the business. Equity funding is also referred to as *risk capital*, because there is risk involved in the investment. Some of the sources of equity financing are personal savings; private investors; partners, friends, and relatives; and venture capitalists. *Venture capitalists (VC)* are individuals or firms that invest money professionally. The way VCs make a profit is through their investments. Therefore, their interest rates and desired return on their investment may be high. Some states offer state-sponsored venture capital funds in order to create jobs and boost the local economy.

CONFIRMATION

In addition to money, what else is considered capital? What is a venture capitalist?

UNDERSTAND MARKETING CONCEPTS

Circle the best answer for each of the following questions.

1. A legal agreement to operate a business under the name of an already established business trade name or brand is
   a. a franchise
   b. a corporation
   c. a management contract
   d. a sole proprietorship

2. The term capital includes
   a. money, legislative action, and equipment
   b. employees, equipment, and tools
   c. property, equipment, tools, and money
   d. all of the above

THINK CRITICALLY

Answer the following questions as completely as possible. If necessary, use a separate sheet of paper.

3. **Research** Think of three of your favorite restaurants. Using the Internet, telephone, or other method, investigate and list the type of ownership of each restaurant.

_____

_____

_____

_____

_____

_____

4. If you were a venture capitalist with a lot of money to invest, what would you want to know about someone who came to you with a great idea for a restaurant? Make a list of information you would want to have before investing a lot of money into the venture.

_____

_____

_____

_____

_____

CHAPTER 7 REVIEW

REVIEW MARKETING CONCEPTS

Write the letter of the term that matches each definition. Some terms will not be used.

_____ **1.** The number of rooms sold expressed as a percentage of the amount of rooms available per month

_____ **2.** Legal agreement to operate a business under the name of an already established business trade name or brand

_____ **3.** Evaluating demand and setting prices that result in maximum revenue

_____ **4.** Expenses that can be directly attributed to a department

_____ **5.** Expenses that are shared among departments

_____ **6.** Selecting and obtaining goods and services from vendors

_____ **7.** When two or more people own a business and share the risks, responsibilities, and profits

_____ **8.** When the demand is low and the rates go down as well

a. breakeven point
b. capital
c. corporation
d. direct operating expenses
e. franchise
f. indirect operating expenses
g. occupancy rate
h. partnership
i. peak season
j. purchasing
k. sole proprietorship
l. shoulder season
m. yield management

Circle the best answer.

9. Hotel room rates are negotiable and subject to change because
   a. room space is a perishable product
   b. property types are variable
   c. the cost of food and beverages is figured in
   d. employee turnover is high

10. In a restaurant, pre-opening specials and promotional items are
   a. a fixed cost
   b. return on investment (ROI)
   c. direct operating expenses covered by the home office
   d. indirect operating expenses shared by all departments

11. The Hubbart Formula is used to calculate
   a. price-quality purchasing value
   b. average room rates
   c. debt capital ratios
   d. occupancy rate

THINK CRITICALLY

12. If you were the purchasing manager for a hotel or restaurant, would you always buy the least expensive items? Explain your answer.

_____

_____

_____

_____

_____

_____

_____

13. Go to a local restaurant and review the menu. See if you can determine which items are the "dogs," the "puzzles," the "plowhorses," and the "stars." List them below and tell why you chose those items.

_____

_____

_____

_____

_____

_____

_____

14. Using the Internet or travel magazines in your library, find and briefly describe three airline companies or three restaurants. Who is the target market for each of the three businesses? What is the price range for each?

_____

_____

_____

_____

_____

_____

CHAPTER 7 REVIEW

MAKE CONNECTIONS

15. Marketing Math   Assume that a plane has 250 seats and all seats sell at the same ticket price. Based on the example given near the end of Lesson 7.2, how many seats will need to be sold to make it economically feasible to make a trip? How many seats will need to be sold to cover the following expenses: employee payroll, jet fuel, owning and operating a fleet of planes, airport maintenance, travel agent commissions, and passenger food?

_____

_____

_____

_____

16. History   Using the Internet, an encyclopedia, or library, look up the history of a legendary hospitality entrepreneur, such as Ray Kroc, J. W. Marriott, or another famous name in restaurant or hotel history. Write a one-page report describing how your subject got started, the nature and characteristics of the business, and the innovations and effects that his or her business had for the hospitality industry.

_____

_____

_____

17. Communication   You are the restaurant critic for your school or local newspaper and have been asked to write a one-page review of a fast-food restaurant near your school. Include the type of menu items, the type of service offered, the favorites, the atmosphere, the price ranges, and the nutritional information of the top-selling items.

_____

_____

_____

18. Technology   Create a spreadsheet to compare the ticket prices of three different airlines to one major destination during three different months. Include first class and coach ticket prices. Explain why you think the prices vary so much.

_____

_____

_____

ENTREPRENEURSHIP PARTICIPATING EVENT

You have decided to open a full-service Italian restaurant in your community. Prepare the participating business plan for your restaurant.

Description of Business Prepare a summary of your business plan. Briefly describe the product/service involved, sources of information, and a brief description of advisors and their involvement.

Analyze Business Situation Prepare an analysis of the business. Include a self analysis that explains your personal business experience and training/education in the field, personal business strengths and weaknesses, willingness to take risks, and plan for personal development. Include a trading area analysis describing the general geographic, demographic, economic, and competitive data for the location of the business, as well as availability, cost, traffic patterns, and proximity to competition. Include a market segment analysis that explains the characteristics of your target market and customer buying behavior.

Outline of Operations Prepare the planned operation of the proposed business. This section should include the proposed organization, proposed product/service, and proposed marketing strategies.

Financial Statements Prepare the financial plan. Include financing and capital needs. Consult a banker or retired businessperson from SCORE. Use charts and tables to show your financial statements.

Conclusion Finish with a conclusion (specific request for financing) using a summary of key points to support your financial request.

http://www.deca.org/
publications/HS_
Guide/guidetoc.html

PROJECT EXTENDED STAY

You and your best friend want to open a new full-service restaurant in your town. You both have a total of 16 years of experience in food service. At different times and locations you have both worked as a busser, then a waitperson, then assistant manager of local restaurants.

1. Select a theme and a target market for your restaurant.

2. Choose a décor, furniture, table linens, glassware, silverware, kitchen, and maintenance equipment. Conduct research to determine the amount of capital you will need to acquire these supplies.

3. Develop a menu with food items, prices, and special promotions for two mealtimes, such as breakfast and lunch or lunch and dinner. Outline a purchasing plan for supplies—both food and maintenance.

4. Outline a marketing strategy. Choose a celebrity to endorse and promote your new business. Whom did you choose? Why?

5. Select a local event or charity to sponsor and promote using your restaurant. Explain why you chose that event or charity and how it relates to your customers and restaurant image.

6. Determine sources of capital. Prepare information to persuade the financing organization your business has a chance for success.

CHAPTER 8

HOSPITALITY MARKETING INFORMATION MANAGEMENT

LESSONS

WINNING STRATEGIES

NEW OLD HOTELS

Amerimar Enterprises is a unique entrepreneurial real estate company that specializes in the redevelopment of real estate, including hotels, office buildings, industrial buildings, apartment complexes, retail facilities, and mixed-use properties. The company has the expertise to evaluate a property, design a plan for revival, and successfully manage the new property for three or four years, until new management, sales, and marketing teams are well on their way to success. Some of the hotel properties acquired and restored by Amerimar include the Doubletree Club Hotel in Harrisburg, Pennsylvania; the Georgetown Inn in Washington, D.C.; the Hotel George in Washington, D.C.; The Rittenhouse in Philadelphia, Pennsylvania; and the Hotel Derek in Houston, Texas.

Capital improvements, service upgrades, and effective management rejuvenate the hotels. The Doubletree Club Hotel in Harrisburg was once a Days Inn. A $1.5-million capital improvement program upgraded the image of the property, and the improved facilities and new image attracted a different clientele to support higher rates. Management also successfully raised the quality of service and improved food and beverage operations to the point of profitability The higher average daily rate achieved as a Doubletree has allowed the property to maintain higher profit margins than were attainable as a Days Inn.

Changing the image of a low-performing hotel requires a management team that can look at current and past trends, determine reasons why a property is unsuccessful, and design management and marketing strategies to turn around an ailing business.

THINK CRITICALLY
1. Why do so many hospitality establishments fail?
2. What marketing strategy would you use to communicate a new image for a redeveloped hotel property?

CHAPTER 8
LESSON 8.1

MAINTAINING A CUSTOMER DATABASE

Describe how technology allows the hospitality industry to keep up-to-date customer records.

Explain how hospitality employees collect information for the customer database.

CHECK IN

Profit in the hospitality industry depends upon high average occupancy rates for hotels and a consistently high number of meals served by a restaurant each day. Hotels are in trouble when occupancy rates are lower than 65 percent. Industry standards indicate that successful hotels have average yearly occupancy rates of 72–79 percent. Management must determine the competition, prices to be charged, and marketing strategies to reach acceptable average occupancy rates and meal counts.

Average occupancy rates depend upon location and image projected by the hotel property. The occupancy rate for a luxury hotel sometimes declines when an upscale economy hotel locates in the same vicinity. Hotel guests sometimes rationalize that a clean, safe room is all they need when traveling. This strategy frees up more of the travelers' money for other activities.

Work with a partner. Determine the competition for a hotel located in your city or a nearby city. Make a list of advantages and disadvantages for each of the competing hotel properties.

THE IMPORTANCE OF INFORMATION

MARKETING-INFORMATION MANAGEMENT

The hospitality industry realizes the financial importance of repeat customers. Service is the key to repeat business, and database technology helps hotel staff provide memorable service. **Guest-history databases** allow hotels to keep up-to-date records on their guests. Remembering a guest's hotel preferences, type of accommodations, previous hotel visits, room numbers, rates paid—and even birthday—helps the hotel team offer services that guests really appreciate.

Today's processor, networking, and data-storage technology make it easy to keep large amounts of information in guest-history databases. What once would have been an immeasurable record-keeping task can now be achieved with a few keystrokes, retrieved instantly for guest-service or marketing purposes, and shared easily with any other company facility anywhere in the world.

AN EXAMPLE IN NEW HAMPSHIRE

The Balsams Grand Resort Hotel is a privately owned property that has been in continuous operation since 1866. The resort, one of two surviving grand hotels in the mountains of northern New Hampshire, does not receive much walk-in traffic because it is far from urban areas. The hotel's continuing success can be attributed to a comprehensive guest-history program. The guest history indicates each guest's rooms, dining room server, food, beverage, housekeeper, and preferred tee times for golf in a personal database. If the guest skis, preferred runs are recorded in the database. Other special preferences are also entered into the guest-history system.

The guest-history database grew out of the idea of creating exceptional service by personalizing treatment of guests. Many competing hotels in the area had failed. The hotel management realized that the resort needed a high ratio of return guests to be successful. In the early 1970s, a guest approached management with the idea of creating a computer program to keep track of all the meals and foods consumed in the main dining room and the other food-service outlets. In the early '70s there wasn't a system that could keep track of 209 individual rooms.

The Balsams management team instituted a guest-history program customized for each guest. Implementation of the system began when the computer program was written, and it is still used today. When a person telephones the hotel, clerks enter the person's name into the system. Each returning guest has a file containing all of the information that has been gathered from the guest's previous stay(s) at the hotel. A major goal of the database is to anticipate and fulfill guest wishes before they are requested. Many of the repeat guests are longtime customers who think of and refer to the Balsams Grand Resort Hotel as a personal tradition. They think of the rooms as their own rooms, and many feel at ease rearranging the furniture in the hotel rooms. Even the preference for furniture arrangement is entered into the computer system. When guests check in for their next hotel visit, the furniture is where they want it.

The practice of using a guest-history database has been tremendously successful. About 85 percent of the occupancy rate consists of repeat guests or first-time guests recommended by a former guest. The upgraded database system is now capable of not only tracking guests but also inquiries, and is fully integrated with other hotel operations. The conversion rate of inquiries to confirmed reservations is approaching 50 percent.

The key to the Balsams' success is how well it uses guest information to provide personal service. One of the owners greets each guest individually upon arrival in the lobby. Each repeat guest is individually acknowledged with a handwritten note or a bottle of maple syrup. The resort also produces a video that is distributed to guests. The video presents the resort from a guest's point of view. Guests show the video to their friends, becoming part of the resort's sales force.

TIME OUT

Highest Average Room Rates

New York, NY	$184
New Orleans, LA	$142
San Francisco, CA	$136
Boston, MA	$134
Honolulu, HI	$129

Lowest Average Room Rates

Bismark, ND	$47
Las Cruces, NM	$49
Billings, MT	$51
Sioux Falls, SD	$52
Reno, NV	$57

CONFIRMATION

What is a guest-history database? List five types of information about guests that would be useful for marketing plans.

THE GROWTH OF DATABASES

MARKETING-INFORMATION MANAGEMENT

Database operations is one of the real growth areas within the technology industry. This growth has had an impact on the hospitality industry as well. Entirely new career fields have opened up in hospitality-related technology that never existed before, and managers of hospitality businesses must have an understanding of how database technology works.

Cendant Corporation is a large, multifaceted company that franchises 6,000 hotels under familiar names. Days Inn, Howard Johnson, Knights Inn, Ramada, Super 8, Travelodge, Villager, and Wingate are all Cendant franchises. Project Power Up is a complex computer network that combines all hotel information functions into one enormous system. Cendant's system includes information from 6,000 franchised hotels. The four main functions of the system are property management, central reservations, Internet communications, and direct marketing.

Cendant management believes that integrating technology into business operations in this way is fundamental to the success of the hospitality business. Major goals include more management control of each property, efficiency and profitability for each hotel, improved communications, and a new level of marketing efforts. Before Project Power Up, only 39 percent of Cendant's hotels were electronically equipped, and in some cases, the hotels turned down more reservations than they booked. Cendant estimated $484 million in reservation turndowns in 1997.

The sales force can use the vast amount of information in the database to conduct targeted direct marketing. Special guest interests are noted in the database, and a hotel can target marketing efforts directly to a group with similar special interests. Returning guests receive VIP treatment such as pre-registration and the fulfillment of special needs or wants.

Inter-Continental Hotels and Resorts has created a global strategic marketing database, called Global 2000. This system contains extensive guest history and consumption patterns for guest stays worldwide. The database contains data on over 13 million guest stays and 9 million guest profiles. Data is collected at the time of departure from all customers staying at participating hotels, not just frequent customers.

Inter-Continental is pleased with the Global 2000 database. One of the advantages of the system is more effective target mailings. Response rates range from 3 to 22 percent, depending on the mailing — relatively high figures for direct mail. The marketing department can reach 5,000 targeted customers with a customized message for less than $10,000.

The Global 2000 database has also helped the company find creative solutions to operational issues as well by looking at data patterns. Improved reservations procedures increase productivity and meet guest needs more effectively. Participation in the guest loyalty program has increased because frequent travelers previously not enrolled have been attracted with special promotions and special membership fees. Benchmarking reports for marketing and individual hotels help senior management make decisions based on better data.

RESPONSIBILITIES OF INFORMATION MANAGEMENT

In recent years, there has been a growing sensitivity to the acquisition of personal information by corporations. Part of that sensitivity comes from the misuse of information by a few companies or individuals, and part of the concern rises from the growth of the systems themselves. With increasing connectivity arises increasing risk of abuse, as groups with no real right to information about individuals may now more easily acquire it.

This sensitivity often translates into consumer resistance. People are more concerned than ever about how information is collected, who collects it, and what will be done with it. Some people refuse to fill out or return surveys for this reason, and some resent automated systems that automatically record information.

Information in a hospitality database is only as good as the input and the uses to which it is put. While a company may have a legal right to record what a customer had to drink with dinner, how he or she paid for the meal, and how frequently he or she visits, those companies that handle this information irresponsibly will find themselves in legal or public-relations trouble. Database and corporate security are extremely important technical and management issues, and every person in the industry should consider ethical issues as well.

Many hospitality establishments sell database information to other businesses. Some people object to the easy exchange of database information. Some do not appreciate receiving bulk mail and telephone calls from companies with whom they have no dealings. Others simply feel that selling personal information is a pure and simple invasion of privacy.

THINK CRITICALLY
1. Do you think that selling personal information to other companies is an invasion of guests' privacy?
2. Should hospitality establishments be required to gain a person's permission before they sell, exchange, or use personal information?

CONFIRMATION

Name two ways that the growth of databases has helped the hospitality industry.

_____

_____

UNDERSTAND MARKETING CONCEPTS

Circle the best answer for each of the following questions.

1. The industry standard for a profitable hotel occupancy rate is approximately
    a. 50%
    b. 75%
    c. 65%
    d. 90%

2. Information in a guest-history database typically includes a guest's
    a. room number
    b. rates paid
    c. dates of previous stays
    d. all of the above

THINK CRITICALLY

Answer the following questions as completely as possible. If necessary, use a separate sheet of paper.

3. **Technology** You have been hired by a major hotel to update the type of guest information that will be entered into the guest-history database. List three kinds of information about the guest that will be helpful for future promotions.

    _____

    _____

    _____

    _____

    _____

4. **Communication** Create a letter to the guests that have stayed at your hotel more than four times during the past year. The letter should thank the repeat guests for their loyalty, and offer them a special two-night weekend package during November and December for $159. Also, create and include a coupon special for the hotel restaurant.

    _____

    _____

    _____

    _____

    _____

MAINTAINING A FAVORABLE OCCUPANCY RATE

CHAPTER 8

LESSON 8.2

CHECK IN

Special incentives and promotions are a way of life in the hospitality industry. Hotels must offer incentives because competition is ready to offer packages that may tip the balance in consumers' minds. The location of some hotels presents an opportunity for developing packages in collaboration with nearby attractions.

Convention and trade show organizers work with the hotel sales and marketing department to reserve meeting rooms, a block of hotel rooms, and meal functions to be catered. Complimentary rooms are offered by the hotel as an incentive for the group to book more hotel rooms. For example, the sponsoring organization may get one complimentary room for every block of 30 rooms reserved.

Work with a partner. Develop a list of ten incentives that a luxury hotel could offer to attract more convention business. Consider the cost of the incentives as you develop the list.

GOALS

Define occupancy rate and yield management.

Discuss two strategies for increasing occupancy rates.

OCCUPANCY AND SURVIVAL

SELLING

Competition in the hospitality industry is good for consumers, but it can be tough on people running hospitality businesses. In order to compete, hotels must find ways to keep as many rooms as possible occupied on any given night. Although there are many ways to evaluate occupancy, occupancy rates determine the fate of hotels.

Occupancy rate is the ratio of occupied to unoccupied rooms, expressed as a percentage. If a 500-room hotel rents 350 rooms, the occupancy rate is 70 percent (350/500). This information is necessary to create **forecasts**, estimates of the number of rooms populated in the future. Forecasts look at past occupancy records for several years and add new information, such as physical improvements, event occurrences, and improved advertising campaigns. Room rates can be adjusted to increase projected occupancy.

Yield management involves calculating strategies to maximize the amount of income or revenue from room sales. Maximum room rates and occupancy rates result in higher daily averages. Computer programs contain sophisticated formulas to assist a hotel manager or the comptroller when they calculate room rates to maximize profits from room sales.

Lowest prices do not necessarily attract the most guests. Prices of hotel rooms are important to guests, but security, cleanliness of the room, and location are even more important. Sometimes the price of a hotel projects an image. A lower price leads the guest to think that the hotel offers less service. Lower prices are also sometimes associated with locations that are less desirable. Dropping prices too far may cost a hotel its normal base of clients.

THINK CRITICALLY
Why might a business manager not want to book his or her employees into the lowest-priced hotels possible?

Room rates usually increase annually. Corporate and government rates may be increased when occupancy rates are expected to rise. Convention and tour group rates are influenced by projected occupancy rates in a given time frame.

People planning conventions at hotels are quoted rates based upon occupancy projections. When an individual is in charge of organizing a convention at a hotel, he or she works with the reservations department to reserve a block of hotel rooms at a quoted rate. The hotel may block off 500 rooms for a $129 rate. Most hotels are aware that the number of hotel rooms that a convention planner projects will be used by conference attendees is inflated. A block of rooms used for specific meetings and conventions definitely has an impact on occupancy rate. For example, if a convention is scheduled for May 30, any of the blocked rooms not reserved by May 1 may be made available to the general public at higher rates.

VARIABLES IN YIELD MANAGEMENT

Yield management must include the number of double- and single-room sales. Commissions paid to travel agent bookings decrease the amount of revenue from hotel room sales. Hotels offer complimentary rooms to groups holding conventions at the hotel when those groups rent a certain number of hotel rooms, such as one or two complimentary hotel rooms for every group of 50 hotel rooms reserved by convention participants. These **non-revenue rooms** are frequently used by the convention group for guest speakers, board members, and special guests. Non-revenue rooms may also be occupied by guests taking advantage of frequent-user programs. These rooms must be included in the occupancy rate formula.

A ten-day or three-day forecast helps the hotel adjust room prices. Some hotels offer lower rates to walk-ins when occupancy is lower than expected. Forecasts are also used by other departments such as housekeeping and food service for scheduling of staff and purchasing. Yield management systems are used to vary room rates according to supply and demand in the hospitality industry.

When a major city hosts the Super Bowl, the demand is high for a limited number of rooms. Prices charged for the rooms rise. During off-peak season, room rates decrease in order to fill more rooms. Yield management is the art of adjusting rates for maximum profit.

CONFIRMATION

How are forecasts important to the hospitality industry?

_____

_____

TWO STRATEGIES FOR INCREASING OCCUPANCY RATES

PROMOTION

Guerrilla marketing is a relatively recent form of advertising that uses unique approaches—sometimes stunts—to draw attention to a company or product. A sort of street theater for a product, guerilla marketing might include everything from T-shirted employees handing out mouse pads with logos on them to decorating vehicles with product names. Ideally, guerilla marketing is inexpensive and creative. Sometimes it falls into the category of publicity stunts, which may have a backlash by disturbing or annoying the public. At its best, guerilla marketing brings attention in fresh and clever ways, without spending massive amounts of money.

The Inn at Essex worked with the city of Burlington, Vermont, to wrap a city bus in a huge vinyl picture of the hotel. The advertisement gave reasons why someone should stay at the Inn. The total-bus advertisement highlighted meeting-room space, convention accommodations, and fine dining facilities. Burdened by its location, restrictions on billboard advertising, loss of a major client, and a highway reconstruction, the hotel did not have a large marketing budget. Although the advertising was not free, the "moving billboard" presented the creative alternative for this situation.

Buses travel hundreds of miles each week, and The Inn received more exposure than any other type of advertisement could provide for that type of hospitality market. The route ran by competitors' hotels and throughout the downtown area where the Essex Inn needed name recognition. The Inn gained visibility among area residents and tourists, and generated a lot of attention and favorable press coverage. Riders on motor coaches traveling in the area wrote down the telephone number from the advertisement and called The Inn for information. The Inn committed to a second bus that served cider and cookies to passengers and distributed hotel brochures and restaurant coupons to attract more business.

The cost to implement bus advertising was $26,000 per year for two buses, and it cost $12,000 to design and install the

Clarion Hotel and Comfort Inn & Suites Prizes to Employees for Generating Sales Leads

$200 First Prize— Employee whose leads produce the most revenue in a two-month period

$150 Second Prize— Employee providing the most leads with potential

$100 Third Prize— Employee whose leads produce the most new accounts

$50 Fourth Prize— Employee using the most creative way to find leads

advertisement's on the buses. The volume of meetings and conferences increased nearly 20 percent after implementing the bus advertising campaign. Restaurant business increased 15–20 percent. The clever transit-ad campaign was a cost-effective way to increase occupancy rate.

GENERATING BUSINESS THROUGH EMPLOYEE LEADS

A Clarion Hotel and a Comfort Inn & Suites are located near the Miami International Airport. The director of sales and marketing for the properties was aware of the seasonal nature of business in the greater Miami area and the extremely competitive nature of hotels in the region. Hotel rooms in Miami are in high demand during the winter months, but sales strategies are needed to increase sales from Easter through October.

The company held a contest, and all participating employees were rewarded for their efforts. All employees at these properties were encouraged to submit names, addresses, and telephone numbers of key corporate players they met during their travels. Winners of the contest received cash prizes and certificates of appreciation.

"Hot Leads in Miami" was the name of the contest. Flyers with spaces for lead names, addresses, telephone numbers, contacts, and sources of the lead were printed for employees to use as recruitment devices. As employees provided leads, the leads were followed up with telemarketing and personal sales calls from a two-person staff.

The costs for implementing the marketing program were minimal. Some printing expenses were necessary for the certificates and flyers. This program was considered a success with 38 employees providing the sales office with 162 leads and $10,749 in related income over a two-month period. Approximately 10 percent of the leads appeared to have significant revenue possibilities according to telemarketing efforts.

TRACKING SUCCESS

However built and maintained, high occupancy rates are the measures of marketing success. All the name recognition in the world is of little value if it doesn't translate into filled rooms. Relating marketing efforts to occupancy rates is critical for evaluation both of the business and its marketing strategies, whether they are conventional hospitality marketing strategies or creative techniques such as guerilla marketing or employee efforts. The tracking function of hospitality marketing cannot be neglected.

CONFIRMATION

What is guerrilla marketing? Why might generating leads through employees yield new sources of customers that other forms of marketing might miss?

UNDERSTAND MARKETING CONCEPTS

Circle the best answer for each of the following questions.

1. Yield management is
   a. the ratio of occupied to available rooms
   b. concerned with maximizing revenue from room sales
   c. not directly related to occupancy rates
   d. a way of ensuring customer satisfaction

2. Creative hospitality marketing techniques are most effective when
   a. they result in higher occupancy rates
   b. they draw a great deal of new attention
   c. they are inexpensive or free
   d. they draw upon employee knowledge

THINK CRITICALLY

Answer the following questions as completely as possible. If necessary, use a separate sheet of paper.

3. Design an advertisement for your favorite restaurant to cover a city bus. Be sure to emphasize the good food and service of your restaurant. The advertisement should be colorful and informative.

_____

_____

_____

_____

_____

_____

4. **Research** Use the Internet to learn more about guerilla marketing. What are the advantages of the practice? Who uses it the most and why? What are potential disadvantages of guerilla marketing?

_____

_____

_____

_____

CHAPTER 8
LESSON 8.3

CUSTOMER SATISFACTION: REPEAT BUSINESS

GOALS

Identify successful strategies used by hotels and restaurants to generate repeat business.

Describe ways in which restaurants can increase customer satisfaction.

CHECK IN

Remember the last time you received exceptional service at a restaurant or hotel? You looked forward to your next visit with expectations of the same superior service.

Quality of customer service frequently determines who gets repeat business in the hospitality industry. The customer-service gap is the difference between what a customer expects from a business and what he or she actually gets. Unfortunately, this gap seems to be growing larger in many businesses. Too many individuals have the attitude, "that's not my department." Employees of the hospitality industry must be multi-faceted guest specialists who take a special interest in every guest. Guest service is everyone's department.

Work with a group. Discuss exceptional and poor customer service that you have received. What made the service exceptional? What was the poor service lacking? Make a list of characteristics of each. As a class, use the lists of all groups to compile ten principles of customer service.

BRINGING CUSTOMERS BACK

PRODUCT/ SERVICE MANAGEMENT

Repeat business is the gold standard of the hospitality industry. Unhappy guests will normally tell at least ten friends about a bad experience. Unfortunately, they don't spread good news to as many people. What do hospitality customers really want? Customers expect hotels, restaurants, and other hospitality venues to provide high-quality service and products. Guests expect to be treated with friendliness and dignity. Most hospitality guests appreciate being treated as part of the hotel or restaurant family.

The most important factor in quality service is employee attitude. Courteous, helpful, neat, and knowledgeable employees generate repeat business. It's an easy thing to say that employees should treat guests well. Sometimes, in hospitality or any businesses, it's another thing to ensure that treatment happens.

TRAINING FOR SUCCESS

Many companies recognize that customer service is not a matter of luck in picking employees. Effective training programs contribute directly to effective service, just as quality service contributes directly to repeat business. An effective training program includes periodic evaluation, retraining, review and revision of standards, rewards for success, and consequences for failure.

The Cincinnati Marriott Northeast created a 12-point guest-service program that encourages staff to treat each guest as if he or she were "part of the family and on a visit to the employee's home." Continuous staff training urges 170 staff members to go the "extra mile" in service so guests will repeatedly return to the hotel. Each employee carries a pledge card identifying 12 points of guest service.

Four Seasons developed a deluxe customer-service orientation aimed at meeting the needs of the luxury market for business and leisure travelers. This program features a higher ratio of thoroughly trained employees to guests. Four Seasons implemented this strategy to ensure the loyalty of its guests and to warrant the five-star or five-diamond rating held by many of its hotels and resorts.

The Four Seasons introduces new employees to the customer value system. Each new employee is interviewed by top management, and then participates in a seven-part orientation program spread over 12 weeks, culminating in an overnight stay in the hotel to experience all aspects of service just as a guest would. Experienced hospitality workers act as mentors to their newly hired cohorts. *Fortune* magazine surveyed employees anonymously and identified Four Seasons as one of the 100 best companies for workers.

Promus Hotels, the parent company of Club Hotel by Doubletree, established "CARE Committees" to boost employee morale and ensure excellent customer service. A CARE Committee has a guest relations subcommittee. The subcommittee is in charge of auditing service standards to ensure that each department is taking care of employees and guests. This committee operates the employee-of-the-month program, monitors the employee-of-the-year program, monitors the Bright Ideas program, organizes quarterly employee parties, and organizes birthday cards (signed by all employees) to be sent to employees. The Bright Ideas program awards employees $25 to $500 for ideas that benefit the hotel.

Four Seasons and Regent Hotels and Resorts hold regular employee meetings to review customer service philosophy and standards. Principles are discussed in weekly department meetings, weekly planning-review meetings, and daily operating-review meetings. The daily meetings inform the hospitality team of VIPs that will be staying at the property. This allows the team to prepare special dinners and other accommodations to meet the guest's expectations. Guest complaints are discussed to improve future customer service.

STRATEGIES THAT WORK

Hotel policies toward both guests and employees help create a climate in which customer service can flourish. Some of the most successful hotels, like the Inn at Essex, maintain a practice of accommodating all guest requests. The hotel has maintained a four-star rating since opening in 1989. Employees are instructed to be proactively friendly and always find a way to say "yes." When employees make a decision for the benefit of the guest, 90 percent of the time they will be right and management will back them 100 percent of the time.

Despite all the talk about customer service and a decade of hundreds of quality plans, Americans still view the quality of service as declining. The University of Michigan's American Consumer Satisfaction Index shows a steady decline in customer satisfaction. In another study, only eight percent of consumers rate companies they deal with as excellent.

The Ritz Carlton Dearborn offers one-stop check-in and registration (OSCAR), a guest recognition program that permits frequent guests to by-pass the traditional check-in at the front desk. Frequent guests have been identified by the Ritz-Carlton's guest-tracking system, CLASS (Customer Loyalty Anticipation Satisfaction System), that records guests' stays and frequency, as well as their preferences. Each day a list of OSCAR members is shared with the hotel staff. A key packet is prepared and a room assigned based upon the guests' known preferences. The doorman or valet receives the OSCAR notebook and the key packets for the day.

When the frequent guest arrives at the hotel, the doorman or valet greets the guest by name and offers a key and extra assistance to bypass any delay caused by normal check-in procedures. The doorman informs the front desk that the guest has checked in, and all other departments are notified. The OSCAR program has proven to be very successful.

Other strategies that work include giving guests more flexibility and assuring them of quality service. With services like Telecheck, Incorporated, accepting checks costs no more than credit-card verification. Free local phone calls, or policies that a particular market segment wants, such as accepting small pets, get remembered and generate repeat business.

One dynamic way of committing to customer service is through a 100 percent satisfaction guarantee policy. Such guarantees are well-known outside the hospitality industry at places such as Nordstrom, LL Bean, and Wal-Mart. These companies support their products with absolute, 100 percent satisfaction guarantees. Choice Hotels, Promus Hotels, and Tarsadia Hotels are among the few hotel companies that have implemented written guarantee policies. If guests are not satisfied with their stay at the hotel, they are refunded their money.

CONSISTENT SERVICE AND A CLEAN ROOM

Hotels that earn high ratings take a systematic approach to establishing and maintaining a high degree of consistency of product and service. These hotels determine exactly how their target clientele defines quality. Then the hotel decides which of these services can be provided in a consistently superior manner to every guest, every time, at any time. Consistency means that a guest receives the same level of service at 2 A.M. as at 2 P.M.

Of course, no amount of courtesy will compensate for a dirty room. One stay at an inadequately cleaned room may end a customer relationship with a particular hotel, or even an entire chain, for life. Here, too, regular procedures for maintenance established in clear and ongoing training make the difference between success and failure.

CONFIRMATION

What is the best way to develop courteous and efficient service for customers?

_____

_____

PLEASING CUSTOMERS AT RESTAURANTS

PRODUCT/ SERVICE MANAGEMENT

Although restaurant customers also insist on high-quality, consistent service, there is another factor involved in pleasing dining customers. Restaurant management requires considerable creativity and flexibility in providing its product. The guiding principle within food and beverage operations is to stay progressive and always remain sensitive to guests' needs. Customers may always want the same hotel room, but they often do not want the same old restaurant food. Tastes in restaurants change.

Four Seasons Hotels and Resorts uses only one food and beverage outlet within a majority of its properties rather than the traditional strategy of multiple venues with varying degrees of service and quality seen in other hotel chains. A second concept implemented by the Four Seasons Hotels and Resorts is a trademarked alternative cuisine that offers nutritionally balanced, homestyle, and vegetarian options to its main food and beverage and room service menus.

The Four Seasons began the practice of having only one food and beverage outlet in the majority of its hotels over 20 years ago with the Four Seasons Hotel in Washington, D.C. Four Seasons rejected the different tiers of quality and menus between high-volume outlets and formal dining restaurants. It has opted for an integrated informal/formal dining strategy. One main dining outlet adjoins a smaller venue nearby. Both venues share the same menu, staff, chefs, and kitchens. The main venue provides more table service formality. The smaller venue is more informal, has quicker service, and offers extended hours. The difference between the two venues is design functionality, not quality of food or service.

CHANGING CUSTOMERS AND CHANGING MENUS

Both hotel and restaurant customers are changing. A new generation of business travelers or even local diners may not want things done as they have been done in the past. Four Seasons believes that fewer customers now want ritual table service and formal atmosphere. They prefer an elegant, yet informal and relaxed environment where they can converse more readily and still enjoy a high-quality menu. This type of dining experience also lends itself to capturing the local market outside the hotel.

The second practice that Four Seasons has introduced is broader cuisine choices. This concept was started about 15 years ago when guests started to become more health conscious. Fitness was becoming more popular among the public who frequented Four Seasons hotels. Four Seasons restaurants began to notice an increase in requests for specially cooked food and healthier menu items. Alternative Cuisine was added as a low-fat, low-cholesterol, low-sodium, and low-calorie menu. Four Seasons hired a dietary consultant to develop an initial list of 100 core "healthy" recipes to be used for the new menu options. After the initial recipes were developed, Four Seasons allowed individual restaurants to create and promote their own Alternative

Cuisine dishes to add variety. Potential recipes are taken to a local registered dietician to be analyzed and certified as nutritionally balanced. The general rule is that the menu item must fit within the food style and concept of the restaurant, and look as impressive as main menu items.

"Homestyle" was the name of a second set of recipes added to Four Seasons' broader cuisine choices. Frequent travelers were tired of traditional "restaurant" food and wanted something simpler, easier on the palate, and similar to home cooking. Each hotel developed recipes taken from favorite recipes of the chef's family or relatives. These items were first introduced in the room service menu and now appear on the lunch menus.

The "Vegetarian" menu was based upon feedback from customers. There was an increasing number of vegetarian guests at the Four Seasons Hotel, and the staff developed a menu to meet this growing need.

Chefs have reacted favorably to the evolving concepts. They are challenged to develop recipes that demonstrate the same level of imagination, food quality, and presentation as other items on the menu. Serving staff and other restaurant personnel understood the value of responding to customer feedback and providing the guests with food that they want.

The strategy of having one main venue for food and beverages has saved labor costs. Four Seasons has remained attentive to guests' needs, and customers have benefited from the unique food and beverage program. High quality food and an elegant, relaxed environment for dining are provided. The smaller venue allows access to the same food with faster service and more hours of availability. The broader cuisine choices provide food that fit individual tastes, without sacrificing quality or increasing prices.

SERVICE IS STILL THE KEY

Today's traveling and local dining public are more sophisticated than ever. Hotel restaurants must dedicate resources to compete with freestanding restaurants. A dedicated chef, an excellent staff, and an unrelenting commitment to consistency, even when business is slow, are the trademarks of successful restaurants. Restaurant management cannot develop a loyal following by operating at irregular hours, cutting staff, or skimping on quality. As in all parts of the hospitality industry, winning personal service often tips the balance between those businesses that do well and those that do not. The key concepts—high standards, consistency, and effective training of personnel—apply at all points in providing products and services that bring customers back.

CONFIRMATION

Why must restaurant managers be progressive in their approach to providing products and services? Identify two trends in restaurant marketing.

UNDERSTAND MARKETING CONCEPTS
Circle the best answer for each of the following questions.

1. Hotels that receive high rankings
   a. recruit good employees who need little training
   b. depend primarily upon the physical facility
   c. establish and train consistent policies of customer service
   d. have employees who focus solely on their tasks

2. A progressive approach to managing restaurants
   a. is usually expensive to implement
   b. is necessary because restaurant tastes change
   c. offsets a lack of well-trained servers
   d. rarely works well at expensive venues

THINK CRITICALLY
Answer the following questions as completely as possible. If necessary, use a separate sheet of paper

3. **Research** Collect menus from three of your favorite restaurants. Do the menus offer healthy meals? What other trends do you see on these menus? Who are the target markets for these restaurants?

_____

_____

_____

_____

_____

_____

4. **Communication** Construct an outline of an employee-training course that you might implement for new employees of a restaurant. Include levels of detail in every heading which show how to include excellent customer service in each task that an employee performs.

_____

_____

_____

_____

_____

MAINTAINING INDUSTRY STANDARDS

CHAPTER 8

LESSON 8.4

GOALS

List basic hospitality standards.

Explain how sales efforts are tied to personal service.

CHECK IN

It seems pretty simple that hospitality guests want friendly service in a clean, secure environment. Why do so many hospitality establishments fail each year with such a straight-forward standard?

The team concept is essential for success in the hospitality industry. You probably noticed the last time you received outstanding service. The head of housekeeping made eye contact and greeted you when you first entered the hotel property. The guest-service attendant greeted you by name and expedited your check-in procedure. The waiter remembered how you liked your coffee or tea and made sure that your glass was always refilled. This attitude and effort is a team undertaking. Increasingly, corporations seek employees who are effective team players to help establish and maintain customer relationships.

Work with a group. Discuss ways to build team relationships among groups who may have different tasks or work in different departments.

FUNDAMENTAL PRINCIPLES

PRODUCT/ SERVICE MANAGEMENT

Standards are the goals or basic expectations that a business must meet to succeed. The competitive business environment requires hotels to maintain basic industry standards. Surprising as it may seem, maintaining basic industry standards poses the greatest day-to-day challenge facing hospitality managers.

KEY STANDARDS

Good housekeeping is the number one standard for the hospitality industry. Hotel and restaurant guests expect a clean establishment. Nothing is a bigger turnoff than a dirty facility. Hotel guests expect clean carpet and bedding, as well as spotless restrooms. Housekeeping and maintenance are extremely important departments for hospitality establishments. The best hotels and restaurants maintain quality standards for cleanliness. Proper training of housekeeping personnel will result in satisfied guests and repeat business. Experienced room attendant trainers called **mentors** are paired with trainees to ensure that a room is cleaned properly. One major hotel expects trainees to clean 17 rooms per day after three weeks of training.

The most effective hotels have a procedure manual for employees to follow. These procedures promote high-quality consistency. Housekeeping procedures range from the proper way to knock on a guest's door to room security procedures. Guests must feel assured that the room attendant is trustworthy and will make a dedicated effort to maintain room security when cleaning a room.

Image is another standard that is imperative to maintain, but all too easy to lose. Members of the hospitality team must take pride in their appearance. Uniforms should be clean, pressed, and accessorized with the appropriate shoes. Employees should always wear their nametags, making them visible to guests. They should also remember that, whether cleaning a room or checking in a guest, projecting a professional image at all times helps the business and one's own career.

Attitude is closely related to image. A similar principle applies. Whatever particular task is being performed, the product of the hospitality industry is the personal experience of the guest. There's a big difference between an employee who is just doing a job and one who is doing a job to help people. Guests appreciate a friendly smile from employees. Customers like to be greeted by employees who remember their name. Managers and marketers who can communicate this attitude to co-workers and employees are the ones who are often the most successful.

Product knowledge is another key standard for the hospitality industry. Hospitality employees are not expected to know all of the answers to all guests' questions, but they must be willing to make the extra effort to retrieve the information from appropriate sources. Success depends on showing that extra effort to take care of guest needs. Managing and marketing in the hospitality industry require training and empowering employees to learn what they need to know to satisfy a guest request, rather than randomly picking information up on their own. Developing and implementing programs to select and train employees well is a critical task for maintaining standards.

MANAGING IN MODERN SOCIETY

The hospitality industry must also keep up to date with the latest laws and regulations. Hotels and restaurants must comply with the Americans with Disabilities Act (ADA). Restaurants and hotel rooms must meet state standards and health codes, and state and national OSHA (Occupational Safety and Health Administration) requirements. It is the responsibility of hotel and restaurant managers to know and enforce them in their own practices.

TIME OUT

The Hotel Inter-Continental in Sydney, Australia, has an unusual housekeeping situation. More than 6,000 wine corks per month are salvaged by the hotel, which is committed to conservation and cost-cutting. The corks are donated to veterans' groups. The veterans' groups raise funds by recycling the corks, which are converted to cricket balls, car gaskets, and floor tiles.

Diversity is an important issue in the hospitality industry. The three largest minority groups in America are African-Americans, Hispanics, and Asian-Americans/Pacific Islanders. These three groups make up 26 percent of the U.S. population, and this figure is projected to grow to 36 percent by 2020 and to 47 percent by 2050. Hotels are providing more programs dedicated to the development of minority managers, with franchise and corporate office opportunities.

CONFIRMATION

What is the most important standard in the hospitality industry? Why is diversity an important issue in hospitality management?

_____

_____

_____

SALES STANDARDS

SELLING

Financial standards also matter in the hospitality industry, and those depend on sales. Sales, of course, are related to customer satisfaction, and tying sales efforts to customer expectations helps keep the relationship clear.

For example, Accor North America developed a six-phase customer-relationship program. Each phase analyzes customer expectations. Key sales activities are established to meet customer expectations for each phase. To ensure that the focus remains on meeting or exceeding customer expectations, sales performance is measured in two ways: (1) completion of the key sales activities, and (2) customer perceptions of how well expectations have been met.

Pre-sale research is the first phase. Gathering information about customer expectations takes place during this first phase. Key sales activities include learning about the customers' business, analyzing sales potential, and developing a strategic sales plan.

Probing and analyzing needs is the second phase of the sales process. Attention is focused on customers' specific needs rather than asking fact-finding questions. Key sales activities in this phase include identifying the decision-making process, examining long-term partner potential, and determining the kind and scope of competition.

Presenting and recommending solutions is phase three. The sales department submits a clear contract tailored to the needs of the customer. This contract is flexible enough to change if specifications change. Key activities during this phase include validating customer needs, creating cost-effective solutions, using endorsements from satisfied third parties, and tracking why business has been lost.

Implementing solutions is the fourth phase. It may also include an attempt to support value-added products that meet or exceed customer needs. Deadlines must be scheduled and met by the sales team. The hotel operation group is introduced to the client, and a thorough communication plan is established.

Monitoring results to ensure profitability and customer satisfaction is phase five. Corrective action is taken quickly to maintain the customer's confidence and business. Continuous feedback and communications are necessary to maximize customer satisfaction. Actual business should be compared with the original commitment.

Maintaining and expanding the partnership with the customer by anticipating future needs and recommending new solutions takes place in phase six. Being knowledgeable about the customers' business allows the hospitality team to help customers make better decisions. Key sales activities include customer appointments to review results and ask for additional business. Thanking the customer for their business is extremely important, and maintaining a customer database enhances the expanded communication process.

THROUGH CUSTOMERS' EYES

Customer-focused sales efforts cannot be just another gimmick or short-term promotion to get business. The efforts must be genuine and require just as much a customer-service orientation as do day-to-day operations. Building a solid commitment to the customer requires measuring the strength of your relationship with the customer. Success depends upon developing strategies to improve business relationships. Satisfied customers are the most important asset of any business. The hospitality establishment's mission is to understand the customers' needs, values, fears, and goals. The best hospitality establishments learn to see through their customers' eyes. Customers who are served with warmth, creativity, compassion, and competence will come back for more.

Building a strategic business alliance focused at all levels of the customer organization develops loyalty and dependence from business partners. The hotel sales manager plays a vital role in the success of customer relations. Some of the most successful managers have switched from the traditional role to a team-alliance approach. The hospitality team practices proactive leadership that depends on consistent two-way communication. The plan is partnership-driven and focuses the resources of the hospitality organization in relationship to all levels of the customer organization.

CYBER MARKETING

The Internet is not only a good place to book a room, it is also a place to find a job or an employee to fill one. Web sites such as Hospitality Jobs Online (www.hjo.net) or Hospitality Online (www.hospitalityonline. com) help both employers and prospective employees find a good career match.

THINK CRITICALLY
1. What advantages might searching the Internet for a career position offer?
2. What limitations does an online job search pose?

CONFIRMATION

How are sales goals related to customer satisfaction? How do specific programs tying sales activities to customer needs help the sales effort?

CAREER SPOTLIGHT

DAVID HILL, MASTER OF CHANGE

David Hill enrolled in college to become an architect. After three years of studying architecture, he changed his major to hospitality management at New York University. Hill acts as general manager for hotels purchased by Amerimar Enterprises to bring about dramatic changes to improve market share.

Hill has served as general manager or director at more than 14 upscale hotels. He attributes his success to a strong work ethic, attention to customer detail, knowledge of trends and market research, and having the organizational skills that a reorganization requires.

His work experiences have included Washington, D.C.; Paris; Houston; St. Lucia, West Indies; Miami; and New York. He never takes a job at a location that is not attractive to him. His network of friends includes hotel professionals throughout the country.

Hill takes on the challenge of changing the image and management of a hotel department-by-department. Decisions about restructuring a hotel are based on the demographics of the area. Sales and management staff are frequently changed to match the new hotel philosophy. It takes about three years from the start of a project until Hill completely turns over management of the changed hotel to the new staff.

The grand opening of a major hotel like The Hotel Derek is a well-planned event. Spending $10,000 on a luncheon for the press can produce $100,000 of free publicity.

Hill believes that the most important hospitality standards are cleanliness of facility and having effective employees. These are people who enjoy delivering service to guests, who are willing to give guests undivided attention, and who have the product knowledge necessary to help guests.

THINK CRITICALLY

How important is a willingness to move frequently in a career like David Hill's? Make a list of advantages and disadvantages to multiple relocations.

UNDERSTAND MARKETING CONCEPTS
Circle the best answer for each of the following questions.

1. Which of the following is not a standard in the hospitality industry?
   a. housekeeping
   b. attitude
   c. salaries
   d. image

2. The earliest phase of a hospitality sales program is
   a. presenting and recommending solutions
   b. monitoring results to ensure profitability and customer satisfaction
   c. researching information about customer expectations
   d. implementing solutions to support value-added products

THINK CRITICALLY
Answer the following questions as completely as possible. If necessary, use a separate sheet of paper

3. **Communication**   Design a Top Ten List of Employee Expectations for a hotel front desk or housekeeping staff. This list should be an easy reference for employees to follow.

_____

_____

_____

_____

_____

_____

4. **Technology**   Prepare a computer presentation that you might use to train new sales personnel on the six phases for making a hospitality sale.

_____

_____

_____

_____

_____

REVIEW MARKETING CONCEPTS

Write the letter of the term that matches each definition.

_____ **1.** Gold standard of the hospitality industry

_____ **2.** Allows hotels to keep up-to-date records on their guests

_____ **3.** Estimated number of hotel rooms populated in the future

_____ **4.** Unique, flamboyant, inexpensive advertising to draw attention to a company or product

_____ **5.** Goals or basic expectations that a business must meet to succeed

_____ **6.** Complimentary hotel rooms given for renting blocks of rooms or as promotions

_____ **7.** An experienced room attendant trainer that is paired with a trainee to ensure that a room is cleaned properly

a. forecast

b. guerilla marketing

c. guest-history database

d. non-revenue rooms

e. mentor

f. repeat business

g. standards

Circle the best answer.

8. Databases
  a. have made it easier to track customer history
  b. make it more difficult to generate bulk mailings
  c. require information only from the sales department
  d. all of the above

9. Yield management
  a. forecasts occupancy rates
  b. adjusts room rates to occupancy rates for maximum revenues
  c. is made easier with computer programs
  d. all of the above

10. Effective guest service
  a. requires good fortune in employee selection
  b. is a function only of the housekeeping staff
  c. requires employee training
  d. none of the above

THINK CRITICALLY

11. Discuss with a partner how hotels and restaurants have adjusted to the latest trends of target markets. Make a list of at least five changes for each type of business since 1990. Share your list with the class.

_____

_____

_____

_____

_____

12. You are the manager of a hotel located in Hilton Head, South Carolina. Use the Internet to find out more about the location. What features of the local area could you tie to sales and customer service for your hotel? What service-related amenities linked to the area might you provide?

_____

_____

_____

_____

_____

13. Go to a local travel agent or use the Internet to find information about three hotels located in three major cities. What information is included in the brochures or on the web site? What features will be attractive to the intended target market? Redesign a brochure or web site to improve the marketing strategy for one of the properties.

_____

_____

_____

_____

CHAPTER 8 REVIEW

MAKE CONNECTIONS

14. Marketing Math   You are the manager of a major hotel in a busy convention city. The standard occupancy rate is 72% for the year, and your hotel has 300 rooms. There are 365 days in a year, and your hotel is filled on 100 of the days. How many rooms must be rented each day to maintain the standard? What percentage of rooms must you rent for the remaining 265 days to maintain the occupancy standard?

_____

_____

_____

_____

_____

15. History   Research the history of a still-operating major hotel that has undergone change over time. Prepare a presentation that shows the changes. In your presentation, show how changes reflected the times and market conditions of their eras. Use the lines below to develop the outline for your presentation.

_____

_____

_____

16. Communication   Prepare a 30-second radio commercial advertising your newly remodeled hotel. Remember to emphasize hospitality standards that guests look for in a hotel property. Record your commercial on a cassette tape. Use the lines below to outline your main ideas for the script.

_____

_____

17. Information Management   You are the manager of a major hotel. You have set up an appointment with a computer specialist to design an effective customer database for your hotel. What information do you want to collect in this database? Give a sales-related reason for each category of information you want to collect.

_____

_____

_____

PUBLIC RELATIONS PROJECT

http://www.deca.org/
publications/HS_
Guide/guidetoc.html

You are a public relations specialist for Houston, Texas. Your goal is to convince the selection committee to choose Houston as the site for the 2012 Olympics. The crime rate in Houston has dropped dramatically during the past five years and light rail service has resolved some of the traffic headaches. New professional football and basketball stadiums, as well as the original Astrodome, give your city the advantage of having three major arenas with roofs.

Assignment 1   Prepare a one-page description, called the Summary Memorandum. Write a Campaign Theme or Focus that includes a statement and description of the issue, rationale for selecting the issue, and description of the target population.

Assignment 2   Describe the local media and other promotional possibilities and the campaign organization and implementation.

Assignment 3   Prepare the Evaluation and Recommendations, Bibliography, and Appendix sections of your public relations plan.

PROJECT EXTENDED STAY

You have been hired to redesign a downtown hotel that has suffered from declining occupancy rates. The hotel, once a luxury palace offering the finest in service and amenities, has declined in quality, though its costs remain high. Its reputation is of a stiff and formal establishment past its prime. What changes would you make to revive this hotel?

Work with a group and complete the following activities.

1. Agree upon a target market for this hotel. Identify characteristics of this market and some demographic profiles of people in it.

2. Write interview questions to use in conducting interviews with people who fit your presumed customer profile. Conduct 20 interviews, and record what your subjects would like to see in a high-end hotel.

3. Agree upon ten interior and exterior facility changes to appeal to your target market. Prepare sketches to communicate your ideas.

4. Decide upon food-service ideas for the hotel's restaurant. Include theme, menu, prices, décor, and other information.

5. Prepare a presentation for the staff about the changes coming to the hotel. Spell out clearly what service expectations you have.

6. Outline a training program to help the staff achieve customer-service goals. Identify visible objectives and specific behaviors for staff.

7. Design a questionnaire for guests to identify strengths and weaknesses of the hotel.

8. Name your new hotel. Present your redesign plan to the class.

CHAPTER 9

PRODUCT AND SERVICE MANAGEMENT

LESSONS

WINNING STRATEGIES

LEGENDS, PINEAPPLES, AND LOGOS

Logos are graphic symbols that represent a business. One of the oldest logos in hospitality arose from a legendary practice in the days of the great sailing ships. Sea captains from New England would return from long voyages to the Caribbean Sea with vessels loaded with fresh tropical fruit, exotic spices, and rum. Legend has it that a captain would spear a pineapple on the fence post outside of his house to signify his safe return. The pineapple was an invitation for neighbors to visit, enjoy food and drink, and listen to tales of adventure from the voyage.

Colonial innkeepers added pictures of pineapples to the signs in front of their inns. Advertisements began to show pineapples as a symbol of hospitality and generosity. Bed posts with carved pineapples became a common sight in New England. Some bed posts had removable pineapples. Stories say that when visitors had overstayed their welcome, the pineapples were removed as a subtle reminder that it was time for them to leave. Places such as The Pineapple Inn, founded in 1838 on Nantucket Island, still use the pineapple as a symbol of hospitality.

Logos are a critical part of a corporate image. Modern companies spend considerable sums to design easily identifiable logos that represent a company's business and stay in consumers' minds. Many logos have a story behind them. Holiday Inn's famous green and white sign began as a whimsical afterthought of a draftsman sketching plans. The large red numeral "6" in the original Motel 6 logo stood for the price of a room, but still conveys a message of simple value. Although many logos today are abstract representations created by professional graphic designers, their work still projects an idea and an image to customers.

THINK CRITICALLY

1. Think of logos you know well. What makes them effective?
2. Identify three ways that logos help market hospitality businesses.

CHAPTER 9
LESSON 9.1

HOTEL PRODUCT AND SERVICE PLANNING

GOALS

Define the product and service mix.

Explain typical rating systems used in the lodging business.

CHECK IN

Hotels often offer amenities that cater to the needs of their specific clientele. Some go as far as creating amenity baskets just for female or male travelers.

Loew's Vanderbilt Hotel in Nashville provides women travelers with baskets containing foot creams, bath crystals, and candles, tied with attractive bows. Gentlemen travelers receive masculine-looking brown and black baskets with shave creams and razors. Men also find cigars and bottles of red wine waiting for them. Women find fresh flowers, fruit, and candy in their rooms. Recently during a conference for 200 female corporate executives, hotel staff members delivered a fresh flower every day in a bud vase to each guest. By the end of the conference, each participant had a full bouquet of flowers.

Work with a partner. Devise a list of other gender-specific amenities that a hotel might provide guests. Try to come up with items that would be useful or appreciated, but avoid stereotyping.

ATTITUDES, AMENITIES, AND ATTRACTIONS IN LODGING

PRODUCT/ SERVICE MANAGEMENT

It takes only two things to keep travel and tourism customers happy—great products and great service. Of course, providing those two is not as easy as it sounds. To identify their goals and to clarify their offerings to customers, hotel operators combine their products and services to offer their customers a total product concept. The *total product concept* is the sum of the marketing and service approaches taken to reach and please a market segment.

Hotel operators constantly research the consumer market to determine what their customers want. As a result of knowing what their customers want, collectively and individually, hotel managers create or update their **product and service mix**, the various products and types of services available for customers.

A limited-service hotel usually has a small product mix, offering mainly sleeping rooms and a few services such as regular check-in/out, wake-up calling service, and regular maid service. The product mix of a full-service hotel, however, may contain a wide variety of services, such as restaurants, banquet areas, recreation and fitness centers, business centers, travel or car rental agencies, and event planners.

GET AN ATTITUDE

Don't confuse the mix of intangible products called *services* with the help and assistance that is true *service*. Whatever the array of services offered, nothing beats a positive employee who gives caring and individualized service. No matter how state-of-the-art the technology is, how plush the towels are, how good the food is, or how comfy the bed is, if the employees in a hotel are unfriendly or incompetent, customers will not return. So how does management ensure that employees provide genuine "service with a smile"? Hiring employees who have strong interpersonal skills and positive attitudes is part of the answer. But, all hotel employees—from management to entry-level—should be trained in and practice some basic guidelines of hospitable attitudes.

- Learn guests' names as soon as possible and refer to guests with the proper title and surname.

- Greet guests and co-workers cordially.

- Make eye contact and smile.

- Offer assistance when needed.

- Use proper and professional language—no slang.

- Be sincere when saying "Thank you" and "Have a nice day."

- Be genuinely concerned for guests and their problems.

- Be creative when solving guests' problems.

- Give guests options when offering solutions to problems.

- Don't take guest complaints personally.

- Be alert to situations that might get out of hand and get help before things get out of control.

- Remember that a hospitality professional remains hospitable and professional regardless of any situation.

When a guest is unhappy, employees should be able to do what they can to make things right for the guest. Giving employees the authority to immediately solve a guest's problem or complaint is called **empowerment**. This means that if a guest has a complaint, the employee who first hears the complaint has the power to take whatever action is necessary to satisfy the customer. That might involve offering an upgraded room for a lower price, not charging the guest for one night, or giving the guest a free breakfast coupon.

AMENITIES

MARKETING-INFORMATION MANAGEMENT

In order to stay competitive, hotels seek ways to provide personalized service and amenities for their guests. Hotels use *guest-history databases* and other types of software to keep a record of guests and their preferences. Imagine how impressed you would be if the front desk agent remembered you from your last visit or the housekeeping staff put the type of bottled water that you requested during your last visit in your room before you got there. Since 1908 when the Hotel Statler in Buffalo, New York, first offered leading-edge amenities such as private baths, full-length mirrors, telephones, and built-in radios, hotels have sought new ways to make their customers feel welcome and comfortable. A list of amenities in the early twenty-first century includes

- Cable TV and in-room movies
- Fully stocked mini bars and refrigerators
- Hair dryers, irons, and ironing boards
- Personal-size bottles of shampoo, lotions, and mouthwash
- Thick, terry-cloth robes
- Personal safes to store valuables
- Cordless phones
- Pillow-top mattresses
- Dataports and/or wireless technology
- VCRs, DVDs, and video game sets
- Jacuzzi tubs
- Complimentary meals
- Concierge services
- Fitness facilities or health clubs
- Express check-in and check-out
- Health-conscious menus
- Jogging trails or jogging escorts for women

ATTRACTIONS

PRODUCT/SERVICE MANAGEMENT

Hotels often develop partnerships and work cooperatively with other travel-related companies to offer special promotions. Many hotels catering to business travelers offer weekend specials that include upgraded rooms and restaurant coupons or breakfast delivered by room service. Hotels in New York might offer rooms, dinner, and tickets to a Broadway show. Consumers like **packages**, or a combination of related services in a single-priced product, because they are easy to arrange and budget-friendly. Companies use package trips or events to increase business during off-peak season as well as to bring in repeat business. Some packages include **programming**, which is a combination of special activities, events, or programs designed to appeal to customers' interests.

- **All-inclusive packages** include round-trip airfare, ground transportation, lodging, meals, drinks, entertainment, recreation, tax, and gratuities.

- **Lodging and meals packages** include at least one night of lodging and a specific number of meals. American plan rates include three meals a day. The modified American plan includes two meals a day, and bed and breakfast rates include one night's stay with breakfast the next morning. The European plan includes no meals.

- **Transportation packages** include fly-drive (airfare plus rental car), fly-cruise (airfare plus a cruise), fly-rail (airfare and train travel), and rail-drive (train transportation and a rental car at the destination).

- **Event packages** are planned around special events, festivals, or sporting events, such as Mardi Gras, the Olympics, the Super Bowl, or the World Series.

- **Special-interest packages** include lodging, transportation, and activities or events such as sports participation and/or instruction in golf, tennis, skiing, or sailing; hobbies such as photography, gourmet cooking, or crafts; education such as literature, history, or money management; or entertainment such as concerts, casinos, plays, or musicals.

- **Family vacation packages** offer something for families with children. Cruise lines and destination resorts often offer programs specifically designed for children.

- **Affinity group packages** are for groups that have similar interests or share a close religious, social, or ethnic bond. Trips are often arranged for service clubs, alumni associations, church groups, choral groups, or social clubs.

- **Convention and meeting packages** usually include accommodations and meals, often with local tours or attractions admissions.

- **Incentive packages/tours** are usually sold to companies or associations that offer the package as a reward for high sales, outstanding performance, or introducing new products.

CONFIRMATION

What is the product and service mix? How do packages benefit both hospitality businesses and consumers?

_____

_____

_____

RATING SYSTEMS FOR HOTELS

How do consumers know whether a hotel or restaurant is good? Rating systems provide a clue. The most commonly recognized ratings are one-to-five stars, used by Mobil Travel Guide, and one-to-five diamonds, used by the American Automobile Association (AAA). Both companies base ratings on findings of inspectors who anonymously stay at a hotel, motel, resort, inn, or lodge. The physical characteristics of a property and the service attitude of the employees are the major areas of consideration. These rating systems help consumers make choices and are valuable marketing tools, and let hoteliers know how they are doing against their target competition.

The Mobil Travel Guide has been advising travelers since 1958 and reviews 22,000 lodgings and restaurants in 4,000 towns in the U.S. and Canada. Each star level has specific criteria. A single star is the lowest rating, and a five-star rating is the highest. Inspectors who have an extensive background in the hospitality industry evaluate a property according to cleanliness, service, and guest safety. Inspectors are concerned with the professionalism and helpfulness of the staff, and the quality and condition of furnishings, guest rooms, and public spaces. The evaluation begins before the guest enters, and includes signage, grounds, building appearance, advertising, and reservation process. Amenities, food and beverage quality, and service and departure are also rated. A complex matrix that includes expert opinions, customer satisfaction and expectations, and the value and quality of the property determines the final star rating. Five-star ratings are rare and usually awarded to only renowned and exclusive properties.

The AAA rating system and accompanying travel guides have been around since 1963, with the one-to-five-diamond rating system beginning in 1977. The first three levels in AAA's rating system indicate whether hotels provide clean, well-maintained, and well-managed accommodations, providing guests a safe and secure facility. While service must be hospitable and professional, it is usually limited. For a property to receive a four-diamond rating, there must be exceptional hospitality, attention to detail, upscale facilities, and a variety of amenities. Five-diamond ratings are rare and awarded to properties that are strikingly luxurious, exemplify impeccable standards of excellence in physical attributes, exceed guest expectations in hospitality and services, and offer a wide array of amenities.

Many hotels prefer to stay in the range of one, two, or three stars or diamonds. It is expensive to provide luxury amenities, and the location and market may not be suitable for such a property. Management must determine the product and service mix that meets the needs and price range of clientele, then train and motivate the staff to provide consistent, professional, and hospitable service.

CONFIRMATION

How do ratings systems help hotels as well as consumers?

UNDERSTAND MARKETING CONCEPTS

Circle the best answer for each of the following questions.

1. Giving employees the authority to immediately solve a guest's problem or complaint is known as
   a. customer-relationship management
   b. empowerment
   c. insurance
   d. management

2. The combination of related services into a single-priced product is
   a. marketing mix
   b. programming
   c. packaging
   d. partnering

THINK CRITICALLY

Answer the following questions as completely as possible. If necessary, use a separate sheet of paper.

3. Assume you are an event planner who is coordinating a three-day conference for a youth leadership organization. What special amenities will you provide in the rooms and in the meeting areas?

_____

_____

_____

_____

_____

4. **Communication** Roberta Vasquez is a guest-services agent in a full-service hotel. Because her attitude is so positive, her manager has just asked her to mentor a newly hired employee to show him the ropes. How would Roberta communicate not just a list of things to do, but the essence of a hospitable, guest-oriented attitude?

_____

_____

_____

_____

_____

CHAPTER 9
LESSON 9.2

SPECIAL HOTEL SERVICES

GOALS

Describe services offered by hotel personnel.

List types of technology available to hotel guests.

CHECK IN

In addition to their regular concierge staff, some Hyatt hotels have concierges solely devoted to assisting meeting planners and attendees during special events or conferences. The meeting concierge is a problem-solving expert trained to anticipate unexpected situations that occur during meetings or conferences. The meeting concierge is in constant contact with the meeting planners, from the initial site visit to the follow-up after the meeting.

The concierge hosts the site visit prior to the conference, accompanies the meeting planners during meeting room inspections, handles all guest relations related to the conference, and assists with group billing to streamline the procedures.

Work with a group. List problems that a dedicated meeting concierge might have to deal with, from initial discussions to the conclusion of a long-planned meeting.

PEOPLE SERVING WELL

PRODUCT/
SERVICE
MANAGEMENT

You know by now that hospitality marketing is all about service marketing. Each hotel employee is in a position in some way to assist guests and make them feel welcome. Some specific jobs in hotels focus on accommodating guests in specific ways.

The hotel **concierge** is best known as a person to recommend a good local restaurant and make reservations for guests. But a concierge does more. A concierge may be asked to

- Suggest local hot spots or attractions

- Recommend and reserve tickets for local theater events, sporting events, or sightseeing attractions

- Give directions to and tips about local shopping areas

- Provide directions to any location

- Send mail or deliver messages

- Assist with travel and meeting plans

- Act as a social advisor and a business expediter

Concierges usually have a network of acquaintances to assist them in getting things done. For example, when a concierge in Chicago was asked by a guest to help him find an emu, the concierge called local animal trainers who provide exotic animals for movie productions. The concierge found the emu, and the guest was thrilled. Concierges have a "can-do" attitude and accommodate any guest request that is legally and humanly possible.

In today's global marketplace, many concierges are multi-lingual and well-versed in etiquette and protocol of multiple cultures. A concierge must have a genuine desire to help others, be able to remain calm in hectic situations, be flexible and creative, and always remain professional, discreet, patient, and kind.

Concierge stations are usually located near the front desk. Some hotels offer special floors with upgraded guest rooms and added services provided by a concierge. In smaller or limited-service hotels, the bell staff often serves as a type of concierge, or in many cases front desk personnel serve as the experts, information sources, and troubleshooters.

BELL STAFF

The *bell staff* is responsible for welcoming guests as they arrive at the hotel. Usually located in front of the hotel or near the front door, bell staff are often referred to as doormen or doorwomen. Since the bell person is the first hotel employee many guests have contact with, the warmth and courteous assistance he or she provides can set the tone for the guests' entire visit. The bell staff

- Assists guests with luggage

- Guides and accompanies guests to their rooms

- Gives guests hotel information such as restaurant locations, available amenities, and hours of services

- Opens drapes, offers to get ice, demonstrates any special features in the room, and generally provides any valet services requested

- Takes luggage to the front desk area for check-out

- Arranges transportation for guests, if necessary

Usually the bell person can determine if the guest is in the mood to chat on the way to the room. If the bell person engages the guest in a light conversation, he or she can listen and discover many ways to offer personalized service. The bell staff are in close contact with guests and can often find out how the hotel can better meet their needs. The guest feedback they receive is often more valuable and easier to collect than information on guest comment cards. For this reason, the bell staff must be good communicators, with a willingness to serve others.

The idea that hotel personnel don't have to mind the business of guests is simply false, as dozens of court cases have shown. Hotel personnel must also function as the eyes and ears of the hotel, remaining alert to any potential problem of or for guests. The measure of proof in a liability case is often what is reasonable to foresee. Hospitality companies have been found liable for what personnel could reasonably be expected to have recognized as trouble, including

- Failing to monitor video security
- Knowing or having reason to know that people in the hotel were not registered guests
- Failing to warn guests of a breach of security or of crime in the area
- Failing to supervise staff properly or to recognize staff imposters
- Refusing to help injured guests, assist crime victims, or protect guests from other guests
- Providing a key to a non-registered person, even when instructed to do so by a guest

When concierges or other hotel personnel are alert to possible problems, guests and the hospitality business itself are more likely to be secure.

THINK CRITICALLY
What personal qualities help make concierges or other personnel effective at both customer relations and at protecting the hotel's interest?

VALET SERVICES

Some hotels provide *valet services* for laundering or cleaning guests' clothes. The hotel usually contracts a separate dry cleaning business to do the cleaning. A front desk agent, a member of the bell staff, a member of housekeeping, or even the concierge may be responsible for taking care of a guest's laundry request. Whoever is responsible completes a valet ticket with the guest's name and room number, noting the amount and type of clothes to be cleaned. The guest is notified when the clothes are returned, and the items are delivered to the guest's room and charges added to the customer's account.

SHUTTLE SERVICES

Hotels often provide *shuttle services*, or transportation to and from airports, train stations, ports, or local attractions. The driver may be a bell staff person, a security guard, or a dedicated transportation specialist. Shuttle drivers are responsible for assisting guests with their luggage and welcoming guests. The shuttle driver may be the first hotel employee guests see and should be helpful, friendly, and knowledgeable about the hotel, the city, and local attractions. The driver must be courteous and make sure guests arrive at their destination in a safe and timely manner. Shuttle services are common when a hotel is not located close to downtown or an airport. The Doubletree Hotel Lakeside New Orleans, eight miles from the airport, not only provides complimentary shuttle service every hour-and-a-half to the French Quarter fifteen miles away, but gives guests a car and driver at no cost for shopping trips within five miles of the hotel.

CONFIRMATION

List the main responsibilities of a concierge.

TECHNOLOGY FOR HOTEL GUESTS

PRODUCT/ SERVICE MANAGEMENT

When the Ritz-Carlton in Chicago saw that many business travelers were asking for assistance with computer-related problems, they created a specific staff position to help guests with technology. The "compcierge" works with guests who are having technical difficulties such as Internet connections, printing failures, or dataport difficulties. Hotels have long known that they are in the business of serving people, and they know that people want and need technology, along with the services provided.

Ten years ago, the latest technology available in a hotel room was voice mail. Three or four years ago, securing a reservation via the Internet was considered innovative. Today, high-tech amenities such as video conferencing, dataports, and Internet access are commonplace.

Hotels are now spending millions of dollars to offer wireless Internet connections for the ease and convenience of their guests. Hotels that offer Internet access through dataports place a major burden on their existing phone lines and PBX systems. Not only will wireless communication systems meet the thriving demand for Internet access, but it will also assure guests that hotels are providing high-tech services.

Hilton Hotels introduced a high-tech concept in 2001 by adding an interactive information and entertainment system to some of its guest rooms frequently used by business travelers. Guests found information about the hotel, business services available, and local dining, entertainment and recreation activities by simply touching a flat-panel, active-matrix screen installed in the desk in the room. The system includes commonly used business software and allows access to individual guests' e-mail, thus eliminating the need for business travelers to lug along a laptop. More than just a computer and info-desk, the system also offers video games, allowing a guest to interact with other players in separate hotel rooms or outside of the hotel. In addition, the system provides travel and reservation assistance, news and weather reports from across the world, and a virtual jukebox of 120,000 musical selections.

In 2001, a developer in Florida started high-tech Matrix eSuites — hotels with a workstation, computer, combination printer-copier-fax machine, and high-speed Internet access in each room. That same year, Hyatt Hotels began placing all-in-one printer-copier-fax machines in the rooms available through its Business Plan program, an upgrade for an additional $20 that provides guests with free phone calls, continental breakfast, and access to the business center of the hotel.

Business travelers are not the only ones benefiting from technological improvements. The Peninsula Hotel in Hong Kong offers bedside panels that control the lighting, air conditioning, radio, television, and curtains. The hotel offers an in-room signal that indicates incoming faxes. Guests who stay at the Peninsula Hotel in New York find a panel near the entry door that gives the outdoor temperature and humidity, the UV levels, and the wind-chill factor.

TIME OUT

The lobby area of each hotel owned by IMPAC has a kiosk containing a touch-screen monitor where guests can answer a series of questions regarding their stay. The touch-screen technology was implemented because management felt traditional comment cards took too long to evaluate and did not allow immediate reaction to guests' concerns. Information is compiled and distributed every morning to the general manager of the property and to the corporate office. Because information about guests' concerns is so readily available, sometimes a problem can be corrected before a guest checks out.

CONFIRMATION

Name two examples of leading-edge technology available to hotel guests.

___

CAREER SPOTLIGHT

THELMA WHITE

Thelma White will greet you with a friendly smile at the Hotel Derek in Houston, Texas. Ms. White has been the head of housekeeping since June 1979. Longevity in today's hotel industry is rare, especially when the hotel has changed ownership at least four times during Thelma's career.

White always knew that she wanted a career that enabled her to help people. She went to nursing school to land a job at a nursing home. She sincerely cares about people and became too emotionally involved with people who were living their last days. White's supervisor at the nursing home suggested that she get a job in a happier environment. The hotel industry provided a great match.

White has seen many changes as the housekeeping director for a constantly changing hotel. She believes that the hotel industry needs dedicated individuals who are friendly, honest, and sincere. These people have a positive attitude that flows through their smiles to guests. Although it has become increasingly difficult to find dedicated individuals for housekeeping positions at a hotel, White believes good training is the key to employee retention. White and her housekeeping department pay careful attention to guest comment cards filled out by 40 percent of the hotel customers. Meeting the needs of hotel guests is rewarding. Personal notes and tips are a result of good customer service.

Thelma White plans to spend the rest of her career at the hotel property where she started more than 20 years ago. Her loyalty has paid high dividends to the hotel. Management relies on White's knowledge of the hotel's history to make sound decisions.

THINK CRITICALLY

1. Work as a group to conduct a survey of local hotel managers. Attempt to find the length of service for hotel employees, categorized by type of job. Calculate the average length of service for each group.

2. Why has Thelma White survived change, while many people change jobs instead? What are the benefits of longevity in a career?

UNDERSTAND MARKETING CONCEPTS
Circle the best answer for each of the following questions.

1. In some hotels, the duties of a concierge may be handled by
   a. front desk personnel
   b. bell staff
   c. housekeeping staff
   d. both a and b

2. Hotels are investing in sophisticated technology because
   a. the cost is relatively low
   b. consumers use it
   c. it helps keep room rates competitive
   d. no special maintenance is required

THINK CRITICALLY
Answer the following questions as completely as possible. If necessary, use a separate sheet of paper.

3. What are some things a bell staff person could do if he or she wanted to advance to the position of a hotel concierge?

_____

_____

_____

_____

_____

_____

4. What risks for hotels are there in devoting a great deal of resources to high-tech equipment?

_____

_____

_____

_____

_____

CHAPTER 9
LESSON 9.3

YOUR HOTEL IMAGE IS SHOWING

GOALS

Describe the importance of hotel atmosphere and furnishings.

Explain the importance of uniforms to the image of a hospitality business.

CHECK IN

Imagine spending time at a five-star hotel in the middle of the African bush, having as close an encounter as you wish with rhinos, elephants, lions, and leopards. For a mere $600 a night, you can treat yourself to one of the twelve luxury suites that feature specially molded stone baths, indoor showers, outdoor showers that overlook a natural water hole, and a round-the-clock private butler. Each room offers state-of-the-art technology combined with traditional and authentic African furnishings and minimalism. The price of the room includes open Land Rover safaris day and night accompanied by qualified rangers and trackers, walking safaris, meals, drinks, transfers to and from Skukuza Airport, and sundowner refreshments and snacks during the evening safari.

Work with a partner. Think of other locales that might offer adventure destinations and packages, based on authentic or native features of the surrounding area.

HOTEL ATMOSPHERE AND ENVIRONMENT

The positive reputation of a company is one of its most important attributes. This is particularly important in the hospitality industry where the customers' perception of the business translates directly into choices

about whether to use it. Many things contribute to the image of a hotel. Vast sums spent on advertising and public relations efforts promote an image, but perhaps nothing does as much as does the service attitude of employees. The atmosphere and environment, physical facility, furnishings, uniforms, and dress code standards are important factors in maintaining a professional and appropriate image of a hotel.

THE EXTERIOR VIEW

The physical facility must be attractive and in good repair. The exterior landscaping of a hotel is the first thing a customer sees. If the hotel doesn't look good from the outside, guests probably won't want to stay there. Appealing landscapes and exterior design distinguish a property from its competition and encourage potential guests to make reservations on first sight. Landscaping can hide unsightly necessities such as garbage containers or electrical equipment. Evergreens are good for reducing the level of outside noise heard inside the building. Flowers and blooming plants offer an unbeatable appeal of color and fragrance as guests approach the front door. Outdoor lighting is important for image and for safety and security. A rock garden and water fountain in front that have 24-hour illumination can be a stunning focal point. If sidewalks and parking lot are not well-lit, guests will feel insecure and anxious.

HOTEL FURNISHINGS

The architecture, décor, furnishings, and indoor illumination of a hotel are also important in creating a pleasing image and atmosphere. When considering the interior of a specific property, designers may ask

- Is there a specific design theme for this property?

- Does the theme reflect the geographical location of the property?

- Do the guest rooms and public spaces reflect the theme?

- Is the lighting ample? Does it complement the ambiance of the property?

- Are the fabrics used in the rooms dated?

- Is technology part of the package offered by the hotel? Are the desk and working area large enough?

- Does this property have any specific overall look that makes it special and different from the competition?

Hotels redesign their guest rooms every five to seven years. Knowing that guests want all the comforts of home, hotel management constantly seeks new ways to give the customer a comfortable place to stay and get a good night's rest. Many hotels are upgrading the mattresses to offer a balance between pillow-top softness and back-happy firmness. Midscale and economy properties are adding better window treatments, dust ruffles, and linens with higher thread counts or satin finishes to improve their image and guest satisfaction level. Upper-tier hotels are also changing the look of rooms by replacing traditional bedspreads with duvets, which are two-piece coverings with a synthetic or down insert and a washable cover. The addition of accent pillows or shams, high-quality linens, and down blankets give any room an upscale feeling.

Hotel lobbies and public spaces contribute to the image and atmosphere of a property. A lobby is more than just the place where guests check in or out. It is mainly used as a gathering place or a "sit-and-wait" place. Lobby furniture should include a combination of sofas and chairs so people can sit and talk in groups or individual travelers can sit comfortably and wait for their friends to arrive. The furniture should be moveable so guests can design their own group-seating arrangement. Many lobbies include game tables or network-access equipment. Places where guests can use cell phones or public phones away from crowds should also be provided.

Hotels are moving far beyond mints on the pillow. Hotels are investing a great deal of money in pillow-top mattresses, goose down or feather pillows, and high-quality linens. The Pan Pacific Hotel in San Francisco offers guests three different sizes and types of firmness of pillows, from small to large and soft to hard. The feather pillows are constantly cleaned and recycled in an onsite machine to ensure guests have a sanitary pillow. The Benjamin Hotel in New York City offers specialty pillows from buckwheat to water- or gel-filled, and even some offering magnetic therapy.

Many hotels are renovating lobbies to provide services in a hospitable setting where guests can meet to work or socialize. The St. Charles Hotel in New Orleans removed its traditional front desk and created a welcome center, complete with a fireplace, deli-style restaurant, and lobby lounge. Instead of checking in at a typical front desk, guests sit at a "reception pod," where guest-service agents interact with customers. The goal is to remove the "bank-teller feeling" and create a pleasant and informal atmosphere.

CONFIRMATION

Identify three critical factors in consumers' perception of a hospitality business.

UNIFORMS AND DRESS CODE STANDARDS

Employee uniforms and dress codes can greatly enhance or totally ruin the image of a hotel. Uniforms must always be clean and in good repair. Name tags help guests feel more personally connected to the staff. Some departments require specific industry-standard uniforms, such as chef coats and hats. Though uniforms in the engineering department will differ from those of front desk agents, all uniforms should reflect a standard that meets guests' expectations. Employees in the back of the house as well as the front of the house should adhere to the dress code standards established by the management or employee teams. There are no casual days in the hospitality industry, and there is no place for the provocative or the sloppy when it comes to creating an image for a hospitality business. Wearing attractive, tasteful, well-maintained uniforms creates a sense of professionalism and team spirit that helps instill confidence in both staff and guests.

Properly fitted, attractive uniforms, name tags, and excellent personal grooming create a professional image that sends a positive message to guests. When employees are neat, alert, and appropriately attired, guests know other details are attended to as well. These details all add together to create an atmosphere of graciousness and genuine hospitality.

CONFIRMATION

What are the essential qualities of hospitality uniforms and dress codes?

UNDERSTAND MARKETING CONCEPTS

Circle the best answer for each of the following questions.

1. One of the most important attributes of a company is
   a. the educational level of management
   b. a positive reputation
   c. the accounting procedures and software used to bill guests
   d. a solid historical background

2. Employee uniforms
   a. may be customized to individual taste
   b. help control employees' behavior
   c. create a sense of order and attentiveness
   d. are legally required for security

THINK CRITICALLY

Answer the following questions as completely as possible. If necessary, use a separate sheet of paper.

3. **Research** Look through travel magazines or web sites to find two examples of advertisements of hotels or other lodging properties. Describe the image that is conveyed by the photographs of the public spaces, outdoor landscaping, guest rooms, fixtures, furniture, and staff uniforms.

_____

_____

_____

_____

_____

_____

4. How do choices made about hotel furnishings and décor reflect choices made about a hotel's marketing strategy?

_____

_____

_____

_____

_____

RISK MANAGEMENT

CHAPTER 9
LESSON 9.4

GOALS

Define types of insurance coverage available for hotels.

Describe common security measures used in the lodging industry.

CHECK IN

Not long ago, an urban hotel in Miami had security officers dressed in dark blue blazers, gray flannel pants, and white shirts. No one could tell they were security officers. However, the hotel was experiencing a dramatic increase in property and guest crime incidents. The director of hotel security changed the officers' attire to easily recognizable security uniforms. The idea behind the change was that if security officers were highly visible, criminals would be deterred.

The officers adjusted well to their new uniforms, most preferring to look like law enforcement officers rather than front desk agents. Hotel guests were happier, too. They felt more secure and comfortable with the officers more visible. Within the first three months, the crime rate decreased significantly. Theft of luggage from the lobby and briefcases from the restaurant stopped completely.

Work with a group. List security measures a hospitality business can take to provide a safe yet comfortable atmosphere for guests.

PROPERTY AND LIABILITY INSURANCE

In a perfect world, nothing would go wrong. There would be no floods, no tornadoes, and no earthquakes. Break-ins, accidents, and injuries would never occur. But there is no perfect world, and hospitality businesses know it only too well. They plan for trouble. Businesses actually refer to "trouble" as risk, and the things a business does to eliminate or at least decrease risk are known as **risk management**. There are several ways that hotels manage the risks inherent in running a business. A hotel or motel can practice *risk avoidance* by locating the property in a safe location to prevent burglaries or vandalism. Some businesses have to assume the loss caused by accidents or poor economic trends. Taking responsibility for a business loss is a form of self-insurance known as *risk retention*.

TYPES OF INSURANCE

Most businesses do more than avoid or retain risks. They purchase insurance to cover losses, which is known as *risk transfer*. A business pays a premium, or fee, to transfer certain risks to the insurance company. Hotels purchase insurance packages that contain several types of insurance policies. An **insurance policy** is a contract between a business and an insurance company to cover certain business risks. Hotels are mainly concerned with property insurance and liability insurance.

Property insurance covers damage or loss not only of buildings, but equipment, machinery, furniture, and fixtures as well. It also includes outdoor property, vehicles, and cash. Property insurance should always include *replacement-cost coverage,* which is the amount it would cost to repair, rebuild, or replace lost property with other property of equal quantity and quality at current prices. Another feature of property insurance that should always be in an insurance package is *business income* or *loss of income coverage.* Business income coverage insures the profit and expenses that would have occurred during the time a business is being restored after a loss. Business income policies should cover 75–90 percent of the property's gross income so that expenses such as mortgage payments, franchise fees, property taxes, and payroll expenses will be covered while the hotel is not generating income. Some insurance policies include another feature, *automatic increase protection*, which automatically adjusts the amount of coverage to allow for rising inflation.

Liability insurance protects businesses from losses or damage claims by customers or guests. If an accident or room break-in occurs on a hotel property causing a guest extensive harm, liability insurance covers medical expenses, lost wages, legal fees, and pain and suffering. Most commercial general liability policies cover $1,000,000 per occurrence, with total coverage of $2,000,000. That amount is considered the "primary" coverage. Most major franchise hotel companies require that a

L awsuits are expensive, and no hospitality business wants to confront one. Some lawsuits seem frivolous, as in the case of a woman who sued McDonald's after she spilled hot coffee on her lap. A jury awarded her $2.7 million—though she was found to be partially at fault.

Other cases are not so frivolous. Through the negligence of a hotel employee, a rising young executive ends up paralyzed after a fall. Should the hotel be responsible not only for her medical costs, but her changed potential income from the loss of her career?

Juries and judges determine the amount of awards, and insurance companies have an interest in defending a business. Often it is better to settle a suit out of court rather than go through an expensive and lengthy trial. Not only may the verdict be in doubt, but the size of an award may be unpredictable.

Consider this hypothetical case: A man slips and breaks an ankle on a wet floor. The worker who was cleaning the floor was present, and yellow bilingual warning signs had been properly placed around the work area. The man has sued your hotel, claiming the Spanish side of the warning marker faced him, and he doesn't read Spanish. He seeks compensation for medical costs and pain and suffering related to his injury.

THINK CRITICALLY
1. In your opinion, does this man have a legitimate case? Why or why not?
2. Would you settle this case out of court or go to trial? What factors would influence your decision?

property carry an extra policy to cover any losses above the primary liability coverage. The average extra, or "umbrella," limit required by major hotel franchises is between $3,000,000 and $10,000,000.

CONFIRMATION

What is the difference between property and liability insurance?

HOTEL SECURITY

Hotels are required to provide reasonable efforts to ensure that guests are safe and secure. Many hotels post a card or list of guest security guidelines that include the following tips for guests.

- Never open the door to strangers.
- Change rooms if the door locks are not secure or seem worn.
- Lock doors and windows at all times.
- Make sure your room has solid doors, locks, and peepholes.
- Use the peephole to identify people who knock on the door.
- If someone claims to be with the hotel and seeks entry to your room, call the front desk.
- Call the front desk or police if you see anyone acting suspiciously.
- Never leave your room key in the room when you are away from the room.

Room key control is one of the most important aspects of guest security. Keyless entry technology has increased guest safety tremendously. Keyless entry is the use of a magnetic card about the size of a credit card that can be re-coded for each new guest. Key cards also track who entered the room and when. This provides valuable information and protection for guests and hotel employees.

Most hotels are increasingly careful about security. From medieval times, lodging establishments have been held responsible for the safety and well-being of guests, and in a society ever more willing to sue, adequate precautions must be taken for the protection of the business as well as the comfort and security of its customers. Here are some standard hotel security policies.

- Guest-assigned room numbers should not be revealed to anyone except the guest at the time of check-in. If a person approaches the front desk and asks for the room number of a guest who is currently staying at the hotel, that person should be directed to use the house

The U.S. Department of Labor estimates that 40 percent of all companies that experience a disaster never re-open for business. Of those that remain open after a disaster, 25 percent close their doors within two years of the disaster. The major problem leading to the ultimate business failure is lack of adequate insurance. The businesses do not have enough cash flow to sustain themselves after a significant loss.

phone to contact the guest or to leave a message. Likewise, no room numbers should be provided over the phone.

- Room keys or key cards must not have the room number on them.

- When keys or key cards are given to guests at room registration, the room number should not be spoken out loud if other people are within hearing range. Front desk agents should show the guests the room number in writing and explain that the key coding system is for their protection.

- Master keys should be kept in a safety box and should be signed out each time they are taken and returned.

- Housekeeping and engineering staff should be properly trained in safe room-entry procedures.

- When cleaning rooms, housekeepers should pull the cart across the entrance door to reduce access to the guest room during cleaning.

SECURITY TRAINING

The people responsible for the day-to-day operations of the hotel are the real front lines of security. A good security director, high-tech equipment, written policies, and the best of intentions mean nothing if hotel staff do not understand or act on what they see and hear. Managers can't expect employees to be responsible for these critical concerns unless they provide adequate training to deal with problems as they arise. Most of the issues involved in security training have to do with people management. That training involves not only how to handle guests or others, but also how to handle oneself in a critical or uncertain situation. Employees must have confidence in their training and ability to deal with emergencies or threatening or potentially dangerous situations.

Hotel guests like to feel comfortable and safe when they are staying away from home. One of the benefits of effective security programs is increased customer confidence and comfort that helps earn repeat business. Lower losses also decrease insurance costs, as well as minimize the risk of catastrophic liability for a tragedy. Wise hotel managers consider safety and security as part of every employee's responsibility and provide training to support that philosophy.

CONFIRMATION

List three examples of security and safety guidelines that hotel employees should practice.

_____

_____

UNDERSTAND MARKETING CONCEPTS
Circle the best answer for each of the following questions.

1. What a business does to eliminate or at least decrease risk is known as
   a. risk avoidance
   b. risk management
   c. risk retention
   d. risk liability

2. A contract between a business and a company to pay for certain business losses is known as
   a. an insurance policy
   b. a liability transfer
   c. a security program
   d. a premium payment

THINK CRITICALLY
Answer the following questions as completely as possible. If necessary, use a separate sheet of paper.

3. Think of a hotel, restaurant, or airport where you have recently spent some time. Identify at last five safety and security precautions or procedures observed or practiced by employees of that business.

   _____

   _____

   _____

   _____

   _____

4. **Research**   Interview the manager of at least one hotel and one restaurant. Find out what risk management and risk avoidance policies they use in their businesses.

   _____

   _____

   _____

   _____

   _____

RESTAURANT PRODUCT AND SERVICE PLANNING

CHECK IN

Food is as important to a theme park as the rides and attractions. As fantasy lands and theme parks open their gates to customers, food-service outlets are there to keep guests fed, relaxed, and happy so they will stay at the park for a longer time period. Food plays a critical role as new parks open, such as Disney's California Adventure; the California-located Bonfante Gardens Theme Park, a 28-acre horticultural theme park; and Orlando, Florida's Holy Land Experience, a $16-million, 15-acre facility with attractions that feature Israel's religious tradition from 1450 BC to 70 AD.

Food outlets in theme parks may be corporate-owned facilities run by operators that run the gamut from McDonald's to Wolfgang Puck. Food services often add to the entertainment value of the park. Goliath burgers, camel-coolers, and milk-and-honey ice cream are featured items at the Oasis Palms Café in the Holy Land Experience theme park in Orlando.

Work with a group. List special goals or requirements that planning food service for a theme park or resort area might entail.

GOALS

Describe basic concepts of product and service planning for restaurants.

List major factors considered when planning products and services for restaurants.

PRODUCT PLANNING

PRODUCT/ SERVICE MANAGEMENT

On a typical day in 2001, restaurants in America averaged sales of $1.1 billion. For the entire year, sales at quick-serve (fast-food) restaurants were projected to reach $112 billion. Snack and non-alcoholic beverage sales were forecast to be as much as $13.2 billion. Total sales in the restaurant industry in 2001 were predicted to reach $399 billion. Clearly, Americans and their touring guests are hungry and thirsty.

So, what should restaurateurs serve? And how should they serve the food they are offering? Deciding what products to sell and what services are necessary to sell those products is known as **product planning**. Some restaurant

Food trends in the early twenty-first century include the following.

- *Nuevo Latino cuisine,* a combination of Latin American and Caribbean ingredients such as corn, plantains, chilies, and tropical fruit
- *Tapas,* small, appetizer-type food served on small plates, often in multi-tier holders
- *Healthy and flavorful versions of favorite recipes,* with focus on vegetables, grains, and fish, using low-fat recipes and sauces
- *Steakhouses* are back as an occasional splurge for customers wanting high-quality beef and willing to pay for it
- *Bistros, brasseries, and tratorrias* are casual, informal dining areas where people can go for a quick meal before a show or other activity

owners will simply talk to their customers as a way of researching their market and making product plans. Other businesses depend on research companies to track food trends. Restaurateurs pay close attention to consumers' eating habits and emerging trends in food products and services to remain competitive. They know that for a "food fad" to become a lasting trend, the food must taste good, look good, and "make sense."

Some restaurateurs incorporate new food ideas slowly into their menu mix. If the new items or food types are successful, they add more. Many restaurants offer short-lived promotions of specific types of food as a test market.

No matter how the information is gathered, several truths remain: the media, food columnists, and television celebrity chefs often have a strong influence on what people want to eat in a restaurant. Other demographic trends that affect culinary trends are

- increased disposable income
- more working mothers with less food preparation time
- aging Baby Boomers who are interested in healthy cuisine
- a population that travels more and has increased interest in varied cuisine

The appeal of ethnic cuisine has grown so much since the mid-1990s that the three most popular ethnic cuisines of 1994—Italian, Mexican, and Chinese—are not now considered really "ethnic." They have become mainstream.

CHOOSING APPEALING PRODUCTS

Chefs and restaurateurs need to know what appeals to their customers as they determine what they will offer as part of their menus. The different products offered by a restaurant are known as its *product mix*. Restaurants vary their product mix, based on what value they seek to engage.

- **Basic family appeal**—familiar, good value for the price, easy to take out, fun for family dining, generally appealing to all customers
- **Festive appeal**—good for celebrations, with drinks that coordinate with hot and spicy food; rich, indulgent desserts; hearty portions; atmospheres that put customers in a good mood
- **Traditional fine dining or Old World traditional appeal**—food for formal or special occasions; not inexpensive; rich, indulgent food and desserts; not for adventurous diners
- **Authentic and mild appeal**—food difficult to prepare at home; mild, pleasant flavors and beautiful presentations; usually preferred by young, upscale consumers
- **Adventurous and spicy appeal**—food is hot and spicy with unique flavors difficult to prepare at home, and is often innovative and authentic
- **Innovative and trendy appeal**—food may be a combination of different ethnic features, not necessarily authentic, lots of variety, menu items are always changing

CONFIRMATION

What is a restaurant's product mix?

_____

_____

SERVICE PLANNING

PRODUCT/ SERVICE MANAGEMENT

The type of food served often determines the methods used to get the food from the kitchen to the customer. Three broad categories of service are counter service, trayline service, and seated service.

- **Counter service**—fast-food or quick-serve restaurants, limited menus, take-out and drive-thru lines are usually available. The counter worker waits on customers as they come to the counter or drive to the speaker. Service is fast, efficient, and courteous, requiring minimal sales skills.

- **Trayline service**—found in cafeterias, all-you-can-eat buffets, and schools and hospitals. The food is prepared and ready when the customer requests an item, and the cafeteria worker _plates the food_, or puts the item on the plate.

- **Seated service**—customers are seated, the wait staff takes the order and delivers it to the kitchen staff. Usually the menu has a wide array of choices requiring the wait staff to have good product knowledge. A full description of seated service is in Chapter 3. Many restaurants offer a combination of types of services. For examples, some all-you-can-eat restaurants have wait staff to take orders but also offer buffets or tray lines. Some restaurants may take your order at a counter, then seat you to wait for your food to arrive.

CYBER MARKETING

Just as the Internet has changed the hospitality industry's reservations systems forever, so has it altered the purchasing process. As with hotel purchasing, finding restaurant supplies online now is as simple as a few keystrokes and mouse clicks. Just type in "online restaurant supply" in any Internet search engine, and a wealth of potential vendors will appear.

Of course, nothing beats a solid relationship with an established and reliable supplier. For equipment, supplies, and some staples, though, there's no reason not to be constantly on the watch for a good deal. Effective purchasing managers have always done so, and the Internet simply gives them a farther-ranging tool.

THINK CRITICALLY
1. What qualities would you use to decide among online vendors?
2. What products might you be reluctant to order online, and why?

FACTORS TO CONSIDER

As restaurateurs plan their products and services, they constantly keep in mind who their customers are and the type of food service and products those customers want and need. Many factors may determine the success or failure of a restaurant. The table below shows some of them.

When restauranteurs consider...	They evaluate...
Location	Convenience for customers, adequacy of parking, historical or design features of the building, surrounding area, competitors
Building	Cleanliness, attractiveness, age and maintenance issues, suitability of design or flexibility for redesign, grounds and landscaping
Signage	Visibility and ease of identification, suitability for image, compliance with local codes
Entrance	Cleanliness, safety, visibility, ease of access, compliance with disability law
Public areas	Adequacy of lighting, attractiveness and serviceability of dining areas, restrooms and lobby, noise level for type of venue
Capacity	Amount of size for projected business, including adequacy of kitchen and waiting areas
Food	Consistency in preparation, attractiveness of presentation, portion size, service at correct and safe temperatures
Service	Promptness, courtesy, professionalism, competence
Staff	Training, experience, knowledge, skill
Price	Value for portion size and type, profit potential

CONFIRMATION

List the three broad categories of service styles and briefly describe each.

UNDERSTAND MARKETING CONCEPTS

Circle the best answer for each of the following questions.

1. Deciding what products to sell and what services are necessary to sell those products is known as
   a. product purchasing
   b. product planning
   c. product modification
   d. menu planning

2. All of the different products offered by a restaurant are known as
   a. service merchandising
   b. brand mix
   c. packaging and promoting
   d. product mix

THINK CRITICALLY

Answer the following questions as completely as possible. If necessary, use a separate sheet of paper.

3. Think about the last restaurant you were in. Describe the product mix and the style of service available.

_____

_____

_____

_____

_____

4. **Communication** Yang Li works in a small, family-owned restaurant. She believes that adding some new products to the menu will bring in new customers and increase sales. Write a memo from Yang Li to the owner describing a food trend that you believe would be a successful and profitable addition to the menu. Explain your reasons.

_____

_____

_____

_____

_____

CHAPTER 9 REVIEW

REVIEW MARKETING CONCEPTS

Write the letter of the term that matches each definition. Some terms will not be used.

_____ **1.** Giving employees the authority to immediately solve a guest's problem or complaint

_____ **2.** Things a business does to eliminate or at least decrease risk

_____ **3.** Various products and types of services available for customers

_____ **4.** Combination of special activities, events, or programs designed to appeal to customers' interests

_____ **5.** Covers damage or loss to buildings, equipment, machinery, furniture, and fixtures

_____ **6.** Combination of related services in a single-priced product

_____ **7.** Protects businesses from losses or damage claims by customers or guests

_____ **8.** Deciding what products to sell and what services are necessary to sell those products

a. concierge
b. empowerment
c. insurance policy
d. liability insurance
e. packages
f. product and service mix
g. product planning
h. programming
i. property insurance
j. risk management

Circle the best answer.

9. Hotels keep records of customers and their preferences using
   a. sales records
   b. business programs
   c. purchased mailing lists
   d. guest-history databases

10. The American Automobile Association uses what symbol to rate the quality of hotels?
   a. diamonds
   b. smiley faces
   c. stars
   d. asterisks

11. Demographic trends that affect consumer food and restaurant choices are
   a. less food preparation time
   b. interest in healthy cuisine
   c. well-traveled population with diverse food interests
   d. all of these

THINK CRITICALLY

12. Spend five minutes discussing with another student how food services and products have changed over the past ten years. Make a list of at least five changes. Share the list with the class.

_____

_____

_____

_____

_____

13. Using the Internet or travel and hospitality magazines, find and briefly describe three travel package promotions. What type of package is each one? To whom and how are these travel packages being marketed? How can you tell?

_____

_____

_____

_____

_____

14. Maria Santos is a sales rep for the manufacturer of a line of environmentally safe fragrance items that includes perfumes, bath salts, candles, moisturizers, shampoo, and bath gels, available in scents that appeal to both genders. Name a hotel corporation to which Maria might promote her product line. Describe the products that she will suggest they use in their rooms as guest amenities. For each product suggested, tell why.

_____

_____

_____

_____

CHAPTER 9 REVIEW

MAKE CONNECTIONS

15. Marketing Math   Raquel Espinosa is a travel agent planning an affinity group package for 15 people. The price is $1,245 per person, plus a tax rate of 17 percent for every ticket. What is the final price per person? Raquel receives an 8 percent commission on the total trip, not including tax. What is her commission?

_____

_____

_____

16. Technology   Design a spreadsheet to compare the prices of two round trips to the same destination. Using a travel web site or magazine, find an all-inclusive package for one trip to any destination of your choice. Design a spreadsheet to include a breakdown of each aspect of the package. Create columns for airfare, hotel prices, and a minimum of five other aspects of the trip. Now look up the prices of each aspect individually and enter that information in your spreadsheet. Compare the two trips to see the difference in prices.

_____

_____

_____

17. Science   Write a one-page report on food-borne illnesses and prevention methods commonly used in restaurants and food-service establishments.

_____

_____

_____

_____

18. Technology   Using the Mobil Travel Guide or American Automobile Association's rating system, create a spreadsheet that compares the services and amenities of ten hotels. Include at least one hotel from each rating level.

_____

_____

_____

_____

TECHNICAL MARKETING REPRESENTATIVE EVENT

http://www.deca.org
/publications/HS_
Guide/guidetoc.html

Bob's Big Burgers is a quick-serve restaurant in Sutherland, population 25,000. The two primary marketing targets are middle class families with one or both adults working and traffic on an interstate highway. Customers demand fast food and friendly small town service. Bob's Big Burgers has a reputation for excellent burgers and great service. It is the only quick-serve restaurant in Sutherland, so Bob's Big Burgers can be very busy, especially on weekends. There are two cash registers inside the restaurant and one drive-through window. The owner wants to improve efficiency to keep happy customers. He is interested in learning about new cash registers and other electronic equipment for taking orders and maintaining inventory. Feedback from cashiers shows a need for a more user-friendly transaction display so customers can easily check price accuracy, and a desire by customers to use credit cards. The restaurant needs to be redesigned to make customer lines move more quickly. The drive-through lane needs revision to decrease long lines of cars. Bob's Big Burgers has budgeted $100,000 for the project. The owner looks at this as a long-term investment that requires a smooth installation for the restaurant to remain open and operating.

PROJECT EXTENDED STAY

Now that you know what goes into planning the products and services of a restaurant, plan one. Use the chart on page 226 as a guide to help you think about your restaurant.

Work with a group and complete the following activities.

1. Identify your target market and competitors.

2. Choose your service. What type of service do you plan to offer and why? Describe the general service operation of the restaurant.

3. Identify your product mix. Determine the type of appeal you will make to your target market. Create a menu that includes specialty items as well as basic and broad-based items including beverages.

4. Use the Internet to locate vendors for products and supplies. Create a spreadsheet to compare vendors for six products. Include such intangibles as reliability, guarantees, returns, and reputation.

5. Identify a good location. Create interior and exterior drawings of an existing building to modify or one you would build. Include parking areas, service and customer entrances, lobbies, waiting areas, restrooms, seating areas, kitchens, offices, and capacity.

6. Write advertisements for the kind of servers and kitchen staff you will need. Calculate the number of employees you will need, and research wages for similar positions in similar establishments.

7. Create a marketing plan with four ways of selling your restaurant. Write a script for a television or radio ad. Design a newspaper ad.

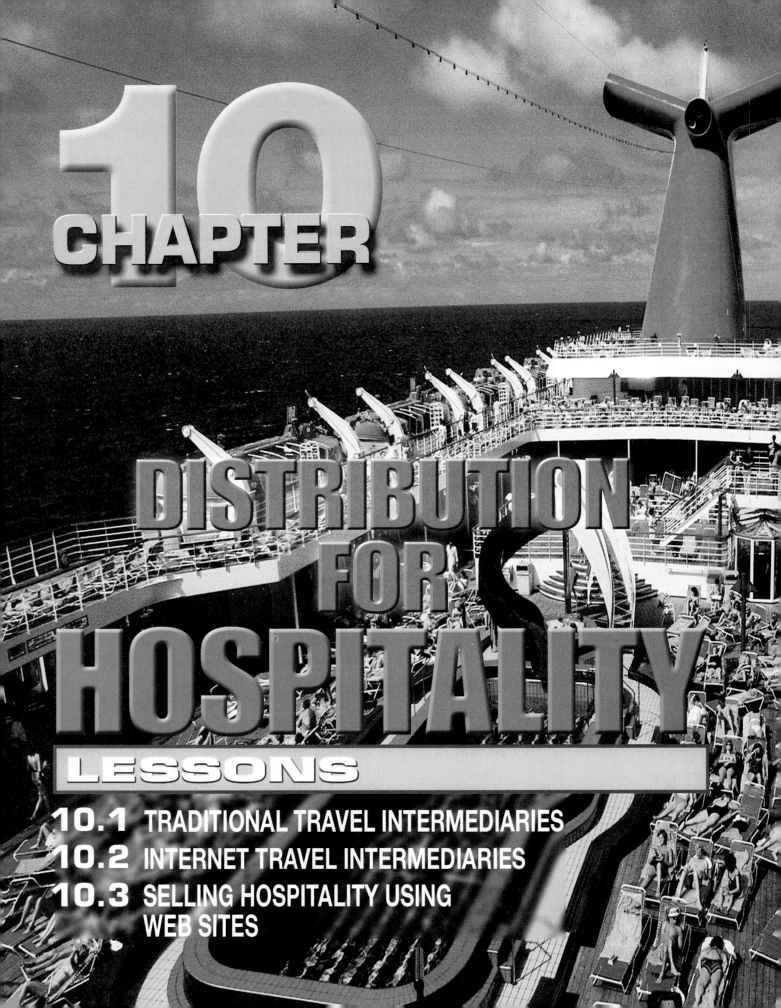

CHAPTER 10

DISTRIBUTION FOR HOSPITALITY

LESSONS

10.1 TRADITIONAL TRAVEL INTERMEDIARIES

10.2 INTERNET TRAVEL INTERMEDIARIES

10.3 SELLING HOSPITALITY USING WEB SITES

WINNING STRATEGIES

INNOVATING FOR SUCCESS

The Marriott International sales team has developed innovative ways to make it easier, faster, and cheaper to book Marriott brands. Marriott recruited sales professionals from other industries to give a fresh perspective, and reevaluated traditional approaches. Salespeople are usually based in the hotel and visit customer locations. Marriott believes its salespersons cannot work in the "factory," and must be more "customer-centric." Customer-centric strategies attach a salesperson to a customer to build customer loyalty.

Marriott sales forces are account based, sell all Marriott's brands, and represent all 1,700 hotels. Marriott also has a network of general sales agents (GSAs) who are not employees, but represent Marriott where it does not have an office. Marriott has 39 sales and satellite locations around the world and 45 GSAs. By the end of 1998, Marriott had 45 Event Booking Centers. These are small-meeting reservation centers used for booking 50 rooms or fewer. Each center handles between 5 and 20 hotels to provide one-stop shopping. The center offers meeting packages, but the customer can negotiate every item.

Marriott employs cross-selling for transient guests. This market is growing, as businesses shorten meetings and conferences for economic reasons. The sales force tries to find space with the requested brand within fifty miles. If nothing is available, the sales force tries to satisfy the guest's need with another Marriott brand.

Marriott helped pioneer single-image inventory, a record that shows the same inventory and rates whether a customer calls a reservation agent, uses a travel agent, checks the Internet, or contacts the hotel directly. Many competitors have recently begun to use this approach.

THINK CRITICALLY
1. What does the term "customer-centric" mean?
2. What problems does having a single-image inventory solve?

TRADITIONAL TRAVEL INTERMEDIARIES

Describe challenges facing travel agencies.

List several sales strategies employed by travel agencies.

Identify other travel-planning outlets.

CHECK IN

Visit a travel agency, and you will see colorful posters advertising exotic destinations. You will also see travel agents providing information, making reservations, and designing travel packages for customers. The travel agency works hard to put together the itinerary for a business trip or a vacation in order to earn its percentage of the prices charged by airlines, hotels, car rental businesses, and cruise lines.

Travel agents must now compete with Internet intermediaries such as Priceline.com and Travelocity.com. Consumers are conducting their own searches to find the best prices.

Is price everything? Work with a group. Discuss advantages and disadvantages of having someone else make all travel arrangements or making them all by oneself. Compile lists on a board.

THE ROLE OF TRAVEL AGENTS

Travel agencies employ travel agents to arrange hotel rooms, meals, transportation, cruises, tours, car rentals, and other travel amenities. The travel agency receives **commission**, a percentage of sales revenue, of all hospitality and travel sales it books.

Most travel agencies rely heavily on corporate or group accounts. The travel agency realizes the importance of establishing a long-term relationship with customers, including corporations, government agencies at all levels, school districts, and other organizations, to maintain business.

A COMPETITIVE BUSINESS

PROMOTION

In the past few years, airlines have cut commission rates to travel agents. These commission cuts have decreased revenue for travel agencies. Travel agents are depending more on booking hotels for revenue. Industry experts estimate that travel agents generate 25 percent of a hotel's sales. Hotel companies are calling top-producing travel agencies to strengthen business relationships. Many lodging web sites feature sections devoted exclusively to travel agents.

Travel agencies realize that marketing is "the engine that attracts business." If agents do not make a commitment to market themselves and the services they provide, they won't get the business they need, because "out-of-sight, out-of-mind" spells doom for travel agents. Dot.com companies are spending big dollars promoting themselves, making it even more important for travel agencies to keep their name in front of customers.

Marketing should be the heart and soul of an agency's business plan, and experts suggest that agencies should allocate between 5 and 10 percent of their total budget for advertising. Promoting a travel agency does not have to cost a lot of money. Some marketing strategies cost nothing. *Guerrilla Marketing Attack*, for example, by Jack Levinson highlights 100 useful tools to promote a business. Half of these ideas are free.

The primary purpose of advertising must be determined. Primary purposes may include bringing in new business, retaining current customers, or building brand awareness of the travel agency. Successfully launching a marketing campaign depends on selecting appropriate outlets—television, print, radio, the Internet, or other media. Decisions will be based on the target market, major goals, and demographics. Lifestyle factors affect the clients' travel purchasing decisions and behavior, so customers should be surveyed to find out which media formats make a greater personal impact.

CONFIRMATION

Why are corporate accounts so important to travel agencies? Why are travel agents challenged to find new target markets?

TIME OUT

A record 39.4 million travelers were expected to visit New York City in 2001, 7.2 million of them international visitors. Tourism remains a driving force behind the city's robust economy. Visitor spending is about $17.1 billion annually.

PROMOTING IDENTITY

PROMOTION

The most successful travel agents market on an individual basis by mail, telephone, or e-mail, notifying clients of travel ideas, bargains, or other travel information of interest. One solid strategy used by travel agencies is writing travel columns or stories for a local newspaper or magazine to enhance the company's image. Web sites provide an excellent outlet to highlight a travel agency and emphasize what makes the company different. Specialty trade shows with preferred vendors are organized by travel agencies at least once a year to spotlight travel products and services.

TRACKING EFFORTS

MARKETING-INFORMATION MANAGEMENT

A travel agency must track advertising efforts to see which methods are most successful. A lot of effort and money can be wasted by pursuing useless strategies. Building database systems that record and analyze information from customer surveys, interviews, and sales records is just as important to travel agencies as it is to other hospitality businesses. Accurate information leads to effective marketing, which should be layered, so that clients will say, "I saw you on cable, heard you on the radio, and read your column in the local newspaper." The challenge to compete in a changing market has never been greater than it is today for travel agents.

SELLING MORE CRUISES

One of the mainstays of travel agencies' business has been cruise bookings, but even that market is changing. Customers want more choices, not only among cruises, but also on what happens on them. Flexible features draw more passengers and should contribute to the success of selling

cruise packages. Free-style dining allows couples to pick when, where, and with whom they want to enjoy a meal. Shore excursions focus more attention on cultural, experiential, and soft-adventure choices. More categories of cabins, many with balconies and other pampering perks, are creating new selling points for accommodations. Clients can shop as long as they wish, enjoy a wide array of spa services, or just kick back and relax. This *flexibility factor* is revolutionizing the way travel agents sell cruises. To take advantage of this, travel agents must have an intimate knowledge of the products being sold and a practical way to communicate that knowledge. Clearly defined marketing plans that spell out goals, objectives, and plans of action are important for the marketing effort.

WAYS TO SELL

Like other hospitality businesses, travel agencies use direct mail, creative advertising, special events, support of charitable organizations, and staff participation in social organizations to promote themselves. Unlike some other businesses, travel agencies can put together the product almost any way they want in order to find a market. Agencies can develop theme or niche-group promotions and advertise them in special-interest publications, such as senior citizen, church, or cultural newsletters. Mailing lists can be based on demographics to target particular markets. Learning the hobbies or cultural preferences of clients allows the travel agency to make a better match when promoting cruises. For example, Baby Boomers seem to like to travel with their children and grandchildren. Knowing this fact gives travel agencies the opportunity to land multiple bookings.

Customer service is the key to survival for travel agencies. The little extras make big differences with clients. Alert travel agents ask if a car rental is needed for every travel transaction. Knowing the needs of the client and the details of a trip's purpose allows the travel agent to serve a customer well. Close relationships with the customer also create the opportunity for upselling the whole experience, from the flight to the car to the cruise. Personal touches work, too. Cards and notes, flowers for big clients, and remembrances of past travel or even social occasions are examples of extras that clients appreciate—and remember when it's time to plan travel.

CONFIRMATION

What is the flexibility factor? Why is customer service the key to survival for travel agencies?

_____

_____

OTHER TRAVEL-PLANNING OUTLETS

DISTRIBUTION

A **tour** is any pre-arranged journey to one or more destinations and back to the point of origin. A **travel wholesaler** is a company that creates and markets complete sets of tours for sale through travel agents. A wholesaler puts tours together and markets the tour product to travel agents at a wholesale price. Travel agents then sell the package at retail price.

Tour operators may sell at retail or wholesale prices. Tour operators usually create their own product entirely and are more likely to perform local services than wholesalers.

Tour consultants are individuals within a travel agency who advise clients about a tour in hopes of making a sale. The consultant is sometimes a salesperson with expertise in escorted-tour sales.

Tour escorts are tour company staff members or independent contractors who conduct the tour. This individual is frequently referred to as the *tour leader* or *tour manager*.

Tour guides take people on sightseeing excursions of limited duration.

TOUR RATES

No tour rate covers all costs, so the terms and conditions of a tour contract should specify exactly what is covered.

All-expense tours offer all or most services—transportation, lodging, meals, transfers, sightseeing, and other expenses—for a pre-established price.

Inclusive tours list the specific elements—airfares, hotels, transfers, and other costs offered for a flat rate.

Tour-basing fares are reduced-rate excursion fares available only to those who buy prepaid tours or packages. Tour-basing fares include inclusive tours, group tours, incentive tours, contract bulk inclusive tours, frequent independent traveler (FIT) tours, and group round-trip tours.

Bulk fares are available only to tour organizers or operators who purchase a specified block of seats from a carrier at a low, non-commissioned price and then must sell for an increased price in order to make money. When a college football team goes to a bowl game, for example, a tour organizer may purchase the seats of several chartered flights and sell the seats at a higher price to fans who attend the game.

OUTSOURCED MEETINGS

Corporations outsource meetings because they don't have the time or expertise to attend to all the details. *Independent meeting planners* fulfill these needs. Most independent meeting planners say that half of their business comes from full-time planners within organizations. The other half originates with people at many levels in the organization—human resources, sales and marketing, and upper management. Needs assessment is the first step in considering which tasks an independent meeting planner will perform. The client specifies the location and the planner presents a variety of choices. Meeting planners frequently take care of registration, housing, and other essentials. Online registration and housing have become increasingly popular, and sophisticated databases offer endless possibilities to planners and clients.

REWARDING TRAVEL AGENTS

Sometimes hospitality businesses establish programs to provide incentives for travel agents to choose their products. Radisson Worldwide's "Look to Book" program rewards travel agents with points redeemable for travel or gifts based on the number of reservations booked online. This "frequent-booker" program is intended to produce and reward brand loyalty. Radisson maintains a database to update points regularly and reward travel agents in a timely manner. Nearly 200,000 travel agents participate, with 125,000 booking multiple reservations in the past year. About 35 percent of Radisson's U.S. room revenue comes from travel agencies.

CONFIRMATION

Name two other travel-planning businesses besides travel agencies.

CAREER SPOTLIGHT

THAO NGUYEN

Thao Nguyen is a successful travel agent at Let's Travel, located in Sugar Land, Texas, a rapidly growing suburb of Houston. Thao has been interested in travel since her spouse worked for an airline in Vietnam. Thao also worked for an airline in Vietnam, then decided to pursue a career in travel and tourism after she moved to the United States. She attended a business school that specializes in travel agent training, focusing on technology used to make airline and hotel reservations. A growing community such as Sugar Land presents many business opportunities for a travel agency. Marketing to new corporations in town is essential to gaining business.

Thao enjoys her career and finds knowing more than one language a distinct advantage in a diverse area such as Sugar Land. Good listening skills are essential, and Thao is not afraid to work a little harder and do the extra things necessary to gain customer loyalty. Her greatest pleasure comes from pleasing customers. Happy customers lead to repeat business. "When customers are happy, they remember you," says Thao.

THINK CRITICALLY

What personal characteristics of Thao make her a good travel agent? Contact a travel agency and find out what qualities they seek in a candidate for a position in the agency.

UNDERSTAND MARKETING CONCEPTS
Circle the best answer for each of the following questions.

1. Travel agents
   a. earn commissions on reservations they make
   b. are not affected by airline rate changes
   c. provide the same service as online systems at a lower cost
   d. prefer individual to corporate clients

2. Tour operators
   a. don't typically provide local services
   b. don't sell at retail prices
   c. often create their own products
   d. usually accompany the tour group

THINK CRITICALLY
Answer the following questions as completely as possible. If necessary, use a separate sheet of paper.

3. **Communication** You own a travel agency in a growing city. Design a brochure or computer presentation that explains why a business or government agency should use a travel agency for its travel plans.

_____

_____

_____

_____

_____

_____

4. **Research** Contact a travel agency to learn about cruises it offers. List your findings and cite examples of the flexibility factor in some packages.

_____

_____

_____

_____

_____

CHAPTER 10
LESSON 10.2

INTERNET TRAVEL INTERMEDIARIES

Define an Internet travel intermediary.

Explain the basic operation of two prominent Internet travel intermediaries.

CHECK IN

How do you use the Internet? Is it an entertainment medium? Is it a reference resource? Is it a marketplace? For many, it's all three. Some consumers have been slow to warm up to the Internet marketplace, fearing risks to credit card numbers and privacy. In spite of these concerns, the use of Internet sites for booking travel is growing rapidly.

Internet travel intermediaries combine the reference and marketplace functions of the Web. Consumers can find information and act on it if they so choose. The Internet has changed the travel-booking business forever, and now hotels and restaurants not advertising and selling over the Internet are losing business to competitors.

Work with a partner. List some Internet marketplace sites that you know. Describe what you like about them. Describe what isn't as effective. How might these ideas apply to sites on the Internet associated with hospitality businesses?

THE RISE OF INTERMEDIARIES

DISTRIBUTION

In the last few years, a new and dynamic force has entered the world of hospitality booking. As in many other cases, new technology has changed everything in ways no one could have fully anticipated. As the Internet developed into an interactive communications medium are an information distribution medium, entrepreneurs looked for ways to expand business opportunities. As a result of these efforts, the entire hospitality industry changed.

The fundamental realization was that every home or office computer could become a reservations terminal for airline flights, hotel rooms, and even car rentals. If a company could provide computer technology to host a dialogue between customers and vendors and to track the exchange, a new way to purchase travel services could arise. Companies providing such services function as **intermediaries** between hospitality businesses and customers, and do so at a lower price per transaction than either the business or a traditional travel agency could provide.

PAYING THE MIDDLE MAN

Part of the reason the time was ripe for a new look at travel bookings was pure economics. In an ever more competitive business, costs for attracting that business were growing. From 1994 through 1999, travel agent commissions and reservations expenses grew at a strong compound annual growth rate of 14.1 percent. Hospitality businesses had to determine if the benefits received were worth the commissions paid to acquire them. It appears that there has been a diminishing return on investment for these hospitality expenditures. During the same six-year period, room revenue grew at a compound annual rate of only 6.1 percent, while hotels experienced an actual decline of 0.6 percent in the number of rooms occupied. The payments made to distribution channels that were supposed to provide increased volume and revenue grew faster than the net benefit to the average hotel.

Into this uncertain climate plunged the new Internet intermediaries. Their idea was not simply to become a home-based automated booking service, but actually to allow customers to do some of the same things travel agents had done—negotiate rates, customize plans, and deal directly with the vendor.

UNEXPECTED RESULTS

The degree of success of Internet intermediaries was unexpected. Part of the success resulted from the dramatic growth of the Internet itself. More people were experimenting with online services, from book-buying to banking, and they grew more and more comfortable with the technology and the concepts. Not only were customers willing to book flights, they were willing to negotiate the deals themselves. Combining database technology, interactive forms for data entry, and search-engine technology to find good deals, Internet intermediaries seem to provide the best of all possible worlds to travelers who know what they want.

Travel agencies were hurt by the rise of do-it-yourselfers, and airlines and hotels found themselves dealing with a new breed of customer. One of the consequences of this change was that hospitality businesses improved their services. In the battle to keep customers, travel agencies became not just booking centers but information outlets as well. A customer who knows exactly what he or she wants may be able to book a single flight, but agencies learned new ways to market their expertise in putting entire packages together. Airline rates became even more competitive, resulting in a high demand for seats. More flights meant more delays and poorer service. Frustrated passengers began making decisions on service as well as price, and the airline industry has responded by making more effort to please customers as well as transport them.

Approximately 43.9 million adults took at least one business trip in 1998. They took 5.4 trips on average and stayed away from home 3.3 nights. Nearly 74 percent stayed in a hotel or motel, and 16 percent belong to a hotel frequent-stay program.

What is an Internet intermediary? What factors led to the rise of Internet intermediaries?

_____

_____

TWO FAMOUS INTERMEDIARIES

Priceline.com and Travelocity.com emerged as giants of the Internet intermediaries. Priceline.com was a pioneer, but diversified far beyond the hospitality industry, venturing even into such markets as groceries, and wandered into financial trouble. A reorganized Priceline.com returned to its original hospitality business and continues. Travelocity.com is the leading online travel web site, providing reservations capabilities for 95 percent of all airline seats sold, more than 47,000 hotels, and more than 50 car rental companies.

PRICELINE.COM

Priceline Hotel Service was launched on October 19, 1998, opening a new world of making reservations for customers. At Priceline, the customer can name any price for a hotel reservation, although the hotel sets the minimum price it will accept and controls its inventory.

Customers visit the web site at www.priceline.com to select their destination cities, areas of the city where they would like to stay, minimum quality star rating, and the price they would like to pay, excluding taxes. Customers without Internet access can call 1-800-PRICELINE (774-2354) and have the concierge service enter the request on the web site for them. Priceline looks for qualifying properties, queries available space and price, and returns data to the customer.

HOW THE SERVICE WORKS

Priceline assigns a hotel to a quality tier based on its own rating system, called the Priceline star rating. Hotels manage Priceline rate and room availability in their revenue management systems. Rate and room availability, subject to restrictions and booking rules, are made available to Priceline as a SecuRate, viewable only to Priceline. Neither the public nor a hotel's competitors sees the bottom-dollar rates from which Priceline selects to match customer bids.

When a customer makes an "offer" for a reservation in a particular hotel market, Priceline tries to match a hotel to that offer, subject to the following considerations.

- Priceline only considers hotels at or above the quality tier the customer has specified.

- Priceline tries to match the offer to the hotel that gives the customer the best value, subject to Priceline receiving an average gross margin of $10 per room night for providing the service.

- Initially, participating hotel companies will each be given an equal number of booking opportunities, or "first looks," to allow Priceline to match a hotel's rate to the customer's bid. At a later date, "first looks" will be determined based on the hotel company's market share.

ADVANTAGES TO HOTELS USING PRICELINE.COM

The greatest advantage to Priceline is that it gives the hotel a way to expand its market. There is no financial obligation for participating in the program. Although some rooms end up renting for less than their usual rate, the discount is not so great that the hotel loses money, and even a low rate is far superior to the zero income an empty room generates. The hotel has complete control of rates and inventory, providing, or *loading*, its bottom-dollar rate to Priceline before the customer ever queries. In addition, Priceline shares part of its revenue with the hotel up front, giving the hotel incremental revenue prior to guest check-in.

Priceline also provides data to help enhance the hotel property performance and allow it to get a respectable share of market demand. Priceline will provide detailed data to each hotel that will outline demand in its particular market and show what customers offer for hotels in the different quality tiers. This feature gives hotels a tool to enhance their understanding of the channel's *price elasticity* in their market. **Price elasticity** indicates the amount of change in consumer demand when prices change. Priceline also acts as a demand collection system, gauging accurately what customers will pay with data that is not clouded by "shopping behavior" because customers pledge their offers with a valid credit card. Priceline complements the existing brand strategy, providing a vehicle to increase price-sensitive business without jeopardizing relationships with existing customers.

Priceline recommends that a hotel property load at least the following rates for its property.

- 20 percent off the Corporate Rate. This is a full-week rate that is net of commission.

- 30 percent off the Best Available Weekday Rate. This is a full-week rate that is net of commission and should be comparable to a non-preferred wholesaler rate.

- 30 percent off the Best Available Weekend Rate. This rate, net of commission, is available for Thursday through Sunday arrivals/stays.

- Deeper discount rates for low occupancy periods.

It is in the hotel's interest to load the most competitive net rates to take advantage of the demand Priceline generates. Priceline makes reservations in "real time" to give the customer an answer within an hour, and agrees to pay the hotel one night regardless of whether a guest cancels, no shows, or departs early. These bookings are handled in much the same manner as advance purchase reservations. Because Priceline will not reveal hotel participation to the general public or to a participating hotel's competitors, hotels maintain integrity of their rate structure by not disclosing their Priceline rates.

A recent survey of 8,600 households by Forrest Research found the following to be the most common ways people located a web site for something they wanted to view.

57%	Search engines
38%	E-mail
35%	Other web sites
28%	Word of mouth
25%	Magazine ads

THINK CRITICALLY

1. What does this research tell you about how people begin to look for travel information on the Internet?

2. What sites would you try to link to if you were running a travel intermediary?

TRAVELOCITY.COM

Travelocity has emerged as the leading online travel web site, providing query and reservation service for nearly all parts of the hospitality industry. Essentially, Travelocity is a giant search engine, allowing consumers to enter parameters of desired hospitality products and returning comprehensive data about options available throughout the hospitality industry. Unlike Priceline, Travelocity does not act as a negotiator, but presents multiple possibilities from which consumers may choose and then book the product directly. By maintaining comprehensive lists of deals, Travelocity also allows hospitality businesses to monitor competition, and the competitive process can result in some great buys for consumers.

One Travelocity feature, the "best fare finder," offers multiple ways to search for economy class travel. The consumer tells Travelocity where he or she wants to go, and Travelocity's search engine seeks the lowest fares offered, presenting fares and dates in an interactive calendar from which the customer can select preferred dates.

- The "flexible dates" option searches for the lowest fares offered and shows dates on which those fares are available.

- The "specific dates, best-priced trips" option searches for the lowest fares offered for specific travel dates entered by the customer.

- The "specific dates, choose flights" option searches for the lowest fares offered for specific travel dates and times the customer enters. The customer enters travel dates, destinations, and times, and Travelocity searches all flights, allowing the customer to build his or her own itinerary. The database then presents the total price, plus offers up to three low-cost alternatives.

- A "modify search" option can be used to change dates, times, and/or connections.

OTHER RESOURCES AND SERVICES

Travelocity even allows customers to select specific seats for their flights. Travelocity offers a World MasterCard; various exclusive offers; partner specials; bargains on flights, cars, hotels, vacations, and cruises; hotel maps and photos; 24-hour customer service; consolidator fares for deep discounts on travel around the world; and a Travelocity business travel center tailored to meet the special needs of business travelers. Travel tools offered by Travelocity include search, custom mini-guides, maps, and up-to-date weather forecasts.

Vacation finder, cruise finder, cruise deals, and vacation deals are tools available to find information on the best vacation deals. Travelocity's fare-watcher feature notifies customers by e-mail about flights and significant fare changes. Flight paging and departure/arrival information are also available through Travelocity.

THE FUTURE OF INTERMEDIARIES

As the travel industry continues to become ever more competitive, it seems likely that Internet intermediaries will continue to grow and prosper. More and more options will be available on numerous sites, and the competitive nature of Internet business as well as the hospitality industry suggests that consumers may have many choices for finding and booking travel accommodations. The failure of many dot.com ventures in general, however, sounds a note of caution. Those intermediaries that can offer services simply and efficiently will survive, and those that cannot deliver in a timely way, or are too complicated and frustrating to consumers, will shortly die. Sound business management of Internet operations is no different from sound business management in any industry.

Competition for the intermediaries will also come from the hospitality industry itself. Almost all hospitality businesses are expanding their Internet presence and services, including travel agencies, which looked originally to be the victims of Internet intermediaries. Already skilled at generating business, agencies will respond with accurately targeted marketing efforts on the Web and elsewhere.

Some consumers simply may not want to book their own travel. For corporations and some individuals, it is simpler, more time-efficient, and cheaper in some cases to hand off the responsibility for travel arrangements. Travel professionals, using intermediaries and other tools, will make their living providing personalized and customized service for their customers, as they always have.

CONFIRMATION

Describe the basic operation of Priceline.com and Travelocity.com. How might these intermediaries change the traditional travel agency?

_____

_____

UNDERSTAND MARKETING CONCEPTS

Circle the best answer for each of the following questions.

1. An Internet travel intermediary is
   a. a Web-based database that distributes travel information
   b. a search engine that returns responses to queries
   c. a forms and purchasing system for economic transactions online
   d. all of the above

2. The main difference between Travelocity.com and Priceline.com is
   a. Travelocity allows hotel bookings
   b. Priceline allows consumers to negotiate prices
   c. Travelocity requires a faster Internet connection
   d. none of the above

THINK CRITICALLY

Answer the following questions as completely as possible. If necessary, use a separate sheet of paper.

3. **Marketing Math** Best Western estimates that 14 percent of its room sales come from the Internet. If a Best Western property rented 12,650 rooms during the year, how many of the rooms were reserved using the Internet?

_____

_____

_____

_____

_____

4. **Technology** Use the Internet to compare Priceline.com and Travelocity.com. Compare the web sites for user friendliness, visual effectiveness, and clarity of directions. Which web site do you like better? Why?

_____

_____

_____

_____

_____

_____

SELLING HOSPITALITY USING WEB SITES

CHAPTER 10

LESSON 10.3

CHECK IN

When television began to arrive in homes in large numbers in the early 1950s, few would have expected the way the new medium would change everyday life. In an astonishingly short time, the Internet has also become a part of mainstream business and private life. Today, almost every television commercial features a web site address for the advertised product, which no one would have even understood a decade ago.

Work with a group. Make a list of ways that the Internet has altered modern culture. Include famous web sites, new language associated with the Internet, and new ways of communicating or finding information. How many of these changes could also affect the hospitality industry?

GOALS

Identify four uses of the Internet for hospitality marketing.

Describe basic principles of effective web site design.

THE POWER OF THE WEB

The explosion of the Internet in the 1990s into everyday consciousness has created a new way of thinking about communication and marketing. Although online sales of some products have been hot and cold, use of the Internet for the hospitality industry has been a success and is growing more all the time. Part of the success of the Internet for the hospitality industry has been through the creative inventions of Internet intermediaries. Companies like Priceline.com and Travelocity.com put data collection, information distribution, and interactivity together in new ways to grab a slice of the market.

A hospitality business need not be a giant information-systems clearinghouse to harness the power of the Internet for effective marketing. Medium or even small-sized hotels and restaurants can make good use of the Internet for advertising, for information distribution, for data collection, and even for reservations and bookings. All it takes is some thought, careful planning, and a good web site design.

ADVERTISING ON THE INTERNET

PROMOTION

At its simplest level, a web site on the Internet can be an electronic billboard for a hospitality business. Some sites begin life that way, until interactive features are fully operational. An attractive, well-designed site works as a sort of TV commercial for the computer generation, attracting attention and providing information about a product. The ability to put pictures on the site, showing various aspects of a facility, allows businesses to show their products in ways that promote the image they wish to convey. Interactivity on the site is a plus, as visitors click through numerous images or select from a gallery of *thumbnails* (small photos that can be enlarged by clicking on them).

Hotels and motels can use this capability to good advantage, displaying their exterior views, rooms, lobby, parking, other front-of-the-house areas, and even "sneak peeks" at back-of-the-house operations. Effective images let consumers feel that they are looking at the property, and a web site is a good way to conduct a tour. It is absolutely imperative for smaller hotels and motels to put pictures of the property on the site. Consumers may have some idea of what they are getting at a national chain without a view of the property, but if you are managing a small or single-property business that customers may not know, you need to reassure them that they will be staying at a clean, secure, and well-maintained place. A great set of pictures on the web site can offset the advantage of familiarity that a big chain has.

Restaurants, too, can use these same principles. It may be less important to display the physical facilities, but shots of diners enjoying their meals or having fun at a theme restaurant, promotional photos of menu specialties, staff "family albums," and other warm and inviting materials encourage the browser to go from a cyber visit to a real one.

Of course, not all Internet advertising needs to be confined to one's own web site. *Banner ads* on other sites, with a clickthrough to the home page, are an effective and usually inexpensive way to advertise on the Internet. The bigger and more trafficked the site, the more cost, but carefully targeted marketing makes as much sense on the Internet as it does anywhere else. If you were managing a vegetarian restaurant, for example, special-interest sites with similar focus would be good candidates for banner advertising.

DISTRIBUTING INFORMATION ON THE INTERNET

One of the chief reasons people use the Internet is to acquire information. Advertising is one form of information, of course, but most users are wary of too heavy a promotional approach. People like to check a web site just for the facts, and they often use the Internet because they can do so independently. Be sure to put every conceivable piece of useful information on the web site that a consumer might want. Web sites can get cluttered if too much poorly organized information is in one place, but a well-designed site satisfies the visitor's need to find what he or she seeks. Some sites include a **FAQ** (Frequently Asked Questions) page. Others place related useful information in well-organized hierarchies of site pages.

For hotel marketing, information distributed on the Web should be similar to that a walk-up customer would get. Room types and configuration, services and amenities, policies, and contact information should be prominent. Above all, though, is location. Provide a map of the location of the property, a map of the facility itself, and a general map of the area, including sites of importance or probable interest. Information and links to local sites that a visitor might be curious about are helpful as well. Create an impression of customer service, a sort of computer concierge, that suggests a thoughtful establishment interested in its guests.

Restaurants can take advantage of the flexibility of a web site. Nothing says a site has to stay exactly the same forever. In fact, it shouldn't, because people will quit visiting the site if it never changes. Feature the menu, or feature a specialty of the house fully described. Include maps and phone numbers, and identify special services such as catering or meeting rooms available at the facility.

Many hospitality businesses are reluctant to put precise prices on the Internet, fearing that rapid change may make the information quickly obsolete. Some managers feel that quoting an exact price will exclude potential customers who might have expected a higher or lower number. Booked reservations, of course, must include a price, but advertising and general information pages on the web site need not. It is a good idea to provide some idea of cost, though, so potential customers have a sense of what they are getting. A phrase like "Entrees range from $7.95–$14.95," for example, suggests a level of expense without pinning down a particular price.

DATA COLLECTION ON THE INTERNET

MARKETING-INFORMATION MANAGEMENT

The interactive quality of the Internet allows businesses to acquire information about traffic on their sites, learn where the traffic comes from, and compile data supplied by the user or customer. This information can be valuable in refining the site for maximum effectiveness and learning more about what potential customers want, both from a site and from a product.

Most web sites are designed with counters that are visible to users as well as to those who operate the sites. These counters indicate the amount of traffic, or **hits**, on the site. Counters can be customized in various ways to provide more information, especially through the use of cookies.

Cookies are messages that the web server, a computer on which a site runs, sends to the web browser that accesses the site. The messages are in the form of files, which transmit information from the browser in your computer back to the site. These implanted files identify you to the web site server. Cookies may be customized to provide other information as well, such as which pages you visit, what links you connect to, and other similar information. Ideally, cookies are helpful in preparing customized web pages for a return visitor. Cookies allow data analysis of web site hits, and some sites bar visitors who do not permit

Concerns over the right to privacy on the Internet have led some users to distrust and avoid sites that use cookies. Some browsers allow users to disable cookies. Options allow the user to reject cookies that get sent to any server but the original one, to be warned before a cookie is accepted, or to reject cookies entirely. In order to collect data, some sites do not allow a user to enter if cookies have been disabled.

Businesses have a legitimate desire for information about customers, but to whom does such information belong? A web site for a hospitality business could lose traffic and potential customers, especially those who are technically oriented and wary of abuse of private information. Privacy issues will increasingly be public-relations issues for all businesses, and in some cases, legal ones if data are not carefully used.

THINK CRITICALLY

1. Would you have your web designer require users to enable cookies to visit your hospitality business site? Why or why not?
2. What other privacy issues might affect how a hospitality business manages a web site?

cookies on their browsers. Because cookies are often invisible to users and vary in kind and amount of information transmitted, some users regard them as an invasion of privacy and disable them in their browsers.

Other forms of data collection on the Internet are much more open. Many businesses put customer surveys right on their sites. These surveys, using interactive forms, may ask users to evaluate either the product or the site itself, or ask for suggestions from potential customers. Such surveys often link to e-mail programs with which visitors can immediately contact the business. Using customer surveys in this way allows businesses to get direct input from customers. Sometimes businesses put polls on sites, asking visitors to pick a favorite item or vote on an issue. Creativity and cleverness in designing surveys and polls can brighten up a web site and add fun to a user's experience.

BOOKING ON THE INTERNET

The ultimate form of data collection on the Internet is collecting orders. However a web site is designed—if it offers the capability of making a reservation or paying online—two fundamental concerns are of the greatest importance.

Accuracy is critical. Poorly designed forms or unclear instructions result in misunderstandings by the user. The process must be simple and clear, with adequate opportunity for the customer to review and accept entered data. The best web sites are those that make it easy for the customer to order and pay.

Security is essential. The number one reason people are reluctant to order online is concern about the privacy of credit card numbers and other information. Most web sites transfer the payment portion of the ordering process to a **secure server**, which uses data encryption and other methods to ensure that customer information is not intercepted. Companies must use the best and latest technology to guarantee the customer's trust.

CONFIRMATION

List four uses of the Internet for hospitality marketing. What is a cookie?

_____

_____

_____

EFFECTIVE WEB SITES

PROMOTION

A web site is no more effective than a billboard if it just sits there. Although the information superhighway has the ability to attract almost unlimited numbers of visitors from all over the world to a site, traffic has to be steered to the site. Visitors don't just drive past the billboard. Hospitality businesses must have strategies to get potential business to the web site.

MARKETING THE SITE

Internet search engines are the largest generators of traffic to a web site. A **search engine** is a program that searches documents on the Internet for particular terms called **keywords**. The program returns the web addresses of documents containing the keywords. Commercial systems like Google.com or Lycos.com can search quickly for terms through vast numbers of web-based documents. A successful hotel or restaurant registers its site with as many search engines as possible. Sites must re-register with search engines regularly, preferably once a month. By adding or changing keywords in a site's underlying HTML code, a hospitality business increases the site's chances of being found as the search engine checks for keywords. The hospitality business's web site can track hits from search engines and other links, so administrators can make changes to key index words in order to coincide with the search terms used most by visitors.

Another way to market a web site is through links to other sites. Marketing a web site effectively calls for creativity in thinking about potential links. Chambers of commerce, government agencies, special-interest groups, and related businesses are all places to which a hospitality site might link. Imagination and effort to find useful links can pay big dividends. Linking to related sites is a form of target marketing.

CREATE A BUZZ

Some dot.com companies will do anything to get publicity, to "create a buzz" for their products. Marketers of web sites need not go so far as to dress in funny suits and harass passersby, but focusing attention on a web site is important. Include the web address prominently in all forms of advertising. Use other forms of advertising to direct potential customers to the site for more complete information. Make the web site entertaining

One study of online shopping revealed that 28 percent of all attempted online purchases failed for one reason or another. Of those who completed an online purchase, 80 percent reported at least one failed attempt at the transaction. About 23 percent of those who experienced a failed transaction gave up on that specific site, and 6 percent quit shopping at that retailer's physical store.

As computer technology and network technology advanced, impressive graphics dominated the displays of new equipment. These attention-grabbing exhibitions, however, are not the keys to sales-winning web sites.

Web site designers sometimes forget users when they put together a flashy site. The key to the Internet is interactivity, not complex special effects. Contrary to what many people think, the best web sites are those that allow users to find what they want quickly, accurately, and simply. When 28 percent of those who experience a failed online purchase stop shopping online, it becomes clear that reliable operation is more important than a light show.

THINK CRITICALLY
What other ways can web site design focus on the user's needs?

and fun as well as informative. E-mails and word of mouth generate a surprisingly large amount of traffic to web sites, and if people enjoy a site, they'll be more receptive to the site's marketing message.

DESIGN A GOOD SITE

The shortest distance between customers and your next online sale should be as close to a straight line as possible. Insist on an attractive, secure, simple-to-use site.

Make sure the site's home page fits a standard browser window. All pages within the site should have a similar look so users don't waste time relearning every page. Identify links clearly and keep them updated.

Navigation bars or other controls must be easy to understand, and the relationship between pages logical. Include "back" and "home" buttons on every page, as well as a site map link. Web sites that force users to waste time pointing and clicking can be frustrating to use.

Go easy on graphics. Too many graphics cause a slow-loading page, and some customers won't wait. Use graphics that add to the message, rather than detract from it. If graphics are animated, make sure they turn off automatically. If the site uses audio, be sure users can control sound.

Use dark type that is neither too large nor too small on a subtle background. Avoid all capital letters or italic type, and proofread carefully. Nothing erodes confidence in a web site faster than misspellings and typographical errors. Assure that the content of the site is accurate and reliable, and that the site continues to work properly. Site maintenance is a form of customer service that can earn or kill business.

Professional web design services are usually worth the money. Make clear to your web designer what you want, and don't get carried away by technology. A clean, clear, helpful web site is more effective than one with a lot of gadgets. Because online business will play a greater and greater role in the hospitality industry, it is important that hospitality marketers understand the principles of effective web design.

CONFIRMATION

What is the greatest source of traffic at most web sites?
What is the most important factor in web site design?

UNDERSTAND MARKETING CONCEPTS
Circle the best answer for each of the following questions.

1. A cookie is a
   a. clearly written privacy policy on a web site
   b. promotional reward for past business delivered via the Internet
   c. relatively inexpensive form of Internet advertising
   d. planted file that returns data about the user to a web site

2. One effective way to distribute information on a web site is through
   a. a secure server
   b. animated graphics
   c. a Frequently Asked Questions (FAQ) page
   d. guerilla marketing

THINK CRITICALLY
Answer the following questions as completely as possible. If necessary, use a separate sheet of paper.

3. List four ways that the Internet can be used for hospitality marketing, and give an example of each.

_____

_____

_____

_____

_____

_____

4. **Communication** Design the home page of a web site for your small hotel or local restaurant. Lay out the page to show links to other pages of the web site, links to other sites, and other helpful marketing information. Use principles of effective web site design.

_____

_____

_____

_____

_____

_____

CHAPTER 10 REVIEW

REVIEW MARKETING CONCEPTS

Write the letter of the term that matches each definition. Some terms will not be used.

____ **1.** Visits to a web site as recorded by a counter

____ **2.** A company that creates and markets tours through travel agents

____ **3.** Amount of change in consumer demand when prices change

____ **4.** Program that searches Internet documents for matching terms

____ **5.** Percentage of sales revenue earned by a travel agent for all hospitality and travel sales booked

____ **6.** Companies providing a service between hospitality businesses and customers, allowing customers to book reservations themselves

____ **7.** Web site that uses technology to prevent data from being intercepted

____ **8.** Term matched by computer programs to find data

a. commission
b. cookie
c. FAQ
d. hits
e. intermediaries
f. keyword
g. price elasticity
h. search engine
i. secure server
j. tour
k. travel wholesaler

Circle the best answer.

9. Hotels that dedicate marketing personnel to meet customer needs are called
    a. customer-centric
    c. franchise marketers
    b. single-image
    d. independent operators

10. Traditional travel agencies
    a. earn commission on sales
    b. provide personal service
    c. have been challenged by intermediaries
    d. all of the above

11. Hotels want to be included in the database of intermediaries because
    a. rooms can be rented for reduced rates
    b. they can collect information about customers
    c. they can reach more potential customers
    d. they earn more commission from Internet business

THINK CRITICALLY

12. You are the sales manager for a major hotel located in the heart of downtown Houston. The competition is stiff, and you are shooting for a 70 percent occupancy rate in your hotel. What customer-centric strategies will you use to attract more group and business clients?

_____

_____

_____

_____

_____

13. Why are privacy issues on the Internet increasingly a part of hospitality marketing?

_____

_____

_____

_____

_____

14. What ways can travel agencies respond to the challenge posed by Internet intermediaries?

_____

_____

_____

_____

15. Why is it important to keep a hospitality web site updated for both function and content?

_____

_____

_____

_____

REVIEW

MAKE CONNECTIONS

16. Marketing Math The Radisson Worldwide "Look to Book" program rewards travel agents who produce reservations. If 60 percent of Radisson's room revenue comes from Radisson's reservations system and nearly 60 percent of that business comes from travel agencies, how much of the $1.65 billion annual revenue is obtained from travel agencies?

_____

_____

_____

_____

17. Technology Visit the American Hotel and Lodging Association site at www.ahma.com. Prepare a computer presentation that highlights ten of the latest hospitality trends.

_____

_____

_____

_____

18. Research View the privacy policies found on six web sites, at least two of which are associated with the hospitality industry. Summarize the policies here.

_____

_____

_____

_____

19. Communication Develop a sales presentation that you as a travel agent will give to a corporate client. Explain why the corporation should contract with your firm to arrange travel, rather than dedicate an employee or two to using intermediaries. Produce handouts, visual aids, or other marketing materials to support your presentation.

_____

_____

_____

_____

FINANCIAL SERVICES TEAM DECISION MAKING EVENT

http://www.deca.org
/publications/HS_
Guide/guidetoc.html

You are the general manager for the Derek Hotel, a new HIP hotel (influenced by European boutique hotels). Your hotel property was previously a traditional full-service hotel with a reputation for frequently changing ownership. The hotel is located in a wealthy area of a large city adjacent to a large Galleria Mall that has over 200 upscale shops for the domestic and international traveler. Three goals for the Derek Hotel include shedding the past reputation, increasing sales from international travelers, and spending more money on creative promotions that include use of the Internet. You and your sales manager must convince the hotel executive team and major investors to spend $200,000 on major promotional campaigns to assure the success of Derek Hotel.

Study the Situation Take 30 minutes to study the situation and outline your marketing strategy for accomplishing the three goals to boost earnings. Organize an analysis of it, using a management decision-making format. During the preparation period, teams may only consult with one another about the management situation.

Present Your Analysis Prepare a 10-minute presentation that describes your analysis of the situation. You may not use printed reference materials, audio or visual aids, and notes made during the preparation time. You may use a laptop computer for the presentation.

PROJECT EXTENDED STAY

Your small hotel or restaurant wants to establish an Internet presence. Plan and design a web site that incorporates the four main functions of hospitality marketing on the Internet. Produce a mockup of the complete site, including a site map, representations of each page, and a description of each graphic or interactive feature on the site.

Work with a group and complete the following activities.

1. Research some current Internet sites of similar properties that have features that interest or appeal to you.

2. Decide on a fundamental approach to the site. Will the site focus on information distribution, customer entertainment, or direct sales?

3. Prepare a detailed site map, showing all pages and the relationships among them. Choose a design for the pages that includes effective principles of web design. Prepare layouts for each page to take to a web designer. Include a list of sites to link to your site.

4. Include a customer survey section on your site that visitors can complete easily and accurately.

5. Design an online reservation section. Plan pages that provide a foolproof way to reserve space. Provide a simple process to allow customers to go back and edit data or exit at any time.

6. Compose a written privacy policy for your site.

CHAPTER 11

PLANNING

FOR THE

FUTURE

LESSONS

WINNING STRATEGIES

HOTELS IN THE SKY

"Look! Up in the sky! It's a bird…no, it's a plane…no, it's a hotel!" This is no joke, no fantasy, and no new space TV drama. Airbus Industrie, the multinational European aircraft builder, has announced production plans for a new super-jumbo airliner to be assembled by fall 2004 and to be delivered to airline companies by winter 2006. The A380 will accommodate 555 passengers. Currently, the largest jumbo jet is the Boeing 747-400, seating 413 passengers.

The new A380 will have room for sleeper cabins, crew rest areas, a business center, and a nursery. The companies who purchase the new giant jets will determine the exact seating configuration and accommodations. There is plenty of space, with four levels per plane. The new jets can have separate restaurants, duty-free gift shops, several galleys, pantries, staterooms with shower facilities, exercise facilities, and plenty of restrooms.

As of December 2000, Airbus had already taken orders for 50 planes from six major international air transport companies, including Air France, International Lease Finance Corporation, Quantas, Singapore Airlines, and Virgin Atlantic. To avoid the financial catastrophe of designing a plane that would not sell, Airbus test-marketed the plane with passengers of their customers. Airbus carried full-size cabin mockups to eight cities across three continents to conduct in-depth interviews with 1,200 frequent flyers.

The A380 has passed government regulations regarding noise, safety, and fit. Although it is larger than any airplane now flying, the new A380 will fit in a standard slot of an airline terminal. It meets strict nighttime noise regulations. Tests have shown that emergency evacuation facilities meet requirements, with wide doors and exit chutes.

THINK CRITICALLY

Imagine you work for a company that has purchased an A380 to use it as a "hotel in the sky." How might you configure it to reach various target markets?

CHAPTER 11
LESSON 11.1

KEEPING AHEAD OF THE COMPETITION

List information hotels need to stay competitive.

Describe customer relationship management systems.

CHECK IN

A 210-room hotel in Boston wants to be "Cambridge's dot.com lifestyle hotel" in order to compete with local big-name hotels such as Hilton and Marriott. To convey the message that this is a wired mini-Ritz for techies, the University Park Hotel at MIT has changed its name to Hotel@MIT, with the words "University Park" appearing in small print. The small boutique hotel is decorating rooms with high-tech themes, marketing special events such as the Boston Cyberarts Festival, and providing guests with tickets to the MIT museum.

Plans are also underway to decorate the lobby area with robotic works of art from MIT's Artificial Intelligence Lab. A web site partly designed by MIT students claims, "If you're already imagining Y3K, this is the place to click." The hotel has high-speed Internet access, multiple phone lines, dataports, and game consoles.

Work with a partner. Brainstorm a list of other ideas that might be used for theme-oriented boutique hotels. Try to come up with an appropriate setting for each.

HOTEL RESEARCH

MARKETING-INFORMATION MANAGEMENT

By now you know that the hotel business is fiercely competitive. Research provides hotel managers with vital information so they can stay competitive. Management relies on consulting companies to provide published reports on the hotel industry on monthly, quarterly, and yearly bases. Smith Travel Research (STR) publishes a monthly newsletter that gives important information about occupancy, room rate, room supply, room demand, and room revenue information for the entire U.S. and specific cities and metropolitan areas. Market segment analyses and future industry outlooks are also available. STR maintains the U.S. Lodging Census database, which includes information such as property name, chain affiliation, year affiliated, address, telephone, number of rooms, published room rates, year opened, and other geographic and market segmentation classifications for over 34,000 lodging establishments equaling about 3.6 million rooms.

PKF Consulting is another international consulting firm that provides trend reports, marketing research, and market positioning services. Hotel managers and corporations keep track of their **market share** (percentage of total sales generated by all competitors) and their **market position** (where they stand in relation to other hotels or lodging properties). Many consulting companies offer research, reports, and analyses to keep hotel executives and managers updated with news and information so that they can make informed decisions about rates, operations, and hiring practices.

REVENUE MANAGEMENT

A major factor in staying competitive is managing revenue in order to keep room rates at a competitive level. **Revenue management**, often referred to as *yield management*, uses past history of bookings and current booking activity to forecast demand as accurately as possible. In an attempt to even out the peaks and valleys of occupancy, hotels increase rates during high demand time and discount rates during slow demand time. Most hotels seek to make this approach more manageable by offering different rates and booking constraints to different market segments, making changes as necessary as bookings come in. For example, if a hotel knew that there was a small group of guests who usually called for a room at the last minute, but were always willing to pay extra for the short notice, it could increase the price without losing the business. Computerized revenue management systems provide high-speed evaluation of a property's history, current booking level, and forecasts, and set minimum rates and length-of-stay limits. Information can be updated every night or even on an hourly basis to avoid delay in deciding whether or not to take a booking.

In 2000, Cendant Corporation was in the top market position with a total of more than 6,400 properties representing more than 552,000 rooms. Brands included in the Cendant Corporation are Days Inn of America, Ramada Franchise Systems, Super 8 Motels, Howard Johnson International, Travelodge, Knights Franchise Systems Inc., Wingate Inns International, and Villager Franchise Systems.

CONFIRMATION

What type of research do hoteliers buy from outside companies?

_____

_____

GIVE 'EM WHAT THEY WANT

PRODUCT/ SERVICE MANAGEMENT

The race to stay ahead of the competition always involves keeping the customer happy. Doing so usually involves consistent service standards, amenities, and in-room technology. A survey completed by Kimberly-Clark for the 2001 International Hotel/Motel & Restaurant Show reported the top priority requests by business travelers.

- A computer with Internet access and a printer in every guest room

- A "smart" phone with caller ID and e-mail capabilities

- Exercise equipment in every room

- A conference room adjacent to guest rooms

- A personal assistant to handle business requests

Priority items for non-business travelers were as follows.

- A code for room access, rather than a key or entry card

- A home theater set-up with an extensive video library

- Spa services, such as aromatherapy and massages, on demand

- Comfort foods, such as ice cream, in an in-room freezer

- Exercise equipment in the room

**MARKETING-
INFORMATION
MANAGEMENT**

In order to know what customers want, hotel operators use **customer relationship management systems**. These databases identify guests' occupancy patterns, lengths of stay, demographic information, types of business, and individual customer profiles. With this information, a hotel can provide better service to its most valuable customers, target customers so that the right offer goes to the right customers, and track return on investment of direct marketing campaigns. Here are some suggestions for using customer relationship management systems.

- Collect information such as the guest's zip code, room type, and spending pattern as a means of customer service. If a guest has no history with your property, he or she'll need information and will appreciate extra attention.

- Don't ask a guest for information unless you are prepared to act upon it. If you ask for a guest's birth date, be prepared to send a card at the appropriate time. If you want to know if a guest prefers feather pillows or foam pillows, have a supply of both types ready.

- Train—and re-train—the front desk staff to read database information and recognize returning guests. Provide incentives and training programs for your front desk staff to make arriving guests feel remembered and comfortable.

- Maintaining and implementing the customer information database should be the full-time job of at least one person and the concern of every hotel employee. Don't just put guests on a mailing list. Give them what they want—and what you know they want based on past information.

CONFIRMATION

What is the purpose of a customer relationship management system?

_____

_____

_____

CAREER SPOTLIGHT

MARIA NINFA RODRIGUEZ LAURENZO

George Bush, Michael Douglas, Reba McEntire, ZZ Top, and Aerosmith loved her food. She sat on advisory boards of numerous prestigious foundations, among them the John F. Kennedy Center for the Performing Arts. These are big accomplishments for a little girl born and raised, along with 11 brothers and sisters, on a small farm in the Rio Grande Valley town of Harlingen, Texas. Some sixty years later, Houston considered Maria Ninfa Rodriguez Laurenzo the first lady of Mexican cooking.

In 1949, Ninfa and her husband, Domenic Thomas, opened a small tortilla factory in Houston and spent 16-hour days rolling out corn tortillas. She continued working even after her husband's death in 1969. By 1972, the tortilla factory was losing money and the equipment needed updating to comply with new regulations. Ninfa decided to turn the factory into a restaurant. Banks turned her down, so she relied on a friend from Mexico City to lend her a few thousand dollars. With a mere ten tables and forty chairs, and the back of the restaurant still a tortilla factory, Ninfa's opened in July 1973. Her famous specialty, Tacos Al Carbon, chopped chargrilled beef filet wrapped in a handmade flour tortilla, was far from the typical Tex-Mex combination plate. Word of the new and different taste soon spread across Houston. The original restaurant soon tripled in size, and Mama Ninfa closed the tortilla factory. Soon she opened a second restaurant where she greeted guests with a warm smile, sometimes a song, and always a watchful eye on the kitchen.

As word spread across Texas, sports figures, musicians, Hollywood stars, and politicians got hooked on her food. George and Barbara Bush often asked her to bring food up to Washington. John Travolta had a private seat in one corner of the restaurant and made special stops to pick up food to go.

By the early 1980s, the Laurenzo family's corporation had nine Houston restaurants. Eventually, the family's RioStar Corporation opened outlets in Dallas, San Antonio, and Leipzig, Germany. In 1995 the Austin-based Serranos Café and Cantina acquired RioStar. Including franchises in Georgia and Louisiana, there are now about 55 independent Ninfa franchises.

Before she died in 2001, Ninfa received numerous awards for community service, including the U.S. Hispanic Chamber of Commerce Business Recognition Award. In 1998, she was inducted into the Texas Women's Hall of Fame.

THINK CRITICALLY

Ninfa's success can be attributed to a unique product. With a partner, list as many possibilities for success stories in food service that might similarly be based on a unique product. Research and report on three of them.

UNDERSTAND MARKETING CONCEPTS

Circle the best answer for each of the following questions.

1. An individual company's percentage of total sales generated by all competitors is called the
 a. market position
 b. market share
 c. sales volume
 d. forecast

2. The use of past booking history and current booking activity to forecast demand as accurately as possible is known as
 a. revenue or yield management
 b. price or planning management
 c. consumer or distribution management
 d. room pricing or rack rate management

THINK CRITICALLY

Answer the following questions as completely as possible. If necessary, use a separate sheet of paper.

3. Assume you want to open a hotel in your hometown. What type of research reports will you want to secure from a research and/or consulting company?

_____

_____

_____

_____

_____

4. **Communication** If you were a front desk agent, how would you greet a guest who had an extensive past history with your hotel? What could you do to indicate that you recognize him or her? Include verbal and nonverbal actions.

_____

_____

_____

_____

_____

THE ROLE OF TECHNOLOGY

CHECK IN

Hilton Hotels International is certainly cyber savvy. In 2001, *InternetWeek* named the corporation the top e-business overall and the travel and hospitality industry winner as a result of a performance-based questionnaire of major U.S. companies. More than 400 candidates were evaluated in areas such as improved relationships with customers and suppliers and the level of involvement in electronic markets.

In the year 2000, Hilton experienced large increases in the volume of online business booked through its brand web sites. The web sites, which include Hilton, Doubletree, Embassy Suites, Hampton Inn, and Red Lion Hotels & Inns, booked more than $300 million total online business during 2000, twice that of the previous year. Hilton Hotels relied on the power of e-business to boost sales, cut procurement costs, and solidify its major market position. Hilton's biggest accomplishment was an extensive web site enhancement that improved Internet information and integrated transaction services for its nearly 1,900 hotels across North America. Information technology teams such as Hilton's are an increasingly large part of hotel management.

Work with a group. List as many possible ways to incorporate technology in hotel and restaurant management as you can.

GOALS

Describe factors to consider when selecting a property management system.

List other areas where technology systems are used in hotel management.

Explain the use of common standards for technology in the hospitality industry.

TECHNOLOGY HERE...

MARKETING-INFORMATION MANAGEMENT

High-speed Internet access, wireless technology, and in-room computers are some of the technological advances available in hotel rooms. In addition to in-room technology, it has been predicted that by the year 2002 there will be more mobile phones and personal digital assistants in use than computers. Keeping that in mind, hotels will increase the use of personal information kiosks in public spaces so users can interface mobile devices to download data and perform other tasks previously restricted to a desktop or office.

CYBER MARKETING

Smart cards are not report cards with straight As. "Smart card" is a term for a card the size of a credit card with a microprocessor chip embedded in it. The chip has computational power and intelligence similar to early personal computers, plus encryption capabilities that protect the information on the cards. Soon hotel guests can use these cards to buy airline tickets and reserve hotel rooms, pick up automated boarding passes, check in at kiosks in hotel lobbies or airport terminals, retreive their guest room assignments, and enter their rooms. As more people use the Internet to purchase merchandise and make travel reservations, they will demand more secure methods of payment that smart cards can deliver. In July 1998, Hilton Hotels International announced that the Hilton New York & Towers, the largest hotel in New York City, would be the first hotel to install a key locking system with smart-card capacity. At least 6,000 travelers carry credit cards with smart-card technology.

THINK CRITICALLY
1. What segments of the market are likely to embrace smart-card technology?
2. Would it be a wise move to convert rapidly and totally to smart-card technology? Why or why not?

Hotels rely on technology to streamline their business and operations in every department from the front lobby to the back kitchen to reservation centers to procurement systems. Prior to the advent of computers, hotel accountants and other staff members spent long hours keeping track of room charges, restaurant charges, gift shop charges, and other fees. Night auditors had to add in extra charges by hand at night so the updated guest folio would be ready every morning for the front desk staff. Computers, database applications, and other programs have dramatically decreased the time and effort required to accomplish these tasks. Property management systems, central reservation systems, room management systems, and energy management systems are some of the types of technology that have made the job of running a hotel easier and more efficient.

Property management systems (PMS) are computer programs used throughout the hotel to keep track of guest registration, reservations, guest folio management, room selections, accounting, supply inventory, and purchasing. It is important for hotels to use programs that integrate easily with software being used among different departments. These programs must be user-friendly and provide the type of information and service required by each individual property. When choosing the property management system to implement, several key factors should be considered.

- How much technology can our computer network support?
- Do we have a lot of group functions that would require flexible booking and billing functions?

- Do we have a large amount of catering that would require specific software functions?

- Do we have a spa or other guest-related activities that would need a special module to track and bill those activities?

- Does our hotel have a high standard for guest services, requiring a strong guest-history feature?

- Is this a roadside motel that simply needs good, solid guest handling with a minimum of fuss?

- Does a large amount of our reservations come from a franchisor, a representation service, or the Internet?

- Does the system provide interfaces to all other systems we have on the property?

Answers to questions like these, closely correlated to the costs of acquiring, implementing, and maintaining the hardware and software, let hotel management select the right applications for the right tasks.

CONFIRMATION

What is a property management system? Name three factors to consider when implementing a management system.

_____

_____

_____

TECHNOLOGY THERE...

MARKETING-INFORMATION MANAGEMENT

In addition to property management systems, other types of technology make it possible to manage the entire business of a hotel. Some of these may be integrated with PMS technology to provide a completely integrated network for the business, from initial marketing to check out.

Point-of-sale (POS) systems are found in hotel restaurants, gift shops, spas or exercise centers, and, of course, at the front desk—any place where guests might purchase an item or service to be added to the folio. As the use of touch-screen technology becomes more common, PMS programs can be concurrent with POS systems, allowing for faster, more effective, and better guest service.

Central reservation systems allow customers to call a central, toll-free number and make a reservation with any property in the system. Large corporate hotel companies, franchises, and managed hotels have company-wide reservation systems that can provide up-to-date information about room availability.

Global distribution systems (GDS) provide electronic connections between and reservation capabilities for travel-related businesses such as hotels, airlines, car rentals, tours, and cruises. For example, eTravnet.com uses a unique technology, develop by REZconnect, that allows companies to take telephone reservations directly from customers who are making online reservations. Travel agents can use this technology, as can independent hotels, bed and breakfasts, and tour operators. Large hotel corporations and franchises often have their own type of GDS.

Energy management systems save massive amounts of money by controlling and monitoring heating and air conditioning units and by automatically turning off lights in meeting rooms, offices, maid closets, public restrooms, hallways, and other areas when unoccupied. In-room monitoring, hot water supply management, outdoor property lighting control, and security procedures are other engineering- and maintenance-related uses of technology.

CONFIRMATION

Name four types of technology systems used by hospitality facilities and give a benefit of each.

_____

_____

_____

TECHNOLOGY EVERYWHERE

MARKETING- INFORMATION MANAGEMENT

Using computerized information and management systems is not as easy as it may seem. Many hotels are unable to take advantage of the labor-saving and revenue-increasing systems because of "communication gaps." The countless new computer and technology programs available in the hospitality industry do not always interface well with each other. To address this challenge, the American Hotel and Lodging Association initiated a project that combined the input of major hotel corporations, consulting companies, and professional organizations to develop universal standards among computer software and equipment. Committees were developed to establish standards for the following.

- **Posting devices**, which include point-of-sale systems, telephone management, voice mail, on-demand movies, mini bar systems, fax systems, in-room Internet/computer systems, and housekeeping and maintenance

- **Food and beverage retail management systems**, which include sales and catering, purchasing and inventory, time and attendance, and labor scheduling

- **Central reservations and yield management systems**, which include central and Internet reservations, yield and revenue management, executive information systems, guest history, and travel agent payment

- **Remote devices**, which include kiosk and hand-held devices, key services, in-room monitoring, and security systems

- **Payment processing and accounting systems**, which include credit card authorization, payment processing, and back office accounting

- **Casino management systems**, which include player tracking, profiles, and folio posting

- **Booking activities/golf tee time reservations systems**, which include tee time management, central and Internet reservations, executive information systems, guest history, and travel agent payment

COMMON STANDARDS

The goal of this initiative, known as the Hospitality Industry Technology Integration Standards (HITIS), is to create common standards for technology in the hospitality industry while lowering automation costs.

All of these software systems have implications for hotel management beyond technical applications. After cost and implementation, the most important aspect of hotel management technology is training. Every person in the facility must be able to use the appropriate software system to perform his or her job effectively. The technical challenge for systems designers is to make the systems easy to use as well as efficient. The challenge for managers is to train a constantly shifting workforce to use the systems well. Without effective training, the most sophisticated software in the world is worse than ineffective. Not only will poorly used systems not do their job, they will frustrate workers, create misleading information, and even cause the loss of customers who deal with inefficient or inaccurate bills, reservations, or workers who haven't been given a chance to do their jobs well.

CONFIRMATION

Explain why it is important to have computer interface standards in hotel technology.

_____

_____

UNDERSTAND MARKETING CONCEPTS

Circle the best answer for each of the following questions.

1. Computer programs used by hotels to keep track of general information such as guest registration and folios, room selections, accounting, and supply inventory are known as
   a. global management systems
   b. purchasing management systems
   c. property relationship systems
   d. property management systems

2. Software programs for use in areas where guests might purchase merchandise or services are called
   a. purchasing software
   b. retail technology
   c. point-of-sale systems
   d. cost-management systems

THINK CRITICALLY

Answer the following questions as completely as possible. If necessary, use a separate sheet of paper.

3. In addition to the cost and effort of buying, implementing, and maintaining management systems, how might training determine whether hotel technology systems succeed or fail in a given business?

_____

_____

_____

_____

_____

4. **Research** Using the Internet or travel magazines, find a web site or an advertisement for a popular hotel franchise or corporation. List as many evident uses of technology that you can find on the web site or in the ad.

_____

_____

_____

_____

REMODELING TO MEET FUTURE DEMANDS

CHECK IN

The 441-room Outrigger Village Hotel in Waikiki recently completed a $3.9 million renovation of guest rooms and lobby area. All guest rooms received new bedspreads, draperies, wall coverings, and artwork. Bathroom fixtures were replaced, and Corian bathroom countertops were installed. New carpet was placed in all guest rooms and guest floor hallways. The front desk was redesigned to include four guest stations. The pool was also completely overhauled, with new pool furniture being added. Lobby spaces were redecorated with Hawaiian quilt wall hangings, new art, and new furniture.

Outrigger Village is a mid-price hotel, a half block away from the beach, in the middle of Waikiki. Rates at the Outrigger Village start at $95 a night during spring and fall and $105 a night during summer. Services and amenities available for guests include room service and a family-style Villager Restaurant. Each guest room has in-room movies, a refrigerator and coffee maker, and kitchenettes.

Work with a partner. Make a list of things that suggest a hotel might be in need of renovation. Include marketing factors on your list.

Describe the effect of technology on renovations.

List the reasons for renovations in hotels.

FUTURE QUEST

Hospitality businesses must stay on the cutting edge of technology and provide comfortable and welcoming environments at the same time. New amenities and services are constantly added to room design and hotel atmosphere as part of an effort to compete with other similar businesses. Hotels must strike a balance between allowing the guest to escape from the pressures of business while also providing high-tech methods of keeping in touch.

Take a quick trip into the not-too-distant future and imagine what travel and hospitality will be like. You are on a jetliner that is taking you to Tokyo, where you will meet with business associates from all over the world. As you sit in your first-class seat, you run your smart card through the magnetic reader and your hotel is immediately aware of your flight status and approximate arrival time. When you arrive at the hotel, there is no need to stop at the front desk since you have already checked in. You head straight to your room where the door opens immediately upon reading a scan of your thumb print.

The room has been prepared to your specific preferences: traditional décor, your favorite selections on CD, the mattress firm with your favorite brand of feather pillows. The temperature is set at 72 degrees, and two framed, high-resolution monitors display your favorite classic art pieces. There is a recumbent bike in the corner of the room for your morning workout. As you turn on the TV, your company's itinerary and updated agenda for tomorrow's business meetings appear promptly. You click on the computer in your room and immediately have access to your e-mail and data to be included in tomorrow's presentation. You change the TV channel to check the stock market and news. Then, just to relax, you switch over to your favorite video game and play a few rounds with another guest a few floors away. You use the videophone to call home and leave a recorded message to let your family know you have arrived safely.

You awake the next morning not to the sound of a jarring alarm buzzer, but to the gradual sunrise of a virtual wake-up light. Your favorite brands of shampoo and bath products await you in the bathroom, as your specialty blend of coffee happily perks away in the individual coffee maker in your room. As you leave the room, the thermostat automatically records your absence and adjusts to the empty room, patiently waiting to readjust the room to your preferred temperature 30 minutes prior to your arrival. You know what the weather is like outside, since the panel near the door displays the outdoor temperature and humidity.

If this scenario seems far-fetched, it isn't. The technology to provide the services described above exists today and is already at work in some hotels. Investment in technology as part of the renovation process is changing the way hotels plan and execute renovations. Although it is sometimes difficult to predict what will succeed in the high-tech arena, it is still necessary to monitor trends and plan accordingly. Videophones have been around since the 1960s, for example, but few consumers prefer them. Taking a costly plunge on technical renovations can be risky, as some technologies become obsolete rapidly, provide their services at too high a cost, or fall to a competing technology. Still, with a profitable business market choosing hotels with high-tech amenities, hotels can't afford not to include technical renovations along with new carpet and new décor.

TIME OUT

The New Otani Hotel & Garden in Los Angeles offers entire rooms in Japanese style, complete with tatami mats, futons instead of beds, shoji screens, low-to-the-ground dining tables, and Japanese robes and slippers. More requests for the Japanese rooms come from American leisure travelers than from Japanese travelers.

CONFIRMATION

Why is planning for technology an integral part of hotel renovation?

_____

_____

REASONS FOR RENOVATIONS

Hotels typically renovate guest rooms and lobby areas every five to seven years. Hotels renovate for several reasons and usually make changes, minor or major, in specific areas on a schedule that will cause the least amount of guest disturbance or inconvenience. Some of the reasons for renovating include the following.

- Renovations or redesigns for the convenience of the customer that involve improved access to technology, better or upscale amenities, open access for disabled guests, added business-related facilities, and increased energy and environmentally friendly systems.

- Replacing or fixing worn-out furniture, fixtures, and equipment in guest rooms, lobby areas, public spaces, and meeting rooms. These replacements usually occur every few years and are considered an ongoing process.

- Equipment upgrades to improve operational efficiency in the back of the house.

- A comprehensive, major renovation to improve operations, reassess infrastructure and facilities, and improve services usually occurs every 20–25 years.

In order for property owners or managers to establish a realistic renovation budget and schedule, they consider the long-term goals for a property and determine the economic feasibility and return on investment. The property owner hires professional and experienced interior designers, or corporations provide their own employees who are experts in hotel interior design. The designs in a hotel must not only be pleasing and comfortable, but functional and durable as well.

JUDGMENT CALL

While concern for guest safety is always a priority in hotel operations, crib safety has not been. A recent spot check of hotels and motels in 27 states found that 82 percent had provided cribs that posed potential hazards. Problems included loose hardware, insecure mattress supports, soft bedding, and use of adult-size sheets. Federal safety standards for cribs have been in effect since 1991, but inspecting equipment has not been a top priority. The U.S. Consumer Product Safety Commission (CPSC) has partnered with the National Safe Kids Campaign to start a crib safety initiative to warn hotels of potential dangers and encourage them to inspect their equipment regularly. Several major hotel companies have inspection procedures in place. Bass Hotels plans to organize a "Crib Safety Week" during which housekeeping and maintenance staff inspect cribs and play yards for safety and condition. Crib safety guidelines are available on Safe Kid's web site www.safekids.org/crib and the CPSC site www.cpsc.gov.

THINK CRITICALLY
1. Why do you think some hotels have paid so little attention to crib safety?
2. Would you favor government enforcement of crib safety standards? Why or why not?

MARKETING MYTHS

Out with the old and in with the new isn't the only way to renovate. Updates of historic hotels that preserve the grandeur of the past while adding amenities and features of the present appeal to customers who seek more than a cookie-cutter hotel. These renovations range from complete makeovers, such as that of the Mark Hopkins in San Francisco or the famous Breakers in Palm Beach, to real historic preservation, such as that of the Mills House in Charleston, South Carolina. There, great care was taken that the renovated hotel closely resemble the original Mills House of the early 1800s. Carpet and draperies were chosen to complement antique furniture, and the antique, two-tiered stairway was carefully restored.

THINK CRITICALLY
Modern legal requirements and market conditions can make restorations expensive and challenging. Do you think such efforts are worth the trouble from a marketing perspective?

DEVELOPING THE PLAN

In order to plan a successful major renovation, hotel management, hotel architects, and interior designers usually meet for several days on the hotel property. The interior design team and hotel management teams visit several surrounding competitor facilities. The manager of the hotel discusses renovation goals, budget, and basic requirements with the design team. The interior design team develops concepts and discusses the strengths and weaknesses of various proposals. The basic blueprint for the renovation project is established. The designers then prepare a summary report and proposal that serves as a basic, coherent plan for the development of the property. The plan may be implemented all at once or in phases, as funds allow.

Designers consider the following when developing a plan for renovation.

- The target market and clientele of the hotel
- Access to lobby, food and beverage outlets, and other retail spaces
- Durability of furniture, fixtures, fabrics, and carpet
- Technology needs
- Disability, safety, and other government regulations
- Physical and geographical location of the hotel
- Historical background and value of the building
- Size of guest rooms and guest bathrooms
- Operations aspects of back-of-the-house departments
- Availability of quality work by local suppliers, vendors, and manufacturers

CONFIRMATION

What are some reasons hotels undergo renovations?
What must designers consider when developing a plan?

UNDERSTAND MARKETING CONCEPTS
Circle the best answer for each of the following questions.

1. Hotels renovate their properties
   a. to upgrade amenities, technology, and guest accessibility
   b. to increase efficiency of equipment
   c. to replace worn or broken furniture and fixtures
   d. all of the above

2. Things to consider when renovating a hotel include
   a. rewriting the hotel mission statement
   b. the turnover rate of employees
   c. types of customers who frequently stay at the hotel
   d. types of name tags worn by employees

THINK CRITICALLY
Answer the following questions as completely as possible. If necessary, use a separate sheet of paper.

3. Create a checklist of questions you would ask the manager of a hotel if you were in charge of a renovation project.

_____

_____

_____

_____

_____

_____

4. Why is some renovation an ongoing part of hotel maintenance? What steps might be taken to minimize disruption for guests?

_____

_____

_____

_____

_____

_____

_____

CHAPTER 11 REVIEW

REVIEW MARKETING CONCEPTS

Write the letter of the term that matches each definition. Some terms will not be used.

_____ **1.** Where a business stands in relation to other similar businesses

_____ **2.** Uses past history of bookings and current booking activity to forecast demand as accurately as possible

_____ **3.** Electronic connections between hotels and other travel-related companies

_____ **4.** Technological methods of efficient property maintenance and management

_____ **5.** Allow customers to call a central, toll-free number to book a room

_____ **6.** Computer programs used throughout a hotel to keep track of guest registration, reservations, guest folio management, room selections, accounting, supply inventory, and purchasing

a. central reservation systems

b. customer relationship management systems

c. energy management systems

d. global distribution systems

e. market position

f. market share

g. point-of-sale (POS) systems

h. property management systems

i. revenue management

Circle the best answer.

7. A company that publishes a monthly newsletter with information about occupancy, room rate, room supply, room demand, and room revenue is

    a. Better Business Bureau   **c.** Consumer Reports

    b. Smith Travel Research   **d.** Fodor's Travel Guides

8. An international consulting firm that provides trends reports, marketing research, and market positioning services is

    a. World Wide Web Travel   **c.** Hospitality Online

    b. JTF Consulting   **d.** PKF Consulting

9. Payment processing and accounting systems include

    a. casino player tracking   **c.** supply purchasing

    b. credit card authorization   **d.** all of these

THINK CRITICALLY

10. Make a list of at least ten ways that hotels use technology to run their properties.

_____

_____

_____

_____

_____

_____

_____

11. List at least five ways a hotel could use guest-history information to customize guest rooms.

_____

_____

_____

_____

_____

_____

_____

12. Using the Internet or travel magazines in your library, find and briefly describe three popular new amenities that guests consider to be basic. To whom and how are these available amenities being marketed?

_____

_____

_____

_____

_____

_____

CHAPTER 11 REVIEW

MAKE CONNECTIONS

13. Marketing Math Gloria Gomez owns an interior design firm that specializes in hotel renovation. The basic fee is $50 per room, plus $20 per square foot of public space covered in the renovation plan. What will be the final bill if Gloria's team of designers plans the renovation of a 327-room property with 5,400 square feet of lobby space, 27,250 square feet of meeting rooms, and 10,225 square feet of hallways?

_____

_____

_____

14. History Using the library or Internet, research the history of a hotel in the mid-twentieth century. Describe the differences of the décor, furnishings, amenities, and technology as compared to hotels in the early twenty-first century.

_____

_____

_____

_____

15. Communication Maria Lopez is a travel agent in the twenty-first century, and she wants to connect her business-traveling customers to hotels that offer the most up-to-date technology. Search the Web or travel magazines to determine which American hotels offer the latest in high-tech amenities. Create a flyer or brochure to give to Maria's clients describing the amenities, technology, and services offered by the hotels you researched.

_____

_____

16. Communication Interview three local hotel managers to find out about the durability of various items and ongoing renovation at their properties. Make a chart that shows what items you included and the results of your interviews.

_____

_____

_____

_____

TRAVEL AND TOURISM MARKETING TEAM DECISION MAKING EVENT

You and a partner are the managers of a major state fair. You are excited about the outstanding entertainment that you have scheduled to perform this year. Top country musicians, pop artists, and comedians hopefully will attract sold-out audiences which will also bring in needed revenue since attendance has been declining for the past five years. The air-conditioned arena holds 14,000 people when a revolving stage is used for performances. Total cost for all of the popular entertainers is $1.5 million. You must design a promotional strategy to sell out the concerts and attract concert goers to the rest of the state fair. How much will you charge for tickets and gate admission?

Study the Situation Use 30 minutes to outline your marketing strategy for accomplishing the three goals to boost earnings. Organize an analysis of it, using a management decision-making format.

Present Your Analysis Prepare a 10-minute presentation that describes your analysis of the situation. You may not use printed reference materials, audio or visual aids, and notes made during the preparation time. You may use a laptop computer for the presentation.

http://www.deca.org/ publications/HS_ Guide/guidetoc.html

PROJECT EXTENDED STAY

Your hotel consulting firm has been asked to develop a customer relationship management system.

1. Describe the type of hotel—full-service or limited-service? Three-, four-, or five-star? Downtown conference center or resort? What are your room rates—rack rates, available discounts, and so forth?

2. Describe the demographics of customers. Leisure or business travelers? Include information on average age, income, gender, and so on.

3. Design a spreadsheet or database. Include name, zip code, employer, and other information that could be gathered prior to a guest's first check in. Create a second level of information that could be gathered after the guest has visited, such as purpose, length, room service orders, and food and beverage preferences.

4. Design a plan to acquire more useful customer information. What tools or means will you use? How will you get customers to participate?

5. Prepare a large chart or poster that shows how the information you collect will be used to provide better, friendlier, more efficient service. What security precautions will you take to protect guests' privacy?

6. Design a training course to teach employees how to use the information collected. Include an overview of the customer relationship management system, benefits to the employees of using it properly, how specific types of information are used in particular jobs, and sensitivity to customer relations and privacy. Design an end-of-course test.

CHAPTER 12

CAREER OPPORTUNITIES IN THE HOSPITALITY INDUSTRY

LESSONS

12.1 PREPARING FOR A HOSPITALITY CAREER

12.2 EDUCATION REQUIREMENTS

12.3 MOBILITY REQUIRED FOR ADVANCEMENT

WINNING STRATEGIES

EMPLOYEE RECOGNITION AND MOTIVATION

Employees need acceptance, approval, and appreciation. Vicki Richman, CFO for the American Hospitality Management Company, suggests nine actions to give your hospitality staff what they need: Communicate, Communicate, Communicate, Recognize, Recognize, Recognize, Thank, Thank, and Thank! Richman has developed more than 50 ideas for ongoing programs to keep employees connected to the hotel or restaurant emotionally, to build excitement, and to protect from competitors seeking to draw employees away. Examples include

- Providing soda, fruit, and snacks to staff all the time

- Bringing a camera to work and taking candid shots of staff to post on a bulletin board for all to enjoy

- Giving all staff a reward when a published goal in revenue or other criterion has been reached

- Awarding a certificate of achievement, lunch, and coffee mug for perfect attendance

- Allowing those with perfect attendance records to enter a lottery to win a $100 or $200 gift certificate

These motivators help keep staff members and encourage them to work hard toward common goals. Companies that implement positive strategies must be sincere and consistent. Hospitality employees are in high demand, challenging restaurants and hotels to create rewarding places to work.

THINK CRITICALLY
1. Why must hospitality businesses create strategies for building excitement among employees?
2. Some activities to motivate employees cost money. Why not skip the activities and save the money?

CHAPTER 12
LESSON 12.1

PREPARING FOR A HOSPITALITY CAREER

GOALS

Describe opportunities available in the hospitality industry.

Identify the four parts of a career-planning strategy.

Describe the characteristics of a successful hospitality employee.

CHECK IN

When you go out to eat or stay at a hotel, how can you spot the best employees? You can usually recognize the best hospitality employees immediately. It may be the host or server in a restaurant who is professional, friendly, and sincere, and who keeps refilling your beverage, attends to detail without distracting, and cares how you like your meal. At the hotel, it's the person in housekeeping, front desk operations, valet service, or catering who makes eye contact, smiles, welcomes you to the property, and goes out of his or her way to please and help you. The ultimate compliment to a hospitality employee occurs when a guest specifically requests service from that individual. The best employees—the ones with the energy, the neatness, the punctuality, and the personality—rise in the hospitality industry, and personal and financial rewards rise with them.

Work with a partner. Discuss the characteristics you appreciate the most from a good server at a restaurant. Share your ideas with the class, and compile a list of characteristics of employees who are winners. Which of your own personal characteristics appear on the list?

A DIVERSE AND EXCITING CAREER

It is typical to think of the servers, the front desk personnel, the reservations agents, and the kitchen staff when you think of the hospitality industry. In fact, many professionals in the industry begin with part-time or lower-level jobs in hospitality. But the field of hospitality is far more than a collection of routine jobs. High-paying careers in diverse specialties from marketing to cuisine planning to technology await qualified and experienced hospitality professionals. Excitement, travel opportunities, and the personal fulfillment of making a difference for a business and its customers are available for those who prepare and are willing to work hard in careers that demand dedication. As service industries in general grow in the worldwide economy, careers in hospitality afford plenty of opportunity for experience, upward mobility, and interesting day-to-day life.

AN EVER-CHANGING BUSINESS

The growth and diversity of hospitality businesses lead to constant change in the industry. Not only do trends and technology constantly move, the staff moves with them. One of the challenges of hospitality management is to keep up with the constant change and its effects on the labor supply. Over the last few years there have been significant changes in numbers employed in certain occupations. Restaurant and catering managers have experienced a significant growth in employment potential. Waitperson numbers have also increased significantly. The number of cooks has declined nationally, opening employment opportunities in this field. Occupations with the most significant projected growth rates include cooks, waitpersons, and kitchen personnel.

The hospitality industry hires a large proportion of part-time workers. Many of these part-timers are young people beginning their careers, or people who have more than one job. A high number of small businesses and the seasonal nature of many hospitality businesses also contribute to the trend toward part-time work. Although there is constant turnover in part-time workers, they are generally less expensive for a business in terms of wages and benefits. It is estimated that by the year 2005 about 45 percent of the people employed in the hospitality industry could be working full-time and 55 percent part-time. Finding, training, and keeping these people and providing great service to customers with this shifting work force are the greatest challenges most hospitality managers face.

WHAT ABOUT PAY?

Salaries in the hotel industry are closely correlated to the number of rooms and services offered. Hotels with more rooms and guest services usually offer higher employee compensation. Such places are bigger businesses and can often afford to attract good workers with compensation. Geographic location of the business also has a direct impact on the compensation. Salaries are generally higher for hotels located in the New England/Mid-Atlantic region and the Mountain/Pacific region as a result of higher costs of living and competition for employees.

Every two years HVS Executive Search conducts the lodging industry's most comprehensive survey of compensation and benefit information, the HCE Hospitality Compensation Exchange. Recent data collected from 135 hotel companies indicated that a vice-president of marketing representing a company with revenues of less than $50 million received an average base salary of $50,020, while a vice-president of marketing at a company with revenues of more than $50 million earned an average salary between $140,000 and $168,400. The average salary for a director of sales and marketing was $53,102 in the North Central United States and $66,394 in the Mountain/Pacific region. A hotel property with fewer than 150 rooms paid a sales manager an average salary of $27,671, while hotels with more than 800 rooms paid the same position $42,400.

National Average Pay for Various Hotel Positions in 2000

Director of sales and marketing $62,387

Director of catering $51,520

Senior sales manager $45,360

Sales manager $35,361

CONFIRMATION

Why are so many hospitality jobs part-time?

_____

_____

PURSUING A CAREER

Every person needs a plan to reach career goals. Pursuing a career and applying for a job involve marketing and packaging your best characteristics. You must, in effect, sell yourself to a prospective employer, and to do that you must organize and empower yourself to make a professional approach, just as you would undertake any professional project. Four parts of a "Career Empowerment Plan" are the planning process, a dynamic career package, a marketing plan, and company research.

The **planning process** creates a roadmap for your professional future. Start with a simple, one-page statement listing personal and professional goals for the next several years. Who are you? What do you want to do? What do you need to know to do it? Answering questions like these allows you to make decisions about which positions you will seek.

A dynamic, hard-hitting **career package** includes a resume that stands out from the crowd and gets employers excited. It also includes a unique cover letter written for each employer and a list of references. Your reference list should sell your experience and business network instead of just listing names and telephone numbers.

The length and format of a resume change according to current market conditions. Employers want factual information on a candidate before they invest the time to make a telephone call, let alone pay for an interview, trips, or relocation expenses. Prospective employers do not have time to call every person who submits a resume, so make sure yours makes the call list. The 1–2 page resumes presented in most resume-writing books are not effective for the hospitality industry. Longer resumes that highlight concrete accomplishments currently generate more interviews. Objectives should be specific. The applicant's objectives, experience, and professional affiliations must be apparent and believable. A clear, impressive, and credible resume puts the prospective employer in a mindset that says, "This person can really help us. We need to impress this candidate. We may have to pay a little more than we planned, but it appears that this person will be worth it."

Next, put together a **marketing plan** for which the product is you. Package yourself to be noticed by a potential employer. Define your own "hot market." A **hot market** is any job with a reputable employer anywhere in the world that will advance your career and improve your salary. Think about yourself and what you like to do and the conditions under which you do things well. Do you prefer large or small cities, hot or seasonal climates, the Plains or the West Coast, Europe or Asia? Answers

to these questions are essential for satisfaction in a career and define your personal hot market.

Once you have defined your ultimate hot market, you must assess your skills and career progression to see if you are ready to restrict your job search to your hot market. For example, your hot market will restrict your career growth if you want to live in a small town in a very scenic part of the world. There are probably a lot of other people who want the same thing. Good jobs in this arena might not turn over frequently, which means promotions could be few and far between. If this describes your personal hot market, make sure your career has advanced far enough that you can afford the lifestyle and don't need rapid promotions.

Networking is extremely important for success in any career, and you can use your network as part of your personal marketing plan. Many professional contacts are made by joining professional organizations associated with the hospitality industry. Most of these professional organizations have annual conferences that focus attention on the latest trends in the industry. Professional conferences not only allow leaders to learn about the latest trends, but also ignite long-lasting professional friendships. These contacts and professional organizations will keep you informed of the best jobs and industry trends.

JUDGMENT CALL

Loyalty was once an important characteristic of the employee–employer relationship. Success used to be measured by how long you were employed by a company. Today's success may depend on career changes necessitated by the changing business environment or desires for career progress. Sometimes employees make changes. Sometimes employers drop jobs, forcing employees to find new ones.

What is the difference between job-hopping and professional mobility? Employers who perceive an applicant as a job-hopper may suspect a person is not a solid employee, and may not be willing to invest training dollars in someone who won't keep the job. On the other hand, employees often feel that they must protect their own interests, because employers have little loyalty to them and might downsize them the moment business looks bad. These conflicting situations pose problems for both employees and managers.

THINK CRITICALLY
1. What circumstances make a job change appropriate? How many changes are too many?
2. As a manager, what types of things could you do to encourage employees to stay with your company?

Doing **company research** before you interview is extremely important to find out exactly what employers are looking for in a candidate. If you can't locate information about a company, remember that all companies want people who can help them improve revenues, reduce costs, improve customer service and training, and reduce turnover. Preparing for the interview involves writing down the most logical questions interviewers will ask and then rehearsing your answers in front of a mirror. Conservative business attire is still appropriate for an interview in the hospitality industry.

CONFIRMATION

What are four parts of a strategy to pursue a career in the hospitality industry?

_____

_____

WHAT EMPLOYERS WANT

It takes more than the right skills to land a job. Personal attributes also play an important role in personnel decisions. Employers may settle for 70 to 80 percent of the skills they want if they find a job candidate they really like—someone who fits the team. Employers realize that it is a lot easier to

help an individual learn additional skills than it is to turn a person into a team player for their company. Employers can read a resume to decide if an individual has the skills, education, and training needed to do the work. Time is spent interviewing to learn a lot more about the candidate.

Flexibility is important to employers. They can evaluate skills, training, and experience, but they are also looking for intangible personal qualities. The bottom line is that the employee must be able to get the job done. Employers want someone who has strong personal characteristics such as honesty, dependability, good work ethic, adaptability, maturity, and mental agility. Self-motivation, verbal ability, and strong listening skills also go a long way in the hospitality industry.

Successful people use creative strategies to get things done. They can successfully delegate tasks to team members. The person who delegates tasks well and gives credit where credit is deserved earns the respect of team members. Sincere and contagious enthusiasm is important too. Positive people are the magnet for team accomplishment. Team members want to help the positive leader accomplish company goals.

Prospective candidates for hospitality positions must be able to back up what they say with actual examples. Gaining experience by working on a team, shadowing the hospitality business, and participating in a paid or unpaid internship while in school will provide you with answers to the questions that interviewers are most concerned about.

CONFIRMATION

CONFIRMATION

What qualities that might not show on a resume are important to hospitality employers?

CAREER SPOTLIGHT

SHARON ESTEP

Sharon Estep is a freelance hotel sales and management specialist located in Florida. Her expertise can be attributed to 20 years in the hotel industry with varied positions including front desk clerk, night auditor, sales and marketing manager, and hotel director. Her keen observation of successful hotel operations has allowed her to become a freelance consultant to hotels looking to improve operations.

Estep attributes her success to hard work, willingness to learn, and dedication to the organization. She regards every job she has had as a learning experience. While working in the Washington, D.C. area, Sharon became actively involved in professional organizations to meet people in the industry and to attract tourism to the Capitol. She landed a position on the Cherry Blossom Committee, charged with providing a comfortable stay for Japanese guests. Working with the Japanese involved relationship building. Impressed, the Japanese invited Sharon to the Cherry Festival in Japan.

Estep has found the international marketplace a fascinating opportunity for the hospitality industry where preconceived notions must be abandoned. The best hospitality businesses determine the comforts for other cultures and provide some of those amenities to international guests. In a global hospitality economy, having translators available is not a bad idea, especially when hosting a sizeable foreign group.

A freelancer since 1998, Estep enjoys the variety that each project provides. An average hotel makeover takes four to six weeks. Sharon normally lives at the hotel property during that time. Her career involves being away from home during most of the year, making it challenging to maintain a balanced family life.

THINK CRITICALLY

What might be some of the difficulties of being a freelancer in any profession? With a partner, make a list of things one might need to know well to be a consultant to the hospitality industry.

UNDERSTAND MARKETING CONCEPTS

Circle the best answer for each of the following questions.

1. A good way to pursue a position in the hospitality industry is to
   a. take any job offered and work hard
   b. prepare a short and dynamic resume
   c. depend on your networked acquaintances
   d. prepare a marketing plan for yourself

2. Compensation in the hospitality industry is most closely related to
   a. networking
   b. location and size of facility
   c. whether the business is a hotel or restaurant
   d. education

THINK CRITICALLY

Answer the following questions as completely as possible. If necessary, use a separate sheet of paper.

3. Write a one-page personal statement of goals as part of a Career Empowerment Plan. Include personal and professional goals for the next five years related to the hospitality industry.

_____

_____

_____

_____

_____

_____

4. **Communication** Write a letter of recommendation for a class-mate. Focus on the qualities that you think an employer would like to see. Give specific examples.

_____

_____

_____

_____

_____

_____

EDUCATION REQUIREMENTS

CHAPTER

LESSON 12.2

CHECK IN

Many high schools in the United States offer "real-world" learning experiences for students. Programs offer paid and unpaid internships to give students an opportunity to learn more about career fields they are considering. Job shadowing allows students to observe a particular career for a period of time.

Innovative high schools are offering hospitality marketing programs in which students actually have some of their classes at a hotel property. This type of learning experience allows students to learn about every department of a hotel. It is an attractive program to major hotels that are constantly looking for well-qualified employees.

Work with a partner. Write down the top three careers you are currently considering for your future. What experiences could you take advantage of now to learn more about those careers in order to make the best decisions?

GOALS

List types of opportunities for education in the hospitality field.

Describe the benefits of hospitality education for both employee and employer.

CAREER CHOICES AND EDUCATION

Hospitality offers diverse career opportunities, ranging from accounting to resort management. There are opportunities for people interested in technology and human resources. People interested in food operations may choose food-operations management or service. Those with powers of persuasion and networking may be good candidates for hospitality sales and marketing. People who have mechanical ability or organizational skills could consider maintenance or housekeeping management. Business communications and organizational behavior are a growing part of the hospitality industry. Individuals interested in legal issues may specialize in hospitality law. Resort management may be the right choice for those who want to provide the best guest experience at a popular location.

No matter what career in hospitality you choose, education and training in direct or related fields are pluses. In careers requiring highly technical skills, specific knowledge and skills are required just to enter the field. In other areas, education enhances your ability and experience. If you are just beginning your career, appropriate education and training distinguishes you from competing applicants and helps offset any lack of experience.

START LEARNING IN HIGH SCHOOL

High school is not too soon to start preparing for a career in hospitality management. A good fundamental education is critical to almost any hospitality career. Basic computation, communication, and business skills are part of the curricula in most high schools. As high schools do more to prepare students for the modern economy with real-world programs and internships, high schools provide better training for a career in hospitality.

Many progressive high schools in the U.S. have hospitality marketing programs that enable students to learn the industry at an actual hotel. The Marriott Hospitality High School is the nation's first four-year public high school dedicated to the hospitality industry. The Marriott family's foundation has pledged $1 million to the school, located in Washington, D.C. The school started with 100 ninth- and tenth-grade students and a new class of 50 ninth-graders will be admitted each of the next two years. This four-year program of academic courses provides workplace-based career preparation. Marriott Hospitality High School is a tuition-free, public charter school open to all interested Washington, D.C., high-school students.

Internships in restaurants, hotels, and other hospitality settings during the 11th and 12th grades enhance students' classroom work. All students who graduate are guaranteed either a job or scholarship assistance. Students at Marriott Hospitality High School have the flexibility to choose a career path that takes them to a university or other post-secondary program after graduation or directly into the workplace. Marriott International Chairman J.W. Marriott Jr. believes that "This innovative charter school will open the door to academic success, rewarding careers in the hospitality industry, and real opportunities for young people to build meaningful and productive lives." Educational and career paths in the twenty-first century will not follow traditional patterns, and the Marriott Hospitality High School will prepare students for a lifetime of learning and working.

COMMUNITY COLLEGES AND TWO-YEAR PROGRAMS

After high school, there are many options for further training and education that will benefit those seeking a career in hospitality. Increasingly popular are junior colleges, community colleges, and other two-year programs at private institutions. Community colleges are usually less expensive than four-year schools and offer two-year associates degrees or certificates in specialized areas. In many cases, basic college work completed at a community college can transfer if a student decides to pursue a four-year degree.

Another advantage of community and local colleges is that they often offer nontraditional programs specifically targeted to particular fields. For example, Columbus State Community College in Columbus, Ohio, offers eight programs or certificates directly related to the hospitality industry. These hospitality management programs are intended to provide the experience and skills not only to get a job, but to enhance growth prospects for one's entire career. Several majors lead to associates degrees in fields such as chef apprenticeship, dietetic technician, foodservice/restaurant management, and travel/tourism/hotel management. Also available are specific courses in dietary management, lodging management, and the travel industry, all leading to certificates.

The coursework attempts to provide a range of *knowledge, skills,* and *abilities (KSAs)* for quality performance in the industry. The general objectives for a major in hospitality management include the following.

- Maintain appropriate standards of professionalism, including ethical behavior and adherence to dress and grooming codes of the industry

- Set and maintain high-quality service standards for satisfying diverse customers.

- Demonstrate effective communication and interpersonal skills with management, employees, and customers

- Demonstrate skills in training, coaching, team building, staffing, motivating, and supervising employees

- Perform basic math skills necessary for the industry

- Use computers, online resources, and software appropriate to the industry

- Demonstrate problem-solving and critical-thinking skills.

- Analyze financial reports and determine appropriate operational procedures

In particular fields, in addition to the general objectives, the goals are more specific. For example, objectives for a major in chef apprenticeship include the following.

- Establish and maintain sanitation and safety standards

- Produce high-quality food products using appropriate ingredients and equipment

- Apply nutrition principles to menu planning and food production for a variety of customers

- Define concepts and procedures for purchasing, receiving, storage, and inventory; and develop specifications for purchase of food and non-food items

- Demonstrate knowledge of and an ability to comply with laws, rules, and regulations governing food-service operations

- Demonstrate basic knowledge of meeting planning and catering services

- Plan, organize, and supervise the production and service of food and beverages to customers

- Demonstrate proficiency in all food production departments in a commercial kitchen

- Work effectively as a first-line supervisor and trainer in food production

Columbus State is not unique in providing such specific coursework in hospitality fields. Many community colleges offer programs accredited by the Commission on Accreditation for Hospitality Management (CAHM) as well as organizations such as the American Culinary Federation Accrediting Commission and the U.S. Department of Labor Bureau of Apprenticeship

and Training. In addition, community colleges offer programs in fields related to the hospitality industry, such as accounting, business management, computer science, and even specific areas such as HVAC training. Because of their targeted curricula, lower cost, and shorter time required to earn a degree, community colleges can offer the most direct and economical route to a career in hospitality management.

FOUR-YEAR PROGRAMS AND UNIVERSITY CLASSES

Hospitality Marketing and Management is a growing field of study at four-year institutions as well. Cornell University, the University of Nevada at Las Vegas, and the University of Houston have been recognized as leading training institutions for the hospitality industry. Each campus has a major hotel. The University of Houston has a Hilton Hotel located on campus. Students gain first-hand experience operating and managing all aspects of a hotel. Some of the finest meals are catered by the catering department at the University's hospitality training school.

Examples of classes taught in a hospitality major include Front Office Management, Hotel and Restaurant Law, Restaurant Operations, Food Service Sanitation and Safety, Hotel and Restaurant Sales and Marketing, and Hotel and Restaurant Supervision and Guest Relations.

- **Front Office Management** exposes students to front-office operations in a lodging enterprise with emphasis on guest relations and accommodations. This class covers proper registering of, accounting for, and checking out of guests. Students learn the administration of the front office by studying forecasting, occupancy statistics, billing, and audit procedures.

- **Hotel and Restaurant Law** covers the fundamentals of law important to innkeepers and restaurant managers. This course examines the duties, rights, and liabilities of the host and guest. Case studies and problem-solving exercises emphasize real-world experiences.

- **Restaurant Operations** is a practical application of principles and practices used in quantity food production. The course provides an opportunity for students to gain training in different food systems. Management of food service, production, and people are emphasized in this course.

- **Food Service Sanitation and Safety** is a course that presents guidelines and concepts to assure a safe food-service facility. Emphasis is on customer protection and maintenance of standards. The course covers accident and fire prevention, food handling and storage, and food-borne illness and prevention. Sanitation certification through the National Restaurant Association Educational Foundation is earned through this course.

- **Hotel and Restaurant Sales and Marketing** is a course that teaches how sales and marketing departments focus on planning and analysis of current competition and markets. Merchandising, promotion, advertising, and public relations are concepts emphasized in this course. Students have the opportunity to design a marketing plan that effectively serves the customer and allows for the greatest amount of profit.

- **Hotel and Restaurant Supervision and Guest Relations** is a foundation-level presentation of supervisory management skill areas. Management of personnel includes employee selection, training, and appraisal. Management areas include management function and theory, leadership methods and styles, quality control and assurance, policy and procedure development, discipline and motivation, and communication and listening skills. The guest relations component of the course provides an in-depth view of guest services, including guest needs and accommodations. Different guest markets are studied to define their desired quality of guest services.

Traditional four-year courses in marketing, business, accounting, engineering, computer science, or pre-law are excellent foundations for hospitality management. Many upper managers hold four-year and graduate degrees in business and management. A CFO of a chain of hotels or restaurants may need to know little of innkeeping or food service, but must be an expert in financial analysis.

CONFIRMATION

Identify two differences between community and four-year colleges.

_____

_____

_____

EDUCATION WITHIN THE HOSPITALITY INDUSTRY

Within the hospitality industry itself, many companies offer education and training for employees and others. With a critical need for accomplished personnel, these firms find it in their own interest to develop programs that teach the skills and services they require.

The Greenbrier is an exclusive, award-winning resort in the Allegheny Mountains of West Virginia that has pampered guests for more than 200 years. The Greenbrier has established a reputation for culinary excellence by instituting several practices, including a formal, three-year culinary apprentice program. Related practices include a culinary school for guests during the off-season, conferences and seminars with food critics and writers as guest speakers, active partnership with the local high school culinary training program, newsletters to 600,000 of the resort's guests, and the publication of _The Greenbrier Cookbook_. These practices increase year-round occupancy as well as highlight the level of service the Greenbrier achieves.

It is not true that customers' problems with alcohol are just personal problems. Several court cases have made the potential for liability of hospitality servers clear. Misuse of alcohol can be fatal, and those who serve it have a social as well as a legal responsibility.

The following facts are provided by "Serving It Right," a program implemented by restaurants and other hospitality venues.

- Alcohol is a factor in up to 70 percent of all drowning deaths.

- Approximately 30 percent of all suicides involve alcohol.

- Alcohol is a factor in many domestic violence incidents.

- Uncounted numbers of serious accidents such as falls are alcohol-related.

- Alcohol can interfere with normal fetal development.

- Drinking alcohol while driving is still the leading cause of death on major highways.

THINK CRITICALLY
1. How might liability of the server be an issue in any of the above circumstances?
2. How is public relations involved with the issue of alcohol abuse and hospitality?

In 1993 a culinary arts program was developed in partnership with the local high school. This program promises permanent employment with The Greenbrier to interested applicants, further stabilizing kitchen personnel. The program is aligned with a national program called "Pro Start," which is endorsed by the National Restaurant Association with support from the state of West Virginia and its hospitality educational programs. The hotel employs 90 percent of its workforce from the local area. This educational partnership highlights the significant community presence of The Greenbrier and its commitment to educating young people interested in culinary careers. The Greenbrier is committed to being a responsible member of the local community.

Four Seasons Hotels and Resorts has created **designated trainer** positions within its far-flung empire of hospitality businesses. The idea is to have people within each department make front-line employee training as effective and consistent as possible. Each trainer is a line employee who holds a regular job assignment, but is selected for knowledge, standards adherence, patience, and communication skills. The designated trainer follows a carefully structured program to teach and coach new employees how to achieve Four Seasons' defined standards of service and attitude. The program encourages leadership and team spirit as well as effective training of new employees.

PROMOTING THE INDUSTRY

HIEAC (Hospitality Industry Education Advisory

Committee) was formed in 1976 by hospitality and tourism associations as a non-profit society. The mission of HIEAC is "To promote the development and delivery of hospitality/ tourism industry training and education programs not traditionally supported by educational institutions." Mandates for the organization include

- Facilitating the development and delivery of educational and training programs for the hospitality/tourism industry

- Networking with local and national industry associations, organizations, and government agencies for the betterment of education and training in the industry

- Encouraging the development and delivery of alternate training not otherwise delivered or offered by schools, colleges, and universities for the hospitality/tourism industry

"Serving It Right" is a program established by HIEAC. It is designed to encourage a responsible, caring, and professional approach by licensees and servers for serving alcohol in their establishments. It gives critical information on the effects of alcohol on people and techniques for preventing over-service. This information helps hospitality businesses develop a more positive environment for their patrons and increased community respect. Programs such as "Serving It Right" provide a common information base for a high standard of responsibility in serving alcoholic beverages.

HOSPITALITY INDUSTRY CERTIFICATION

Hospitality and allied industry managers who demonstrate expertise, competence, and experience in the hospitality industry are qualified for professional certification and recognition from the American Hotel & Motel Association's Educational Institute (EI). This honor is recognized worldwide as the highest industry honor of professional achievement. EI's certification and recognition programs elevate the professionalism and image of both the recipient and the hospitality industry. Over 15,000 people throughout the world have become certified through EI. Each certification program requires that applicants be currently employed in a qualifying industry position or in teaching hospitality courses. Certification gives hospitality professionals a competitive edge with proof of their abilities, knowledge, and level of skill. Many hotel companies are moving in the direction of certification. Holiday Inns Worldwide and Sunburst Hotels require that all general managers be certified within 12 months of obtaining their management positions.

BENEFITS OF TRAINING

Education, training, and certification within the hospitality industry not only helps employees perform better in their current jobs, but sparks motivation and prepares them for advancement as well. Those companies that train well or sponsor education through tuition-reimbursement programs build the type of loyalty that encourages staff to stay with the sponsoring company. Employees feel that their company cares enough about them to invest in them. Training itself can be a relaxing break from day-to-day routine, and many employees return from training sessions with renewed enthusiasm to do their jobs well. Employees who care about a company that they feel cares about them are less likely to become part of the retention problem that plagues so many hospitality businesses today. Employees with training and skill have more confidence in delivering quality service. The result of job-specific training is more knowledgeable, competent employees, who in turn provide better customer service.

CONFIRMATION

What is a designated trainer? Why is training within the hospitality industry a good investment for companies?

_____

_____

UNDERSTAND MARKETING CONCEPTS
Circle the best answer for each of the following questions.

1. Which of the following is not currently providing education and training for the hospitality industry?
   a. middle schools
   b. high schools
   c. private institutions
   d. four-year colleges

2. Designated trainers are
   a. employees who counsel customers about alcohol abuse
   b. employees who train employees
   c. new employees who are not yet certified
   d. interns who job-shadow experienced employees

THINK CRITICALLY
Answer the following questions as completely as possible. If necessary, use a separate sheet of paper.

3. **Research** Visit the National Restaurant Association's education web site at www.restaurant.org/careers/schools.cfm. Pick three schools reasonably near you and compare and contrast their hospitality management offerings.

_____

_____

_____

_____

_____

4. **Research** Contact three local hospitality businesses and find out how they train their employees. Discover what these employers feel are the essential knowledge, skills, and abilities that their employees need. Write a summary of what you learn from each employer.

_____

_____

_____

_____

MOBILITY REQUIRED FOR ADVANCEMENT

CHAPTER

LESSON 12.3

Your grandparents may have worked at the same career for a lifetime. They were part of a generation that placed great value on stability and employee loyalty. The dynamic nature of modern business makes it highly unlikely that you will have the same career or job during your entire working years.

Statistics show an average of seven career changes during today's working lifetime. Changing technology, company ownership, and economic trends have influenced a mobile workforce. Among these seven job changes, relocation will likely be a part of your career.

Work with a group. Make a list of the advantages and possibilities that relocation offers. Make another list of the challenges that relocation poses. How might these challenges best be met?

GOALS

Explain the need for mobility in the hospitality industry.

Describe how the Internet has affected hospitality career searches.

CHANGE ON THE HORIZON

Hospitality industry sources estimate that total industry employment in 1998 was 12 million people. Job growth through 2006 will require at least an additional 200,000 employees to be added to that total annually. The American Hotel and Lodging Association (AH&LA) has created a hospitality workforce initiative task force called AH&LA Experience Lodging. The goal of this task force is to create an expanded, enlightened workforce for the U.S. lodging industry. They created a "Checkinn" tool kit for hotel owners and managers to develop relationships with schools and other organizations in their local communities. The kit includes step-by-step instructions as well as posters, brochures, and a presentation on CD-ROM—all promoting careers in lodging to high school guidance counselors, teachers, students, and parents. The many changes in the hospitality business will require a mobile workforce. Those who understand the need to go where the opportunities are will find that advancement, compensation, and quality of life can offset the challenges posed by relocation.

NEW JOBS

Part of the reason mobility is such a factor in a hospitality career is the growth of jobs. Although some growth is local, career professionals find that their companies need them in new branches or franchises. A desk clerk could work in a single city and move from hotel to hotel, but beyond a certain career level, opportunities in a single location are limited. The pyramid gets more narrow near the top, and those who wish to progress

The U.S. Bureau of Labor Statistics predicts an 18 percent increase in tourism and hospitality employment by 2005. Current figures rank the travel industry as one of the top three employers in 32 states, and it is the country's third-largest retail industry.

may find it necessary to relocate. New markets are a source of fresh opportunities for employees, and the price of promotion is often relocation.

IMPLICATIONS OF PROMOTION

People who make their mark in the hospitality industry are not afraid of work, generate new and progressive ideas, create strategies to improve occupancy and customer satisfaction, and implement the team approach to accomplish company goals. Many times success means working over-time hours while being paid a set salary. The reward for hard work and success is promotion. Many promotions or new job offers are proposed to people who have proven themselves to be leaders. The promotion or new job often means moving to a new domestic or international location.

Sharon Estep, a freelance hotel sales and management specialist, indicates that longevity in a hospitality position can speak for or against you. A minimum longevity of two years for a hospitality salesperson shows credibility. Having the same sales position for more than seven or eight years may indicate stagnation. Changing jobs too frequently may be viewed negatively as job hopping. Hospitality businesses realize the cost of training a new employee and do not want to invest training dollars for an individual to stay with the company for a year or less.

While single people may have more flexibility to relocate, they need to consider the relocation carefully. How will the price of real estate compare to where they currently live? Is the climate substantially different? Those with growing families have additional considerations. What effect will this move have on a spouse and children? Will the school system of the new location provide a high-quality education for children?

Many companies pay relocation costs for management positions. Those who are not in management must find out if the cost of moving is covered. Moving costs a lot of money. Imagine what it would be like to pack up and move 1,000 miles. Think about what it would be like to move to another country. These decisions must be made often by people moving up in the hospitality industry. Sometimes opportunities come up quickly and a move must be made in less than a week. It takes a special personality to deal with the stress and excitement associated with relocation.

MAKING THE DECISION

If a company offers you a new job with a good salary increase, you still have to consider all factors. Is the new job a stable one? Will you receive the company support that you enjoyed at your current job? Is the new company willing to pay moving expenses? Will the new location meet the needs and expectations of you and your family? Will you be able to start anew with friends and community life? It is important to maintain a favorable relationship with all previous employers—in other words, do not burn any bridges. Previous employers may resurface in the future with excellent job offers.

If you accept a position in a new company, you are the new person on the block, and you will have to prove yourself to the rest of the staff, which is likely neither to know nor care about your successful past. Almost all organizations tend to resist change, so a new manager has a double burden. If someone within the business also applied for the position, you may find you have a disappointed

individual not inclined to cooperate with your strategies. Your actions and leadership skills must earn you the respect that got you the new job.

NEW CAREERS

You may do more than change jobs in your life. You may also change careers—many people do so more than once. Sometimes career change is not voluntary. Jobs go away, and people must find other options. Sometimes people simply change their minds about what they want to do, such as a long-time chef founding a cooking school. Some of the happiest career changes come when a person outgrows one job, and through hard work and extra effort moves to a new level. Perhaps a housekeeping employee takes hospitality management classes and makes her way to general manager of a hotel, or a desk clerk who understands the reservations system becomes a computer expert. Although change brings stress, including relocation, those who do well demonstrate the personal flexibility to make the most of an opportunity.

CONFIRMATION

Why does an individual need to be flexible when considering promotion within the hospitality industry?

_____

_____

CAREER SEARCHES ON THE WEB

The "new economy" revolutionized the recruitment of employees. Internet web sites have changed the way professionals look for work, and the hospitality industry is no exception. Internet sites can assist those who are actively or passively looking for a job. Some sites share important job trends that affect employment possibilities in the hospitality industry. Individuals can post a resume, search job databases, obtain career advice, learn compensation information, improve their resume and interviewing skills, research companies, and read the latest industry news.

INTERACTIVITY IS KEY

The interactivity of the Internet allows customization far beyond mere job listings. Sites such as careerpath.com and hospitalitycareernet.com include a built-in "career agent" that searches job databases 24 hours, seven days a week and forwards an e-mail when positions meet the individual's determined criteria. This type of "push and pull" technology stands apart from more passive sites. Some of the better sites have resume-builders that present work history in the most marketable format. A feature called 20/20 Skills™ at hospitalitycareernet.com is useful for people looking for hospitality positions. Job seekers complete an assessment profile and, if it is similar to an employer's specifications, the job seeker and the employer

CYBER MARKETING

The hospitality industry increasingly uses the Internet. Web sites help employers as well as employees in an industry that is constantly seeking qualified workers. Some of the best sites include

careerpath.com
hospitalitycareernet.com
vault.com
hotelreports.com
monster.com

THINK CRITICALLY
Visit one of the career web sites. Locate five hospitality careers listed on the site. What qualifications are needed for each position? Is willingness to relocate a requirement?

receive e-mail messages regarding potential compatibility.

Prospective candidates should conduct research on the potential employer prior to interviewing. Vault.com and hotelreports.com have excellent tools for research, such as compensation data, interviewing tips, and relevant statistics for the industry. The Internet allows prospective employers to take a more proactive approach to recruiting employees. Some of the best career sites offer employers the ability to search databases and post help-wanted ads. Many sites have search capabilities based on industry-specific criteria such as industry segment, job classification, and job title. The Internet also makes background checks, referencing, and credit checks easier to conduct, although privacy policies must be followed.

Some sites, such as monster.com and hospitalitycareernet.com, have relied on strategic partnerships with hospitality businesses and educational institutions. Site partners deliver a wide range of services to users. Partnerships with educational institutions, such as Cornell University, New York University, and the University of Houston, make the sites more relevant.

There are hundreds of web sites devoted to employment. Many are specifically for hospitality employment. Associations, organizations, and individual firms also maintain pages devoted to employment.

Don't confuse career planning with looking for a job. Job hunting comes to a conclusion while career planning never stops. A "cradle to grave" career plan will be the basis for winners in the new economy. Although the Internet is a new and exciting tool, it is no substitute for careful self-analysis and diligent effort. Ultimately, the individual person determines the success of a job search and a career plan.

CONFIRMATION

How has the Internet changed the search for hospitality careers? List three features of employment web sites.

UNDERSTAND MARKETING CONCEPTS
Circle the best answer for each of the following questions.

1. Relocation is often required in the hospitality industry because of
   a. personal choice
   b. promotion
   c. downsizing
   d. all of the above

2. The interactivity of the Internet
   a. ends responsibility for privacy concerns
   b. allows a greater number of customized features
   c. makes it possible to see job postings from distant places
   d. both b and c

THINK CRITICALLY
Answer the following questions as completely as possible. if necessary, use a separate sheet of paper.

3. **Technology** Use the Internet to look up one of the web sites described in this lesson. List the main functions of this web site on the following lines, and then write a one-page paper about the services provided by this web site. Be sure to tell how the site is beneficial to the employee and the employer.

_____

_____

_____

_____

_____

_____

4. **Research** Choose three major cities in the United States some distance from where you live. Use the Internet to get an estimate of costs to move you from your current location to those cities.

_____

_____

_____

_____

_____

REVIEW MARKETING CONCEPTS

Write the letter of the term that matches each definition. Some terms will not be used.

_____ **1.** Roadmap to a professional future

_____ **2.** Includes a resume, cover letter, and references

_____ **3.** Finding out as much as possible about a company

_____ **4.** Packaging oneself to be noticed by a potential employer

_____ **5.** Company employee assigned to work with new employees

_____ **6.** Non-profit organization created to promote development and delivery of hospitality/tourism industry training and education programs not traditionally supported by educational institutions

a. career package

b. company research

c. designated trainer

d. HIEAC

e. hot market

f. marketing plan

g. planning process

Circle the best answer.

7. The percentage of hospitality employees estimated to be working part-time by the year 2005 is

    a. 25 percent   **c.** 55 percent

    b. 45 percent   **d.** 85 percent

8. A resume for the hospitality industry should

    a. be kept to a single page

    b. highlight concrete accomplishments

    c. attract attention with unique typefaces

    d. have general objectives for a wide audience

9. Job shadowing is

    a. following a worker to learn about his or her job

    b. usually a paid internship

    c. an Internet privacy issue

    d. not available for high-school students

10. Community colleges offer

    a. harder courses than four-year universities

    b. few hospitality management courses of study

    c. a shorter and more economical path to fields in hospitality

    d. all of the above

THINK CRITICALLY

11. How do in-house training and development programs benefit both employers and employees?

_____

_____

_____

_____

_____

_____

_____

12. What major sections are the most important to include on a resume? Give a reason for including each section.

_____

_____

_____

_____

_____

_____

_____

13. Interview someone who has relocated for professional reasons. Prepare a list of questions about the move, its reasons, and the challenges and rewards presented both in personal and professional terms. Report your findings to the class.

_____

_____

_____

_____

_____

_____

REVIEW

MAKE CONNECTIONS

14. Research Conduct research regarding the number of part-time and full-time employees in four hospitality businesses in your area. Find out from employers their greatest needs and what knowledge, skills, and abilities they would like their employees to have.

_____

_____

_____

15. Marketing Math In 1998 it was projected that there were 12 million people employed by the hospitality industry, and that the number would grow by 200,000 each year until 2006. How many people will be employed by the hospitality industry in 2006?

_____

_____

_____

16. Technology Enter the terms "hospitality employment" in an Internet search engine. Summarize what you find, and describe two or three of the most interesting or useful sites.

_____

_____

_____

17. Technology Prepare a computer presentation that explains the four-step procedure for pursuing a career. This presentation should provide enough information to help young people achieve success. Use the following lines to first outline your main points.

_____

_____

_____

18. History The Marriott Corporation has proven itself to be an educational leader with the Marriott Hospitality High School in Washington, D.C. Use the Internet to learn about the history of the Marriott Corporation. Report your findings in a one-page paper.

_____

_____

ADVERTISING CAMPAIGN EVENT

You and a partner are in charge of the advertising campaign for a time-share condominium located in a tropical climate. You must describe the timeshare program and your client. Clear objectives for your campaign must be stated and identification of your target market (primary and secondary) is essential. List all advertising media you intend to use in order to achieve your goals. Your budget should include detailed projections of actual cost. Schedules of all advertising planned and sales promotion activities must be included with your campaign. You must convince your client with your statement of benefit to them.

Prepare Fact Sheets   Advertising fact sheets should be prepared in outline form and limited to 9 pages (not including title page). No artwork is to be included on the fact sheets. The fact sheets must include all items being evaluated in this project.

Present Your Advertising Campaign   Prepare a 10-minute presentation (including visual aids) that describes your advertising campaign. You are allowed five minutes to set up visual aids and the judges are allowed to ask questions for five minutes following your presentation.

http://www.deca.org/
publications/HS_
Guide/guidetoc.html

PROJECT EXTENDED STAY

Now it is time for you to package yourself for a job. Prepare a personal portfolio following the guidelines suggested in this lesson. Complete each assignment separately and then put them together in your professional portfolio.

Work with a group and complete the following activities.

1. Draft a planning process for your career. This one-page statement should list personal and professional goals for the next several years. It should serve as a roadmap for your future. Include personal goals and education that you might seek.

2. Prepare an interesting career package that includes an effective resume summarizing experience and detailing concrete accomplishments. Also prepare a cover letter for an employer for whom you would like to work. Write the letter so that it can be easily adapted for other potential employers, yet still seem as if it were individually constructed.

3. Prepare a marketing plan for your career search. The marketing plan should detail how you plan to package your qualifications, procedures you will follow to pursue a career, and steps you might take to search for and win a position at an interesting company.

4. Research three companies where you would like to work. Write a half-page summary for each, highlighting information that would be useful for a prospective job applicant.

INDEX

PHOTO CREDITS

Chapter 1   2, 5, 9: © PhotoDisc, Inc.
Chapter 2   22, 24, 26, 30, 34, 37, 43, 44: © PhotoDisc, Inc.
Chapter 3   50: © CORBIS; 52, 54, 58, 61, 62, 63, 64, 65: © PhotoDisc, Inc.
Chapter 4   74, 77, 79, 83, 89: © PhotoDisc, Inc.
Chapter 5   96: © CORBIS; 99: © Reuters New Media Inc/ CORBIS; 111: © CORBIS; 101, 104, 106, 109, 110, 111: © PhotoDisc, Inc.
Chapter 6   118, 120, 122, 123, 127, 130, 133, 137, 138: © PhotoDisc, Inc.
Chapter 7   160: © CORBIS; 144, 147, 148, 150, 152, 155, 159, 164, 165: © PhotoDisc, Inc.
Chapter 8   172: © CORBIS; 181: © Jeremy Horner/ CORBIS; 176, 180, 185, 187, 188, 191, 193: © PhotoDisc, Inc.
Chapter 9   209: © CORBIS; 200, 202, 203, 204, 205, 208, 211, 214, 216, 221, 223, 226: © PhotoDisc, Inc.
Chapter 10 232: © CORBIS; 235, 236, 241, 242, 245, 247, 248: © PhotoDisc, Inc.
Chapter 11 268: © CORBIS; 258, 260, 262, 265, 267, 269, 272: © PhotoDisc, Inc
Chapter 12 280: © Patrick Ward/CORBIS; 282, 284, 286, 290, 291, 293, 295, 298: © PhotoDisc, Inc

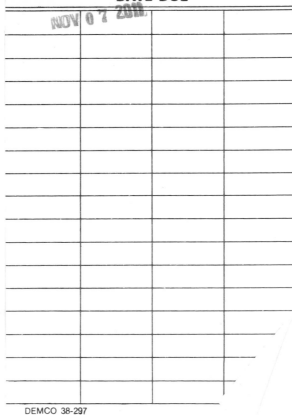

DATE DUE

NOV 0 7 2011

DEMCO 38-297